The Which? Guide to Choosing a Career

About the author

Barbara Buffton is a freelance writer and former careers adviser. She has written *Career Planning* (careers education materials for pupils in years 9 to 11) and has contributed to many publications, including *Careers Encyclopaedia* (Cassell), *The Job Book* (CRAC/Hobson) and *CareerScope* (the magazine of the Independent Schools Careers Organisation), and has written information for the Careers and Occupational Information Centre (COIC) of the DfEE. She is a member of the Institute of Careers Guidance and the Careers Writers' Association.

Acknowledgements

Advertising Association, Architects and Surveyors Institute, Armed Forces Careers Office (Bournemouth), Association of Accounting Technicians, Association of Chartered Certified Accountants (ACCA), ATB-Landbase, Bank of England, British Acupuncture Council, British Bankers' Association, British Chiropractic Association, British Dental Association, British Dietetic Association, British Display Society, British Homoeopathic Association, British Horse Society, British Institute of Architectural Technologists, British Medical Association, British Printing Industries Federation, British Psychological Society, Building Societies Association, CACHE (Council for Awards in Children's Care and Education), CAPITB Trust, Catholic Media Office, Central Council for Education and Training in Social Work (CCETSW), Charles Clifford Dental Hospital, Chartered Institute of Environmental Health, Chartered Institute of Housing, Chartered Institute of Management Accountants, Chartered Institute of Transport, Chartered Insurance Institute, Chartered Society of Physiotherapy, Church of England, CITB (Construction Industry Training Board), City & Guilds, Civil Aviation Authority, Coastguard and Marine Safety Agency, College of Occupational Therapists, College of Radiographers, Community Service Volunteers, Crown Prosecution Service, Council for British Archaeology, Dental Auxiliary Schools (London, Cardiff), Department for Education and Employment – Briefing Division, Department of Public Health and Epidemiology – University of Birmingham, Edexcel Foundation, Engineering Careers Information Service – Engineering and Marine Training Authority, English National Board for Nursing, Midwifery and Health Visiting, Environment Agency, Fire Services Unit – Home Office, General Council of the Bar, General Optical Council, Graduate and Schools Liaison Branch – the Cabinet Office, Hairdressing Training Board, HCIMA (Hotel and Catering International Management Association), Hospitality Training Foundation, Information Technology Industry Training Organisation, Institute of Actuaries, Institute of Biology, Institute of Careers Guidance, The Institute of Chartered Accountants in England & Wales (ICAEW), Institute of Legal Executives, Institute of Packaging, Institute of Personnel and Development, Institute of Physics, Institute of Public Relations, Institute of Revenues, Rating and Valuation, Institute of Sport and Recreation Management, Institute of Translation and Interpreting, Institute of Travel and Tourism, International Association of Conference Interpreters, International Health and Beauty Council, ISVA (The Professional Society for Valuers and Auctioneers), Kodak Ltd, Law Society, Law Society of Scotland, Library Association, Local Government Management Board, London Stock Exchange, Merchant Navy Careers – Chamber of Shipping, Museum Training Institute, National Association of Funeral Directors, National Centre for Volunteering, National Coaching Foundation, National Council for the Training of Journalists, NSEAD (National Society for Education in Art and Design), National Youth Agency, Nuclear Electric Ltd, Office of the Chief Rabbi, Periodicals Training Council, Police Personnel and Training Unit – Home Office, Post Office, Prison Service – Home Office, Probation Unit – Home Office, Publishing Training Centre, Qualifications and Curriculum Authority, Recruitment and Assessment Services – the Civil Service, Royal College of Speech and Language Therapists, Royal College of Veterinary Surgeons, Royal Forestry Society, Royal Institute of British Architects, Royal Institution of Chartered Surveyors, Royal Society of Chemistry, Royal Town Planning Institute, Scottish Office – Education and Industry Department, Scottish Qualifications Authority, Shiona Llewellyn Associates, Skillset, Society of Archivists, Society of Chiropodists and Podiatrists, Society of Occupational Medicine, Society of Teachers of the Alexander Technique, St Quintin Chartered Surveyors, Teacher Training Agency, Travel Training Company, United Kingdom Institute for Conservation of Historic and Artistic Works (UKIC), Universities and Colleges Admissions Service, University of East London – the Psychology department, University of Liverpool School of Dentistry.

The Which? Guide to Choosing a Career

Barbara Buffton

CONSUMERS' ASSOCIATION

Which? Books are commissioned and researched by
Consumers' Association and published by
Which? Ltd, 2 Marylebone Road, London NW1 4DF
Email address: books@which.net

Distributed by The Penguin Group:
Penguin Books Ltd, 27 Wrights Lane, London W8 5TZ

First edition May 1998

British Library Cataloguing in Publication Data
A catalogue record for this book is available from the British Library

ISBN 0 85202 713 3

For a full list of Which? books, please write to Which? Books, Castlemead,
Gascoyne Way, Hertford X, SG14 1LH
or access our web site at http://www.which.net

Cover and text design by Kyzen Creative Consultants

Typeset by Paston Press Ltd, Loddon, Norfolk
Printed and bound in Great Britain by Clays Ltd, Bungay, Suffolk

Contents

For the sake of brevity qualifications are given only in terms of the English GCSE, GNVQ and A-/AS-level. See pages 28–32 for Scottish equivalents.

Introduction

Starting out on the right foot and in the right direction is important for any school- or college-leaver who wants to get established in a career. But it is no easy task to make the choice when the possibilities range so far and wide, yet may be, in the main, completely unfamiliar to you. One thing you have probably discovered at school or in higher education is what your aptitude is in different subject areas and which subjects you enjoy. Now the challenge is to match that aptitude and that interest to a career in which you can fulfil your potential. That is where this book can help you.

Part 1 explains in detail the National Curriculum, the education systems in England, Wales and Northern Ireland and Scotland, and the many different types of qualifications currently available. It also gives information on further and higher education and how and when to apply for courses. If you or your parents are confused by the number and type of new training initiatives, such as Youth Credits, National Traineeships and Modern Apprenticeships, you will find detailed explanations here.

The book then takes you through the decision-making process at two key stages during your time at school: in year 9, when you have to choose which GCSEs or GNVQs to study; and in year 11, when you must choose what A-levels to study if you wish to stay on at school, and what to do if you decide to leave.

In addition, it explains what you should do while you are still at school to make yourself more employable in the future, such as gaining work experience.

Finally, Part 1 advises you about what to do if your circumstances change or if problems arise.

Part 2 of the book is a careers guide offering general information about 43 different career areas. Each entry contains information about opportunities, advice about which subjects to study to follow a particular career, what training is necessary, details of other factors to consider (such as anti-social hours, weekend shifts, stamina and so on), a list of organisations to contact and useful books and leaflets that can take you a stage further.

The guide can be used in two different ways. If you already know what you want to do you can look up the career in the book and find out all the above information; alternatively, if you do not have any ideas at present, you can look up the subjects you are good at and find out which careers they lead to.

At the back of the book you will find a section called 'Other sources of information', which gives details of careers encyclopaedias, directories and software databases, and a large 'Addresses' section which lists organisations to contact for information about individual careers.

Your choice of GCSE and A-level subjects will have implications for future career options, so this book emphasises the importance of keeping your options open by studying as wide a range of subjects as possible for as long as you can; this means that you can be more flexible when making career choices in future. Part 1 explains the implications of particular subject choices and gives advice about the best combinations for leaving your options open. However, it is important to remember that all is not lost if you change your mind later about the career you had decided on but find you do not have the right qualifications for your new choice. The book explains about the conversion/foundation/introductory courses available to enable people to make a career switch. Although the advice in Chapter 2 is not to specialise too early, the book recommends that you start to think about careers from the age of 13 (year 9) and suggests that you begin keeping a careers file (examples are given for you to copy).

The jobs market has changed dramatically over the last decade or so from secure, full-time jobs that could be expected to last a good number of years, towards more part-time, contract and flexible work. It is highly likely that you will have more than one career in your working life. This is one reason why the emphasis in the careers market is increasingly on transferable skills (for example, teamwork and 'interpersonal' skills – that is, the ability to get on with others). Employers want people who are flexible and self-reliant and who have a broad range of skills including communication, computer literacy, numeracy and problem-solving. They frequently complain that school-leavers, despite the government's stated commitment to 'the highest standards of basic skills and a secure foundation for lifelong learning, work and citizenship', do not have the necessary skills for today's workforce. Skill requirements within occupations are rising, and current trends in employment suggest that the demand for higher-level skills will increase during the next five to ten years. Part 1 of this book outlines exactly what employers are looking for in their recruits.

A string of impressive examination results alone is no longer enough. Employers want people who can demonstrate personal and social development as well as academic attainments – likable personalities, the ability to think clearly and the confidence to 'sell' themselves. They look for any experience, achievements and commitments students have beyond their formal studies. Employers are also increasingly looking for employees who can demonstrate that they have some knowledge of business and industry in addition to academic qualifications. This book emphasises the importance of these skills and gives advice (in Part 1) about how to gain them.

The emphasis in this book is on how to choose a career and what you can do to help yourself from year 9 onwards. It is not just a directory of different careers. It also encourages you to think laterally. For example, the 'Finance' section describes accountancy, actuarial work, banking and building society work, insurance and stockbroking, so if you have a flair for figures you will be able to pick an area of activity that not only uses your talents but which you will find interesting and challenging. The book helps you to think about jobs at different levels within the same industry or profession, too. For example, you might be keen to work with animals and might have thought about becoming a vet. If you then discover that you are unlikely to gain the appropriate entry qualifications, you can still consider the other jobs in the same field that do not demand such high qualifications.

Whether you are a student wanting help with decision-making and looking for facts and figures for all types of career, or a parent wanting to know what career choices are available for your son or daughter, this book gives you valuable advice and information you cannot afford to miss out on.

Throughout this book, for 'student' read 'student or pupil' and for 'parent' read 'parent, guardian or carer'.

Part 1

Background and preparation

Chapter 1

The education system and government initiatives

England, Wales and Northern Ireland have traditionally had a system of education that is different in some respects from that of Scotland. (see pages 28–33 for information on the Scottish education system).

England, Wales and Northern Ireland

This section explains the secondary education system, the requirements of the National Curriculum, the various qualifications which currently exist and all about further and higher education.

The secondary education system

Significant changes have taken place in the education system over the past few years, affecting how schools and colleges are run and what subjects students are taught. These are described below.

- As a result of the **1988 Education Act**, local authorities handed over control of school budgets to schools (Local Management of Schools – LMS); they can now make independent decisions about how they spend the money they receive from their Local Education Authority (LEA).
- In the 1990s the government introduced **charters for many of the public services**. In the education sector these included the Parents' Charter, the Charter for Further Education and the Higher Education Charter. They were intended to make public service providers more accountable to their users and to clarify standards and people's entitlement to services and information, for example, under the

Parents' Charter, parents are entitled to receive an annual report on their child's progress. The Charter for Further Education guarantees basic rights for students, such as access to examination and assessment results. Individual institutions are encouraged to publish their own charter.

- **The Disability Discrimination Act (1995)** requires colleges to take account of the needs of students with learning and other disabilities. Each college should have a disability statement outlining its policy towards such students and giving information on the facilities, access, specialist equipment and counselling available.
- **Each school is now required to publish its public examination results** in the governors' annual report to parents, usually in the autumn.
- The **National Curriculum** – introduced in 1988 in state schools – stipulated which subjects children should study.

Students have to make important choices at various stages during their school career. At the age of 13/14 (in year 9) they must choose which subjects to study for examination (for example, GCSE or GNVQ). At the age of 15/16 (in year 11), they need to decide whether to stay on in education, go into training or start work; if they are staying on at school, they must choose which subjects to study post-16 (for example, A-level, AS-level, Advanced GNVQ, BTEC awards). At the age of 17/18 they can choose between higher education or work/training. About 85 per cent of 16- and 17-year-olds participated in some form of full-time education or structured training in 1996 (*Labour Market Skills Trends 1996/1997*).

Compulsory education is divided into four key stages (KS):

- KS1   5- to 7-year-olds
- KS2   7- to 11-year-olds
- KS3   11- to 14-year-olds
- KS4   14- to 16-year-olds

The National Curriculum

All state schools have to follow the National Curriculum, so do students have any choice at all? When it was first introduced, the subject choice for students aged between 5 and 14 was more limited than it had been before 1988. This was because the syllabus and content of study for every child was clearly defined. Compulsory subjects took up most of the timetable. In 1993 Sir Ron Dearing, Chairman of the Schools Curriculum and Assessment Authority (SCAA), carried out a major review of the National Curriculum, and in 1995 his recommendations to allow more time for other options came into operation.

As a result of his study, the National Curriculum has been slimmed down. The mandatory requirement at Key Stage 4 (age 14–16, in year 10) has been reduced to about 60 per cent (from 100 per cent) of curriculum time. This is intended to:

- make the National Curriculum less prescriptive
- simplify its assessment and administration
- give schools more opportunity to develop the three key skills of communication, numeracy and information technology
- free up more time for schools to use at their own discretion
- increase flexibility and choice for 14- to 16-year-olds. Students now have a choice of subject options at GCSE. Alternatively, they can choose to study GNVQs or other vocational qualifications in subjects such as health and social care, business, leisure and tourism. The choice of subject and type of examination depends greatly on the individual school.

The aim of the National Curriculum is to give students a broad general education, so each student must study the core subjects:

- English, mathematics, science (and Welsh in Welsh-speaking schools in Wales) from 5 to 16 years of age. These subjects are most frequently required by employers and must be studied.

In addition, each student must:

- be taught physical education from 5 to 16 years of age
- take at least a 'short course' GCSE in both design and technology and in a modern foreign language at Key Stage 4 (age 14–16).

Short course GCSEs were introduced in many schools in September 1996 to add breadth and balance to the school curriculum. The benefits are that students can gain extra qualifications in subjects they are not studying as full GCSEs; in addition to keeping their options open they can learn subjects that are becoming increasingly useful and desirable to employers. These courses take half as long as a full GCSE to complete and are worth half the award.

Religious education and sex education are not National Curriculum subjects, although they are mandatory. All schools (all secondary schools for sex education) must teach them, although parents can withdraw their children from these lessons if they wish. In addition, all secondary schools must provide careers education.

The foundation subjects of history, geography, music, art and Welsh (in non-Welsh speaking schools in Wales) are studied up to and including Key Stage 3 (age 5–14). Students also have the option of studying these foundation subjects at GCSE alongside other qualifications such as GNVQs. In non-Welsh speaking schools in Wales from 1999 students aged 14–16 will also be required to study Welsh to GCSE level. Independent schools are not required to follow the National Curriculum but are expected to adhere to the curriculum principles (breadth, balance, relevance and differentiation – planning for pupils of different abilities) as one of the conditions of registration.

Information technology is a National Curriculum foundation subject up to Key Stage 4 (up to age 16). It may be taught as a separate subject or via other subjects, for example, in science, computers may be linked with physics experiments, and pupils may work with software packages to explain chemical bonding; in geography, databases may be set up to help with field trips; and in art, desktop publishing packages may be used.

Students must study eight subjects between the ages of 14 and 16 and can take examinations in all of them if entered for them. Most students take a minimum of five subjects (English, science and mathematics usually at GCSE, plus two others – either GCSEs or other examinations, such as GNVQs or short course GCSEs).

A word about science

Students must study all areas of science (chemistry, biology and physics) until they are 16 years old. Most of them do this by taking a balanced science GCSE course. Science can be taught in three different ways:

- as a coordinated subject with separate strands of biology, chemistry and physics
- as one integrated subject
- as modules exploring different topics.

Certainly, students thinking of following a career using science should consider taking a balanced science GCSE course. They can then take any combination of sciences at A-level or in further education. Some schools offer sciences as separate subjects but most offer balanced or combined science, which can be taken as a single science worth one GCSE or as a double worth two.

Qualifications (see Scottish 'Qualifications' for the equivalent)

Sir Ron Dearing carried out a review of the framework of qualifications for 16- to 19-year-olds in 1996 for the Secretaries of State for Education and Employment, for Wales and for Northern Ireland. The aim of his recommendations in March 1996 was to bring greater coherence into the numerous qualifications and training initiatives for young people in schools, colleges and workplaces. Some of his main recommendations included:

- encouragement of depth and breadth of study
- development of a strengthened GNVQ as a major alternative to A-levels and as a means of providing the fundamental knowledge and understanding for broad occupational areas, and for progression to NVQs (see 'Part One GNVQs')
- encouragement of people of all abilities to consider the range of options now available for combining work with part-time study for NVQ qualifications from the age of 16.

It is possible to combine different kinds of qualification in a single course, depending on what is available in the school or college. For instance, you may be able to take A-levels immediately after completing an Intermediate GNVQ, or one Advanced GNVQ and two AS-level qualifications in different subjects at the same time.

GCSEs

General Certificates of Secondary Education (GCSEs) replaced O-levels and CSEs in 1988. They help students develop knowledge, skills and understanding in subjects and are the main examinations for 14- to 16-year-olds. Students are tested by means of a final examination as well as assessment of various pieces of work completed throughout the course. GCSE pass grades are from A★ (the top grade awarded to about 3 per cent of candidates) to grade G. Grades A to E are generally regarded as passes by educational institutions and industry, although there is officially no fail grade. Four or five GCSEs at grades A–C is a common starting point for many careers, or for going on to take A-levels.

A-levels

About one in three 18-year-olds takes Advanced-levels (A-levels) as the main route into higher education; four or five good GCSEs (grades A–C) or equivalent (for example, GNVQs) are generally required for entry to A-levels. A-level qualifications are a recognised way into many jobs, and two or three A-levels are usually necessary for entry into higher education. Students are tested mainly by final examination.

AS-levels

Advanced Supplementary level (AS-level) qualifications were introduced in 1987 to broaden the curriculum for A-level students by allowing them to take more subjects. The work is of the same standard as an A-level, but the courses have half the content, take half as long to complete and are worth half an A-level. They are usually taken alongside A-levels. Although AS-levels can be taken in most of the subjects offered at A-level, exactly what you can study will depend on your school. The Dearing Report (1996) recommends that AS-levels be renamed Advanced Subsidiary levels and provide an interim accreditation (acknowledgement for work studied) for those students not wishing to complete a full A-level course. The intention is that it would enable students to study more than three subjects at this level, thereby broadening their education.

GNVQs

General National Vocational Qualifications (GNVQs) were introduced in September 1993. They are taken (in broad vocational areas) mainly in full-time education alongside GCSEs, A-levels and NVQs although they can also be studied part-time in colleges. They provide an alternative to academic qualifications for students who want to keep their options open until they decide on a specific career or continue in further education. They are designed to show what students know and what they can do. Testing is by both regular short examinations and periodic assessment of work (projects and assignments), which are completed during the course. Students also learn the key skills required by employers:

- communication
- information technology
- numeracy (called application of numbers).

They also acquire the skills, knowledge and understanding they need for a range of different jobs rather than being trained to do a specific job.

GNVQs can be taken at three levels:

- **the Foundation level GNVQ** is equivalent to four GCSEs at grades D and below and is usually taken as a one-year, full-time course
- **the Intermediate level GNVQ** is equivalent to four to five GCSEs at grades A*–C and is usually taken as a one-year, full-time course
- **the Advanced level GNVQ** is equivalent to two or more A-levels at grades A–E and is usually taken as a two-year, full-time course. Many universities accept Advanced GNVQ (sometimes combined with an A-level) as admission to a wide range of degree courses. It is important to check with admissions tutors which qualifications they will accept and which qualifications most candidates have.

GNVQs are currently available in:

- Art and Design
- Business
- Construction and the Built Environment
- Engineering
- Health and Social Care
- Hospitality and Catering
- Information Technology
- Leisure and Tourism
- Manufacturing
- Science.

Other areas operating as pilots or being planned are:

- Land and Environment
- Media: Communication and Production
- Performing Arts and Entertainment Industries
- Retail and Distributive Services.

Most students who take GNVQs do them as part of a package that includes GNVQs, GCSEs, A-levels or other vocational qualifications. Students who do not finish a full GNVQ qualification may still get certificates for course units they have completed.

Part One GNVQs

In his review of qualifications, Sir Ron Dearing recommended that GNVQs should be brought into Key Stage 4 (age 14–16) to broaden the curriculum and provide students with an understanding of the world of work. Part One GNVQ is intended to be studied over two years and takes up about 20 per cent of curriculum time. It is available at two levels: Foundation Part One is equivalent to two GCSEs at grades D and below, and Intermediate Part One is equivalent to two GCSEs at grades A*–C. They are not yet available in all schools but are being piloted nationwide in some of them in a range of subjects including:

- Art and Design
- Business
- Engineering
- Health and Social Care
- Information Technology
- Leisure and Tourism
- Manufacturing.

It is anticipated that all secondary schools will be able to offer them to 14- to 16-year-olds from September 1999.

NVQs

National Vocational Qualifications (NVQs) are job-specific qualifications. They set the national standard against which your ability to work in any job can be measured. You can choose from over 800 subjects covering almost every area of work. Some NVQs have five levels; others are available only at the lower level: levels 1 and 2 are basic craft, level 3 is technician and levels 4 and 5 are broadly, but not exactly, equivalent to higher education qualifications. It is not necessary to take each level in turn. It is up to you or your employer to decide which level is appropriate. NVQs are open to people of all ages – from students to adults reaching retirement. You can work towards an NVQ at work, at home or at college. You are assessed on what you can do in workplace conditions so there are no examinations.

As a general guide, NVQ level 2 equates to four GCSEs at grades A–C and NVQ level 3 equates to two A-levels.

Many of the qualifications are awarded by City & Guilds, the RSA (Royal Society of Arts) or the Edexcel Foundation.

BTEC awards

These are still available in a variety of occupational areas and provide you with the skills and knowledge to do a real job. The qualifications are nationally recognised and are awarded by the Edexcel Foundation, which was formed in April 1996 to incorporate Business and Technology Education Council (BTEC) and London Examinations. Employers value them because they include hands-on practical experience and help students develop the ability to be proactive and work both independently and with others. They are offered by schools and colleges in England, Wales and Northern Ireland and take between one and two years to complete, depending on the level. Certificates are normally studied part-time and diplomas full-time.

One of the great attractions of the BTEC course programme is that it enables school-leavers with few or no GCSEs to climb the qualification ladder. They can start with a course at a basic level, work their way up and finish by taking a degree.

BTEC First Certificates and Diplomas normally take one year to complete and are on a level with GCSEs (grades A*–C), Intermediate GNVQs and NVQ level 2. They are an initial vocational qualification for those entering work – at 16 years of age or later. There are no formal entry qualifications, although a record of achievement of school work or GCSE passes are very useful.

BTEC National Certificates (NCs) and National Diplomas (NDs) are for students aged 16-plus. They usually take two years to complete and are equivalent to A-levels, Advanced GNVQs and NVQ level 3. Entry qualifications are not specified but it is helpful to have a BTEC First or four GCSEs (A*–C) or NVQ level 2 or an Intermediate GNVQ or relevant work experience.

BTEC Higher National Certificates and Diplomas (HNCs/HNDs) are for students aged 18-plus. They are generally two-year courses and are seen as being on a level with a pass at degree level. People with an HND often move on to the second or third year of a related degree course. Preferable entry requirements are a BTEC National or at least one A-level or an Advanced GNVQ or relevant work experience.

Other qualifications

Students can study towards a variety of other qualifications either at school or college, full- or part-time. These are listed below.

City & Guilds

City & Guilds is one of three major awarding bodies of further education qualifications in England and Wales; Edexcel Foundation and The Royal Society of Arts (RSA) are the other two (the Scottish Qualifications Authority – SQA – provides a similar service in Scotland). It offers a wide selection of nationally recognised vocational qualifications, including NVQs, GNVQs and SVQs (the Scottish equivalent to NVQs). It also offers progression awards, which bridge GNVQs and NVQs in a range of vocational areas from bakery to information technology.

Some 16-year-olds start a job immediately after leaving school and acquire craft or trade skills while working for a company by attending part-time courses at further education colleges. These vocational qualifications are available in a huge range of subjects covering nearly every aspect of working life. They test the detailed knowledge and practical skills required for a particular job. Assessment is by a combination of evidence of work, assignments, projects, oral questioning and written papers.

RSA (Royal Society of Arts)

These courses lead to GNVQs or RSA certificates in vocational areas such as business, finance, information technology, languages, office skills, manufacturing, retailing, wholesaling, warehousing and many more.

International Baccalaureate

This is an academic alternative to A-levels offered by about 30 schools in the UK. The course is broader than the A-level course, covering six subjects over two years. It leads to an international university entry qualification.

Equivalence table

GCSE D-G		Foundation GNVQ	NVQ 1
GCSE A*–C	BTEC First Certificate/ Diploma	Intermediate GNVQ	NVQ 2
A-level	BTEC National Certificate/ Diploma	Advanced GNVQ	NVQ 3
First degree	BTEC Higher National Certificate/Diploma		NVQ 4
Postgraduate			NVQ 5

Further education

The staying-on rate for school-leavers is at its highest ever. The further education (FE) sector is made up of colleges of further education, some higher education colleges offering further education courses, adult education centres and some private further education colleges. They may be called any of the following:

- **further education colleges**, which offer GCSEs, GNVQs, A-levels, BTEC awards, City & Guilds, RSA and many other vocational and non-vocational courses; they may also have degree and HND courses associated with local universities
- **colleges of further and higher education**, which provide a similar range of FE courses to those at further education colleges, degree and HND courses associated with local universities
- **colleges of art and technology**
- **colleges of art and design or schools of art**, which specialise in art and design subjects (for example, media studies, performing arts, communication studies and many different design alternatives such as graphics, furniture and fashion)
- **sixth-form colleges**, which specialise in A-level subjects and some vocational courses (mainly for students aged 16–19)
- **tertiary colleges**, which combine elements of sixth-form colleges and further education colleges in those areas where there is no sixth-form provision
- **colleges of horticulture, agriculture, building, printing, furniture, music, drama**, which are all specialist colleges
- **adult education centres**, which offer courses locally for adults returning to work or seeking special skills in an adult environment (much smaller than colleges)
- **independent further education colleges**, which offer fee-paying rather than free or subsidised courses and attract overseas students.

In 1992, as a result of the Higher and Further Education Act, FE colleges and sixth-form colleges left the control of local authorities and became independent.

Application to FE
Careers libraries in schools and colleges and careers offices have reference copies of prospectuses, but you will need to obtain your own

application form by contacting the college direct, usually at the beginning of the autumn term in year 11. Make sure that both the course and the college suit your requirements before returning the application form (see pages 49–51).

You may apply for more than one course and to more than one college to keep your options open. However, many LEAs do not now pay travel expenses to students who do not attend their nearest college. Check this with your local authority before making any decisions.

Your educational background, interests and abilities, together with your choice of course will all be taken into consideration by the college, and you may be asked to attend for interview.

Although there are no national closing dates for courses, it is best to apply as early as possible – preferably in the autumn term, and certainly no later than the spring term of year 11. If you are applying for a popular course you should apply early in the autumn term before all the places are filled. Your careers adviser can give you information and advice about deadlines for applications to courses in your area.

Why choose FE?

You may want to go on to FE because:

- it provides an adult environment
- colleges provide a social as well as an academic environment: they have sports, social, political and other kinds of clubs and societies, student unions and often a wide ethnic mix
- their GCSE and A-level programmes offer the opportunity to take resits in subjects that are unlikely to be offered in schools with a restricted curriculum
- your local college may offer new subjects that are not available in your school, for example, communication studies, media studies, sociology, computing, engineering, electronics, and so on
- colleges provide a wide range of City & Guilds, BTEC, RSA and NVQ courses in many vocational subjects such as agriculture, horticulture, engineering, business, hospitality, health and community care, art and design, sciences, humanities, media studies, performing arts, and so on
- some colleges have courses leading to degree and HND awards
- attendance can be part-time or full-time to suit your needs.

All these factors mean that there is a mixture of people of varying ages – as there is at work – and many students appreciate and enjoy this adult atmosphere.

The different ways to study at FE level are described below:

- if you are undertaking vocational training through the Youth Credits scheme, or as part of your work-related training as an apprentice, trainee or employee, you can obtain **part-time day-release from work for off-the-job training at college**
- many employed young people study at college by taking **block-release from work** (a block of full-time college attendance such as six or eight weeks). Block-release can be over a one-, two- or three-year period and in some cases can be combined with day-release
- some people take **short full-time courses** of up to four weeks' duration
- if you become unemployed you can attend college voluntarily **on a part-time basis** in order to improve your skills and qualifications. Remember, though, that certain rules and regulations apply if you wish to claim benefit and study at college. Ask at the Jobcentre or Benefits Agency office for details when and if appropriate.

Higher education

Higher education (HE) comprises courses that usually require one or more A-levels or equivalent for entry. There are over 40,000 HE courses in the UK, either at degree or diploma level; they are offered at universities, colleges of higher education and some specialist institutions such as colleges of art, agriculture, drama, and so on. The distinctions between the types of institutions have become increasingly blurred over time. Do not assume that universities are better than colleges. All have strengths and specialist areas.

Degree courses usually take three or four years on a full-time basis to complete. Some take longer if they involve some kind of industrial work experience. For instance, sandwich courses can last four years if a full year is spent in industry between years two and three. Diplomas last for two or three years.

A wide variety of subjects are on offer in higher education, including those that are studied at A-level/Advanced GNVQ level as well as a multitude of new ones. Many courses do not necessarily lead to a qualification for a specific career so further professional training is often required.

The minimum entry requirement for a degree course is two A-levels or equivalent course, and for an HND it is one A-level or equivalent, although normally you should have studied two. Equivalent qualifications are BTEC National awards or Advanced GNVQs. Grades vary according to the course; standard offers are usually printed in prospectuses, either as grades or as points. A-level grades are worth the following points:

- A = 10
- B = 8
- C = 6
- D = 4
- E = 2.

Having completed an HND course, you can progress to a degree course. The proportion of young people going on to higher education has increased from one in eight in 1980 to nearly one in three in 1996. Many students take a year out (gap year) between school and university to travel or do paid or voluntary work. Deferred entry (where students are offered a place at university for the following year) is increasingly being accepted by higher education establishments.

Application to HE

Application is via UCAS (the Universities and Colleges Admissions Service). This is a central agency which handles all the higher education applications for first degrees, Diplomas of Higher Education, HNDs and some university diploma courses. You will be given an application form and a *UCAS Handbook*, usually by your school or college (careers offices also have them). The handbook gives details of the procedure, the deadlines for submitting forms as well as the institution and course codes. UCAS sends a reduced-size copy of your form to your chosen institutions which will then send you their offer decisions via UCAS; these are usually conditional on your examination results.

If you do not have a confirmed place or hold any offers once you have received your examination results, you automatically have the chance to go through the 'Clearing' system during August and September. The system works by putting you in touch with the universities and colleges that still have places that need to be filled and that may ask for lower grades.

It is important that you do not go away on holiday during the period after you have received your examination results. This is because you have to confirm within seven days that you wish to take up your place at your chosen university/college; if you do not, your offer may be withdrawn. If you use the Clearing system you also must be available to talk to someone at the various institutions and attend interviews.

The lowest unemployment rate is still that among graduates. Forty per cent of employers advertising jobs do not specify degree subjects. They are interested in graduates of any discipline who can demonstrate that they can communicate and are willing and able to learn.

Some degree courses are vocational, such as medicine or dentistry. Others, such as English or history, do not lead directly to a specific job but are useful for many different careers; these are still highly rated by a range of employers because they require intellectual qualities.

Art and design applications

Since 1997 art and design course applications have been made via UCAS not ADAR (Art and Design Admissions Registry), which no longer exists as these two systems merged in 1996. There are two entry routes and both have equal status: Route A, and Route B (later applications). Under Route A the application is considered simultaneously by all your choices (up to six) – in the same way as the main UCAS scheme. Route B applications are sent sequentially to each college – up to a maximum of four. An applicant may choose courses from both routes, allowing up to six choices in total, with a maximum of four Route B choices.

Modular courses

These courses enable students to choose a specified number of options (modules) from a range; this system provides choice and flexibility for both students and lecturers. However, it may be difficult to obtain a grant or loan if studying part-time on a modular course, as priority for funding is given to students on full-time courses.

Acceptance of qualifications by HE institutions

It is important to refer to individual prospectuses for the precise entry requirements for a degree course, although most HE institutions recognise equivalent qualifications to A-levels, such as BTEC National awards, Advanced GNVQs or the International Baccalaureate as being suitable entry qualifications. However, many ask for additional qualifications alongside these, for example, either GNVQ units or A- /AS-level passes. A merit or distinction grade in an Advanced GNVQ is also often required – particularly for courses where demand is high. The publication *University and College Entrance – the Official Guide* (UCAS) gives details of the expected entrance qualifications for all UK institutions.

A special database called 'GATE' (GNVQs and Access to Higher Education) provides details of admissions requirements using GNVQs. GATE is accessible through the Qualifications Curriculum Authority (QCA).

Students with Scottish qualifications equivalent to A-levels are accepted at universities and colleges in the whole of the UK.

All institutions accept overseas qualifications. However, there is no hard and fast rule, and applicants should check the acceptability of their qualifications with admissions tutors.

Scotland

This section explains the secondary education system, the various qualifications including the proposed Higher Still, the remit of the newly formed Scottish Qualifications Authority (SQA) and further and higher education in Scotland. Throughout the book for the sake of brevity qualifications are given in terms of the English GCSE, GNVQ and A-/AS-level. The equivalent Scottish qualifications are also relevant.

The secondary education system

In many respects Scotland's education system is different from that of the rest of the UK. Unlike England, Wales and Northern Ireland it does not have a compulsory National Curriculum but instead a curriculum that is based on a broad range of subjects taught throughout primary and secondary education. The decision about what is taught in each school is made by the local authorities and head teachers.

To ensure consistency across Scotland, head teachers and local authorities refer to circulars from the Scottish Office Education and Industry department, guidance from the Scottish Consultative Council on the Curriculum (SCCC), and national guidelines for teachers on curriculum programmes for 5- to 14-year-olds.

Compulsory education begins at the age of five, and the programme last seven years up to the transfer age of 11 or 12. Secondary schooling begins at age 11 or 12 (a year later than the rest of the UK).

In 1997 there were 401 publicly funded Scottish secondary schools; all have a comprehensive (non-selective) intake and 93 per cent offer compulsory education covering four years, from age 11/12 to 16, and two additional years from 16 to 18.

In the first two years of secondary education students take a broad-based curriculum course made up of eight subjects ('subject modes'):

- language and communication
- mathematics
- science
- social and environmental studies
- technology
- creative and aesthetic activities
- physical education
- religious and moral education.

Students can also study a modern foreign language. In practice most schools insist that students take English, mathematics, a modern language and often science too. Science is usually taught as three separate sciences (biology, chemistry, physics) beyond the second year.

At the end of their second year, students choose subjects to study during the following two years; the subjects are chosen from all the modes to ensure a broad and balanced curriculum. At the age of 15/16 students usually take examinations for the Standard Grade (S-grade) of the Scottish Certificate of Education (SCE).

In the fifth and sixth secondary years students can currently opt to study subjects for examinations at the SCE Higher Grade (Highers or H-grade). Not all students are able to complete the Highers they require in one year and may take two years to do so. Those pupils who have already passed the H-grade in the subject concerned can study the Certificate of Sixth Year Studies (CSYS) in the sixth year; students may also take A-levels (occasionally) or SQA National Certificate courses (see page 31). They can study H-grade or CSYS subjects or a combination of both. From the age of 15 to 17 students can carry on studying a wide and balanced range of subjects instead of specialising. See under 'Higher Still' for proposed changes to Scottish education.

Qualifications

- **The S-grade of the SCE** This is suitable for students of all levels of ability and has replaced the Ordinary Grade examination. It is equivalent to the GCSE in England and Wales (grades 1–3 are equivalent to GCSE grades A–C). It is graded on a scale of 1–7, where 1 is the highest.
- **The H-grade of the SCE** Highers are the typical university entrance qualifications in Scotland and are usually taken one year after S-grade (in the fifth year of secondary school) when candidates are aged 17 and over. Highers are the equivalent to A-levels (three to five Highers, grades A–C, are broadly equivalent to two to three A-levels). For most higher education courses, four Highers or three A-levels are required. Students usually take five subjects – to ensure breadth of study – over one or two years, depending on their ability. Highers are due to be replaced by the Higher Still in 1999/2000.

The Certificate of Sixth Year Studies (CSYS)

CSYS is an in-depth study of subjects including a dissertation on one or two subjects. Candidates for CSYS examinations must have a pass in the same subjects at H-grade or equivalent. The CSYS award is graded A–E. Performance in CSYS is taken into account for university entrance in Scotland, and a number of universities elsewhere in the UK recognise suitable performance for admission purposes. It is due to be replaced by the Higher Still in 1999/2000.

General Scottish Vocational Qualifications (GSVQs)

These are vocational alternatives to academic qualifications and are equivalent to GNVQs in England, Wales and Northern Ireland (see page 18). They are offered at three levels: level I, which is a broad introductory qualification; level II, which is a more focused qualification in various occupational areas; and level III, which is a more demanding qualification in all occupational areas covered by GSVQs:

- Arts and Social Sciences
- Business
- Care
- Communication and Media
- Construction
- Design
- Engineering
- Hospitality
- Information Technology
- Land-based Industries
- Leisure and Recreation
- Science
- Technology
- Travel and Tourism.

Scottish Vocational Qualifications (SVQs)
These are equivalent to NVQs (see page 20).

SQA National Certificates, Higher National Certificates and Higher National Diplomas
The principal awarding body for vocational further education in Scotland used to be the Scottish Vocational Education Council (SCOTVEC) – the equivalent to BTEC in England and Wales – but it has now been replaced by the newly formed SQA (see overleaf). Awards are made at non-advanced and advanced levels for a wide range of courses in the technical and business sectors. At the non-advanced level students can take National Certificate courses either full- or part-time. Advanced courses – Higher National Certificate (HNC) and Higher National Diploma (HND) – are available in modular form.

Higher Still
In 1994 the government announced that it would introduce a new unified curriculum and assessment system – Higher Still. From 1999/2000 this new system of courses and qualifications will be introduced into schools and FE colleges for students in the fifth and sixth year of secondary education. The Higher Still will replace the current Highers, CSYS and SQA National Certificate courses and will be offered at five levels.

The Scottish Qualifications Authority (SQA)

A new qualifications body – the SQA – has been set up to replace the SEB (Scottish Examination Board) and SCOTVEC, and will administer the new Higher Still. The SQA is the certificating body for qualifications in the national education and training system in Scotland, the main awarding body in Scotland for qualifications for work and Scotland's accrediting body for SVQs.

Further education

There are 46 further education colleges in Scotland. Forty-three of these are incorporated colleges which are responsible for running their own affairs and are directly funded by the Secretary of State for Scotland. They have a wide range of courses at non-advanced and advanced levels similar to those offered in the rest of the UK. Some offer degrees in their own right or in association with HE institutions. Most courses lead to SQA awards, or to SVQs (which can include modules from SQA awards).

Higher education

Scotland has thirteen universities, and nine higher education colleges which mostly specialise in a narrower area, for example, music and drama, art and architecture. A feature of Scottish higher education is that full-time, first-degree honours courses normally last four years, allowing for both depth and breadth of study. Application is through UCAS in the normal way. Four Highers are required for most courses, although if a course is very popular, five Highers may be asked for. Five Highers with good grades are usually required for the most competitive courses, such as medicine or veterinary surgery. A pass in English – at least at S-grade – is necessary for a large number of courses. For many degrees and diplomas, applicants are expected to offer some evidence of ability in mathematics (minimum Standard grade).

Continuing education (for the whole of the UK)

There are many ways for you to continue your education at a later stage if you missed the opportunity to gain all the necessary qualifications at school. However, you should remember that this is not an easy route. Inevitably, it is harder to study once you have left school and become an adult with commitments.

- **'Access' courses** are available through further education for adults (usually aged 21 or over) who do not have the formal qualifications necessary to enter higher education. Access courses last one or two years (full- or part-time) and either prepare you for entry to a specific course or for a variety of different ones. Course titles may vary so if you specifically want a course to give you access to higher education, it is important to ask course admission tutors for any kind of access or preparatory course for higher education.
- **Adult Residential Colleges** (seven in England and Wales) provide fee-paying full-time courses of varying lengths (depending on the subjects) to help prepare people for higher education.
- If you cannot attend college or university you could do a **home-based course**. These are often now called distance- (by correspondence) or open-learning (flexible attendance) courses. They give you the opportunity to learn independently at a time and pace that suits you. Many colleges offer home-study facilities to students who are unable to attend regular college classes.
- The Open University, the Open College and the Open College of the Arts offer a wide range of **distance-learning courses**.
- **Adult education courses** are offered by LEAs and some university Continuing Education departments. You can choose between attending them during the day or in the evening, and they can be advanced (leading to a qualification) or non-advanced (for interest only).

Your local library is a good source of information about these options. Some have a computer database called TAP (Training Access Points), which gives details of local (and occasionally some national) courses. TAP may also be available in your local college or careers service.

Educational bodies and institutions

- **The Qualifications and Curriculum Authority (QCA)** came into being in October 1997 'to promote coherence in education and training.' It brings together the work of the Schools Curriculum and Assessment Authority (SCAA) and the National Council for Vocational Qualifications (NCVQ). SCAA advised the Secretary of State for Education and Employment on the curriculum for maintained schools, school examinations and assessments; NCVQ was set up by the government in 1986 to introduce the NVQ framework and to ensure that qualifications met particular criteria and were broadly comparable across different sectors. NCVQ also developed and accredited GNVQs. The prime duty of QCA is to advise the Secretary of State for Education and Employment on the school curriculum, pupil assessment and publicly funded qualifications offered in schools, colleges and in the workplace.
- **The Office for Standards in Education (OFSTED)** was established in 1992 and is responsible for the quality and standard of education in schools. Inspectors regularly visit schools and colleges, inspect them and provide a written report for parents. This inspection has become part of the guarantee of quality, as promised in the Parents' Charter. Although OFSTED works closely with the Department for Education and Employment (DfEE), its inspection team is independent and not part of an LEA; it includes at least one person who does not work in education. The members of this team are expected to seek parents' views when making the report. The inspection standards are set by Her Majesty's Inspectors (HMI).
- **GMS (Grant-maintained schools)** – some schools have chosen to become self-governing and receive funding directly from central government instead of through LEAs. They generally received more funding than LEA-controlled schools to reflect their additional responsibilities. However, the government is likely to abolish grant-maintained status and create three new categories of school: community, aided and foundation.

The Careers Service

Following a change in legislation, the duty of providing careers services transferred from LEAs to the Secretary of State in 1994. Subsequently, the DfEE awarded contracts to careers companies to provide a careers information, guidance and placing service to young people.

The White Paper *Competitiveness: Helping Business to Win* (May 1994) stated that young people are now entitled to careers advice throughout their time at school, and if they go to college until they are 18. Schools invariably have a careers library and a teacher responsible for advising on opportunities in employment, education and training. Your local careers service company can help you with your career choices by giving you expert information, advice and guidance at key stages in your life:

- when you start thinking about which subjects to choose for GCSE and other examinations
- when you are deciding which type of qualification you want to aim for or which course to take
- when you are choosing which career route to take
- when your examination results are not what you expected
- when you are considering further training or looking for a job.

Careers advisers can also give you practical help and support, for instance in arranging interviews and preparing for them and completing application forms for education, training or employment. Careers service companies work closely with schools and colleges, usually for students in at least year 9 onwards (aged 13/14), so ask your careers teacher for information (for example, who is your careers adviser? when is he or she in school? how and when can you have an interview? and so on). Your parents are entitled to be invited to your careers interview (usually in year 11 when you are aged 15/16) where you may discuss the various career opportunities open to you. They are also entitled to be sent a copy of the report of that interview and of the action plan to be carried out. Careers service companies have careers offices in many towns (the telephone number is usually under 'Careers' in the telephone directory).

Government initiatives

There have been many new government initiatives for education and training since 1988. Although the initiatives are national (unless otherwise stated), arrangements for delivery in Wales and Scotland may be slightly different from those in England.

National Targets for Education and Training

The revolution in education and training, brought about in the 1990s by the introduction of charters, NVQs and greater access to higher education, was continued when the Confederation of British Industry (CBI) persuaded the government to adopt what we now call The National Targets for Education and Training (NTETs). These state what the UK will need from its workforce in order to maintain and improve its competitiveness in the twenty-first century; they also provide a target level of qualifications that the UK's workforce should have by the year 2000. They have been set as a guarantee of standards to reach for foundation and lifetime learning but are subject to review and may change, particularly as a result of the government's Investing in Young People strategy. The current targets are listed below.

Foundation learning

- By the age of 19, 85 per cent of young people in the UK are to achieve five GCSEs at grade C or above, an Intermediate GNVQ or a full NVQ level 2.
- Seventy five per cent of young people are to achieve NVQ level 2 competence in communication, numeracy and information technology by age 19; and 35 per cent are to achieve NVQ level 3 competence in these skills by age 21.
- By age 21, 60 per cent of young people are to achieve two A-levels, an Advanced GNVQ or a full NVQ level 3.

The percentage of 19-year-olds achieving the first target had reached 63 per cent in 1995 and the percentage of 21-year-olds achieving the third target had reached 44 per cent. This means that there is still some considerable way to go before the present levels of achievement of a large number of students are raised.

Lifetime learning

- Sixty per cent of the workforce should be qualified to NVQ level 3, Advanced GNVQ level or have two A-levels.
- Thirty per cent of the workforce should have a vocational, professional, management or academic qualification at NVQ level 4 or above.

- Seventy per cent of all organisations employing 200 or more employees, and 35 per cent of those employing 50 or more should be in a position to be recognised as Investors in People. This is an award that employers can aim for; it demonstrates their commitment to training their staff.

Figures for 1995 show that about 40 per cent of the workforce in the UK had achieved NVQ level 3 or equivalent and just over 20 per cent had achieved NVQ level 4 or equivalent.

The National Record of Achievement (NRA)

This was introduced in 1991 to record individual student achievement and planning of future learning. It is made up of a number of standard sheets in a folder, covering personal details, qualifications, achievements and experiences, education and employment history and an individual action plan. Exactly what you put on these sheets is up to you, although you should discuss it with a teacher, adviser, college tutor or work supervisor.

The commitment of schools and colleges to the NRA is variable, and not many employers know much about it. Dearing (1996) recommended that it should be restructured and relaunched. He believes it should be used as a tool throughout a lifetime of learning, not just for use in job applications and interviews but also as a means of encouraging people to take responsibility for their own learning.

Traineeships for young people

Dearing (1996) recommended that Youth Training (YT) be relaunched as a system of National Traineeships providing progression to Modern Apprenticeships (see overleaf) and a work-based route to qualifications and training. As of September 1997, National Traineeships offer a broad and flexible learning programme for young people aged 16–19, helping them to achieve NVQ level 2 and acquire competence in the key skills of communication, numeracy (application of numbers) and information technology. Trainees are paid an allowance or a wage if employed. National Traineeships are designed by National or Industrial Training Organisations (NTOS/ITOs) and Training and Enterprise Councils (TECs) and delivered in partnership with further education providers (for example, colleges). Trainees usually attend college on a day-release basis to gain the necessary qualifications; other training is on-the-job. The length of traineeship depends on a trainee's ability and the area of work.

Youth Credits

These are vouchers for training (often in the form of credit cards) and are known by different local names all over England. They are available to all 16- and 17-year-olds leaving full-time education in England and are used to buy training which leads to a recognised qualification such as an NVQ. They are not a loan – there is nothing to repay. They were introduced to give students a greater sense of ownership of their training and of being more involved in planning their future. Each Youth Credit has a financial value which varies according to the type and duration of the training you undertake and your individual needs. You can present it to an employer or training provider in exchange for training to recognised qualifications. Youth Credits are currently on offer from TECs throughout England and are available from your local careers office. The work-based vocational training is usually off-the-job, involving attendance at an FE college. Arrangements for Youth Credits in Wales and Scotland are slightly different from those in England. More information is available from TECs in Wales and from Local Enterprise Companies (LECs) in Scotland.

It is likely that Youth Credits will be phased out gradually and incorporated into the learning entitlement (see below).

Learning entitlement for young people

As part of the government's Investing in Young People strategy, as of January 1998 young people in year 11 (age 15/16) in England receive a 'learning entitlement' (in the form of a 'Learning Card') which enables them to enter education up to the age of 18. This learning will be suitable for their needs and will enable them to achieve the highest qualification they can reach (at least to the minimum of NVQ level 2). Prior to leaving compulsory education, young people will receive up to two weeks' work experience with an employer and impartial advice, guidance and information (from careers advisers) to help them choose their preferred method of learning or training.

Modern Apprenticeships

These were launched nationally in 1995 to attract young people (mainly 16- and 17-year-olds) to a work-based route to qualifications, training and employment. They are different from traditional apprenticeships, in that the emphasis is not on time-serving and they are not restricted to certain industries. Employers also require their employees to be adaptable, multi-skilled and trained to higher levels than they have been previously.

The aim of Modern Apprenticeships is to improve the supply of technical, craft and junior management skills at NVQ level 3 or above through work-based training. So they are for people with the ability to gain high-level qualifications and skills.

They are not just for occupations with a tradition of apprenticeships but are also available for all businesses thought to be able to benefit from them. Modern Apprenticeships help trainees to develop a wide range of skills to prepare them for a career, including team-working and problem-solving. Other skills, such as learning a foreign language, may also be on offer in certain areas of industry. The training is in the skills specifically wanted by the employer. Modern Apprenticeships are demanding and need commitment from all those involved. A training agreement between the young person and the employer sets out what is expected from both parties.

Nearly every apprentice on this scheme is employed and paid a wage; they are not trainees on an allowance. Modern Apprenticeships are not time-bound. How long you take to complete one depends upon your individual needs and the progress you make.

By the end of March 1996 over 25,000 young people in England and Wales had started on Modern Apprenticeships.

Further information

BTEC (Edexcel), Edexcel Foundation
City & Guilds
COIC
CRAC
Future Prospects
QCA Customer Services
Qualifications and Skills Strategy Division of the Scottish Office, Education and Industry Department
RSA Examinations Board
Scottish Qualifications Authority

Books and leaflets

Copies of the charters can be obtained from the DfEE Publications Department.

Information on the National Curriculum and on the Dearing Report can be obtained from QCA.

For information about the opportunities available in your area, students should contact their careers teacher, local careers office or local TEC. Students in Scotland should approach their local LEC. Addresses can be found in the telephone book.

The Complete Parents' Guide to Higher Education. 1996. Trotman in association with UCAS
Entrance Guide to Higher Education in Scotland. 1997. COSHEP
Framework for Inspection. OFSTED
Guide to Student Support Arrangements (annual). The Student Awards Agency for Scotland
School Inspection: Understanding the New System. OFSTED
Student Grants and Loans – A Brief Guide for Higher Education Students (annual). DfEE, available from schools or LEAs
University and College Entrance – the Official Guide (annual). UCAS

Chapter 2

Preparing yourself for a career

Throughout your school life you will have to make a number of important decisions. The major choices are:

- **in year 9 (aged 13)**: which GCSE/GNVQ subjects to choose
- **in year 11 (aged 15)**: which A-levels, AS-levels or Advanced GNVQs to choose if you decide to study after year 11.

Before you choose your subjects you should find out which ones are available in your school and write down which ones you like and/or are good at.

Subject choice in year 9

When you are deciding which GCSE or GNVQ subjects to do you should choose a mixture of science, arts and practical subjects (in addition to the compulsory core subjects, see page 15). By doing this you will leave your options open when you are choosing courses and careers later in life. To make sure that your choice is balanced you might find it helpful to arrange all the possible subjects under different group headings then choose one or two from each category (your school may group subjects differently or have more subjects on offer), for example:

- **humanities** – history, geography, religious education, modern foreign language
- **sciences** – physics, chemistry, biology, zoology
- **practical** – home economics, design and technology
- **business** – business studies, typing, economics, computer studies
- **arts** – art and design, music, dance, drama, media studies.

Note that some higher education institutions do not accept certain practical GCSEs and A-levels as academic qualifications, so make sure that the majority of your subjects are considered to be academic.

Below is a list of questions to ask yourself before you choose your subjects.

Which subjects motivate you most? List your subjects in order of preference. What are your hobbies or interests? Are they associated with any subject? For example, you might decide to do music GCSE because you are good at and enjoy playing a musical instrument.

What are you particularly good at? In which subjects do you get good marks? Where do you think your strengths lie? Think about yourself honestly and then ask other people – such as your teachers – for their opinion.

What are your options? Although some subjects are compulsory (see page 15 for National Curriculum subjects), others are optional. Not all schools offer all subjects. What is available in your school? Are you able to do GNVQs as an alternative to or in addition to GCSEs? Is the school willing and able to be flexible enough to allow you to study the subjects of your choice? If not, are there any alternatives you could consider, such as other subjects or even moving to another school?

What subjects do you need to study? If you have a career in mind already, do you know what the necessary entry qualifications are? If not, turn to the Careers guide in Part 2 of this book to do some research. Does your school offer a GNVQ that is related to your chosen career? Ask your teachers if you do not know. If you are interested in a broad career area look at the Careers guide to find out which the useful or compulsory subjects are. If you do not have a specific career in mind you should keep your options open by studying as broad a range of subjects as possible.

Remember that you will be studying your chosen subjects for at least two years, and you will be more motivated and more interested in learning if you enjoy what you are studying.

Careers – what to do now (Year 9)

- **Begin a careers file** (and keep it throughout your school life) – follow the example shown below and jot down any ideas you have. Fill it in as and when you have the information (some of which can be found in the Careers guide in Part 2 of this book). Remember that your ideas may change.
- Find out where your **school careers library** is, what is in it and when you can use it for researching your career ideas.

Example careers file

Career idea: Civil engineering (CLCI: UN)

Related/alternative areas: surveyor; technician (surveying or engineering)

Reasons for this choice: I like the practical aspect of science subjects

Qualifications: GCSEs in mathematics, English, physics are preferable; mathematics and physics plus one other subject at A-level; engineering degree

Training: Four years' higher education, including work experience, plus continuous professional development

Questions to consider: How do I feel about another four years of study after A-levels or Advanced GNVQs? Do I want to work in a predominantly male environment? Have I got the self-discipline for the academic side of the work? Do I have the right personality – am I analytical, a good communicator, practical, resilient, good at solving problems?

What do I think I would like about this career?: The varied opportunities, including work abroad; the mixture of working both on site and in the office

What might I not like so much?: Being away from home for periods of time; being in a predominantly male environment.

Subject choice in year 11

In year 11 the process for choosing which subjects to study during the next two years is the same as that for choosing your GCSE/GNVQ subjects. You should consider:

- which subjects you may require for a future career (if you have career ideas)
- which subjects motivate you most
- how likely you are to succeed in a particular subject.

You must also decide which type of qualifications you need to have. Many schools and colleges offer qualifications other than A-levels, such as AS-levels, Advanced GNVQs and BTEC awards.

If you are interested in a particular career area and both A-levels and Advanced GNVQs, for example, are acceptable, consider:

- **what your best method of learning is**. Academic courses (A/AS-levels) are usually taught through lectures and culminate in a final examination; vocational courses (Advanced GNVQs/BTEC awards), on the other hand, are taught in a more practical way, usually through continuous assessment, with projects and assignments. You may be better at doing course work than sitting examinations, or *vice versa*
- **what type of training you want to do**. Do you wish to study courses that do not train you for a specific job but which give you skills and knowledge for various future careers (A/AS-levels) or do you wish to study courses that are directly relevant to the world of work or to a specific job area (advanced GNVQs or BTEC awards). Both types of qualification enable you to go on to higher education.

Should you specialise?

Your choice of subjects in year 11 narrows future career options because you are choosing fewer of them so it is important that you are fully informed about the implications of the various choices.

Most students tend to choose either arts or science subjects, although a mixture is more common than it was in the past. Specialisation is appropriate only if you are convinced you know which career you want to follow or if you are going on to do a higher education course that requires certain subjects. However, many degree courses do not require specific A-levels (see below). Remember that by combining AS-levels with A-levels you can take more subjects and gain a greater breadth of study.

Science combinations

If you take three rather than two science A-levels you will be able to choose from a wider selection of careers. The most common combinations are:

- mathematics, physics and chemistry *or*
- physics, chemistry and biology.

If you select mathematics, physics and history A-levels, for example, you will not be able to follow any careers using chemistry. Alternatively, if you study chemistry, art and sociology you will be able to follow a wide range of careers but you may not be able to go straight to university to do a science degree course without first doing a foundation science course. The combination of biology with chemistry is good for a wide range of careers, such as pharmacology, bacteriology, and in food industries. The combination of mathematics, physics and chemistry opens up a wide range of possible degree courses and careers, including those in the fields of business and commerce. Students with science A-levels are sought after for many professional careers.

Arts and humanities

The term 'Arts and humanities' covers a wide range of subjects, including English, history, French and geography; a combination of any of these at A-level will lead to a wide range of degree courses and careers. In fact, very few institutions require specific A-level subjects for humanities degrees. However, if you want to study a foreign language at higher education level you will need to have studied at least one foreign language at A-level.

A-levels for specific degree courses

Many degree courses, such as business studies, law, computer studies, psychology, accountancy, statistics, archaeology or economics do not require an A-level pass in the same subject. However, English, maths, chemistry, physics and modern foreign languages are usually compulsory A-levels for degree courses in these subjects.

Remember that information dates rapidly. Check in *University and College Entrance – the Official Guide* (UCAS), which A-levels are required for the degree course in which you are interested.

Careers – what to do now:

- **Begin a careers file** (if you have not started one already) and note down any ideas you have (see example opposite). Think about the reasons for and against your career choices. Your work experience may give you more information. Refer to the careers guide in Part 2 and ask yourself if you can imagine doing any of the jobs.
- **Write down your list of resources**, i.e. the names of people who can help you (careers teacher, teachers, careers adviser, family, friends) and the names of useful books and software (see pages 288–92)
- **Start your research**: talk to students in the years above you and at college; talk to people who are doing jobs that interest you (why did they choose what they are doing? what is good/not so good about what they are doing?); familiarise yourself with the resources in your careers library; discuss any ideas you have with your family, careers teacher and careers adviser; list what information you still need, such as entry qualifications or training details
- **Note what you need to do when,** for example, with respect to college, sixth-form, training or job applications; college open days; and careers interviews
- **Consider more than one career idea** (refer to Chapter 3).

Which route should I take at the end of year 11 and (if applicable) year 13?

At the end of year 11, your options are:

- **to continue with your study** (at school or college) – the majority of young people choose this option
- **to go into training** (traditional apprenticeship, National Traineeship, Modern Apprenticeship)
- **to get a job** (with or without training).

At the end of year 13, you are faced with additional options (in theory you can do these at the end of year 11 but most organisations prefer you to be older):

Example careers file

Career idea: Accounting technician (CLCI: NAB)

Related/alternative areas: banking; accountancy

Reasons for this choice: I enjoyed my work experience in an accounts office

Qualifications: English and maths GCSEs (grades A–C) are preferable

Training: Via day-release, part-time study, evening classes, distance-learning or on-the-job

Questions to consider: Would I cope with studying part-time as well as working? Do I want to work in an office? Do I want to travel to clients' premises? Which area of accountancy am I interested in? Do I have the right personality – am I accurate and neat in my work; a team worker; able to work on my own initiative; organised; willing to carry out meticulous, routine work (for example, checking records); a good communicator?

What do I think I would like about this career?: Good promotion prospects; studying for professional qualifications; working with figures and computers

What might I not like so much?: Talking to clients.

- **to do voluntary work**
- **to study or work abroad**.

Below are profiles of the routes other young people took.

Sam

I decided to stay on at school to do A-levels – French, biology and chemistry – since I had been at the same school since year 7 and had enjoyed it. It seemed natural to stay on at my school rather than go to college, particularly as I knew all the teachers.

Sixth-form life has helped me develop academically and has given me many opportunities to improve my communication and leadership skills.

I thought A-levels would be easier than they are, given that I had performed well in my GCSEs. They require a much higher level of understanding, and you need to be very well organised and able to work on your own. Although the work is very intense at times, the atmosphere is friendly here, and I've got quite a bit of freedom as a sixth-former.

I am looking forward to pursuing my chosen career in medicine.

Sam wanted to remain in a familiar environment so staying on at his school in the sixth-form was the choice for him. He knew he wanted a career in medicine and so sensibly decided that two science A-levels would give him a stronger scientific foundation than an Advanced GNVQ in Health and Social Care. His A-level subjects will enable him to choose from a variety of healthcare or nursing careers (to be a doctor, his A-level subjects should ideally be chemistry plus two others from biology, physics or maths). As he is finding A-levels intensive he needs to consider carefully whether he has the stamina to take him through the years of study and training for a medical career.

Vidma

When I finished my GCSEs I had three options: to stay on at school, find a job or go to college. I couldn't find a suitable job and I wasn't keen to return to school but still wanted to get some more qualifications. So I decided to do an Advanced GNVQ in Engineering (equivalent to two A-levels) at the local college. The course is excellent. As it is so practical, it suits me better than a purely academic course. I can also go out on placements (to employers), which enable me to put into practice what I am learning. Being treated like an adult has been good and has, I think, helped to prepare me for work. When I finish the course I could either consider further study (perhaps an HND) or try to get a job.

Qualifications are important to Vidma. She chose an Advanced GNVQ rather than A-levels because she recognised that she learns better if the course has a more practical content. She also found that she is interested in engineering, having spent her year 10 work experience with a local engineering firm. An HND would give her a better chance of progressing in an engineering career than going straight into a job with an Advanced GNVQ, and she may be able to find a company that will both employ her and sponsor her study.

Stefan

I prefer to be outdoors rather than in a classroom so when I heard about a training scheme that involves four days out on placement at a countryside park and one day in college I decided that should be the next step for me. I spend my days outside with an estate worker, helping to mend and erect all kinds of fences, learning stonewalling, maintaining the hedgerows and learning all the different countryside skills. At college I learn more skills which will help me achieve my NVQ level 2 in Agricultural Estate Maintenance. When the course ends I hope to get a job as an assistant estate worker and maybe work towards an NVQ level 3.

Stefan learns best through practical experience and so a course where he can immediately put into practice what he learns in the classroom is ideal for him. Gaining qualifications and work experience at the same time means he is making himself more employable because employers have clear evidence of his abilities and skills.

Now ask yourself the following questions:

- what is my preferred way of learning?
- do I want to gain qualifications and work experience at the same time?
- is any route for my chosen career preferred by employers?
- am I sure I have chosen the subjects I need?
- am I anxious to start work or do I want to gain more qualifications first?

Discuss the answers to these questions with your teachers, family and careers adviser before deciding on the best route to your career.

College or school?

If you have decided to continue studying full time, you may now be faced with yet another choice: is school or college best for me? Your decision will depend on which you think provides the best learning environment for you and on factual information, such as what each offers in terms of courses. So first of all think about:

- **your time at school** – what was good about it? what could have been better?
- **whether you want to stay in a familiar environment or prefer to go somewhere different** – for what reasons? What makes one environment better for you than another?
- **what each environment can give you** – consider who your peers and teachers will be, what facilities – for example, library, sports, drama – are available, how your future career needs may be met, and so on.

Then, before you make up your mind obtain more information:

- **look at school and college brochures/prospectuses to find out exactly what the courses are** – does your favoured environment offer the course that interests you?
- **visit your local college and imagine yourself in that environment** – what might it be like?
- **go into your school's sixth-form area and again imagine yourself in that environment** – what might it be like?
- **talk to the teachers at your school and the college lecturers** – what will the teaching be like? What will be expected of you in terms of commitment to the subject/course? How many students were successful the previous year? What happened to the ones who did not complete the course?
- **talk to some college and sixth-form students** – ask them about the benefits of their environment? what do they particularly enjoy?

You may discover that the course you want to study is offered in only one place. This may not matter, but, equally, it may mean that you have to study in a place that you feel will not suit you (it might be too big or too small or too near or too far from home, for example). If this is the case you should consider what steps you might take to help you to fit into that environment. Think about how you might be able to motivate yourself to study there. For example, you could focus on your reasons for choosing the course and what you will get from its successful completion. Alternatively, you may find that the course you want to do is offered in more than one place, so consider which environment might suit you best. Based on the answers you received to the above questions, make your choice.

Should I have a gap year at the end of year 13?

Many students take a year out before continuing with study at a higher education level. This is commonly known as a 'gap year'. During this year you could do a temporary job, then travel or combine the two by doing voluntary work abroad. Voluntary work not only helps others but is also a good way of gaining work experience; in fact, it can be very useful experience for some careers, such as social work. It also looks impressive on a CV.

Things to remember

- Remember that **you should not make any decisions based on what your friend wants to do**. There is no guarantee that you will remain good friends with someone in the future so do not choose a subject just to be with him or her. You could be stuck doing something that does not interest you. Remember you can be with your friends outside of lessons and you will probably make new ones as well.
- **How well you know yourself will help you to make decisions**. Many self-awareness guides and software programs are available (see pages 288–92 for details). These ask you questions to help you find out more about yourself, for example, about your likes and dislikes, what you are looking for in a career, what you are good at, and so on. You should be absolutely honest with yourself – for instance, although you might like and be good at science and think a career as a veterinary surgeon is for you, you might not be able to stand the sight of blood, in which case you may need to think again. Ask your careers teacher what is on offer in your school.
- **Ask as many questions as you can**. The more information you can gather before you make a decision, the more likely you are to make the right one. Speak to your careers teacher, careers adviser, family, people doing jobs you are interested in and students studying the subjects you are considering.
- If you are still unsure about which subjects to choose, **aim to keep your options open**. Choose a broad range of subjects. It is best to have a balance of arts and sciences if you are unsure so that you have a grounding for either area. In addition, try to gain as many

qualifications as possible. The more qualified you are, the more opportunities you will have.

- **Make sure you have a contingency plan**. If you are prevented from pursuing your first career choice – due to bad health or insufficient or inappropriate qualifications, for example – it helps if you have already thought of an alternative. It may also be that your ideas alter as you develop and change.

- **It is never too late to change course**. If, later on – in year 11 or even after you have left school – you find that you need to study different subjects for your chosen career, it might be possible to do so either in year 12 or at college. Transferring from one higher education course to another is also easier now than it was in the past. Students who lack the required qualifications to undertake a science or engineering degree course can take a science/engineering foundation course first.

- **Refer to relevant sections in this book for more information**. If you want to know more about further or higher education, see pages 23–28 and 32; also read the Careers guide in Part 2. You will come across information to help you make decisions and might find some ideas about careers that you had not thought of.

- **Have you got what it takes**? Some careers have strict health and physical requirements – do you fit them? Others require lengthy and intensive training – have you got the stamina? Be honest with yourself. Having the right personality for the job can be as important as having the correct qualifications.

- Above all, stay calm. **Help is always available** from teachers, careers advisers, family, friends and the many books and software programs in your careers library or public library.

Work-related transferable skills

You should be aware that it is highly likely that you will have more than one career during your working life. This is one reason why the emphasis in the jobs market is increasingly on transferable skills.

The nature of the jobs market has changed dramatically over the last few years: secure, permanent, full-time jobs for life are decreasing, and part-time, contract and flexible work is becoming more common. According to the Institute of Management and Manpower, almost nine out of ten employers now use part-time and temporary workers. A large proportion (70 per cent) of companies are contracting out non-core operations (peripheral work). There are far fewer traditional industries, and new technology has changed the working lives of millions of people. The effect of all this is that more people are being made redundant, changing jobs more frequently and are experiencing at least one period of unemployment in their lifetime. During their working life it is expected that most people will change their jobs at least seven times, re-train at five-year intervals to be employable and retire earlier.

It is important that you continue to add to your skills and qualifications throughout your working life so that you can adapt to the demands of the ever-changing jobs market. Although assessing the sorts of skills needed now and over the next few years is not easy, it is possible to look at how the factors influencing skill requirements are changing and how this is affecting the demand for various skills.

Technical and industrial change has meant a shift towards higher-calibre jobs and a broader range and higher level of skills being required in most jobs. Overall demand for blue collar, manual occupations is declining and an increasingly wide range of general work skills are being asked for in many jobs.

Employers have responded to these changes by seeking to attract people with good qualifications and transferable skills. These are general work-related skills, such as:

- the ability to communicate well
- interpersonal skills
- leadership ability
- the ability to work well in a team
- problem-solving skills
- computer literacy
- numeracy
- time management skills
- business awareness.

The GNVQ qualification (see page 18) is intended to help students develop some of these skills – particularly communication, computer literacy and numeracy – and other abilities, such as planning, information handling and evaluation of their own work. Employees who have such skills are highly valued because they are seen to be flexible in what they can do and able to be effective in the workplace. Employers also look for the development of similar skills to these among A-level students and graduates. You will be taught some of these at school but you can practise others during your time at school, college, university or at home by doing some or all of the following:

- working and cooperating with other people
- being supportive of others
- managing your time effectively (do you get your assignments in on time? do you plan your work schedule?)
- being interested in what is happening in the outside world.

Employers are interested in any experience, achievements and commitments students can exhibit beyond their main studies, for example, voluntary work and being part of the girl guides/scouts or a choir and so on. These demonstrate personal and social development as well as academic attainments. Many employers also consider a good standard of communication in a foreign language to be an advantage.

Quotes from employers

A good qualification is a valuable start to a career. Also important is a high level of personal skills including the ability to communicate and liaise effectively and to appreciate different perspectives. We seek people who can achieve excellent results through close and supportive interaction with others. (Director of Human Resources, Nuclear Electric).

We find that A-level grades tell us a lot about an individual's intelligence, but the style and quality of presentation of both their covering letter and CV will determine whether they make the initial 'possibles' or disappear in the 'rejects' pile. Candidates then obviously have to live up to the expectations we have of them from their CV and letter! This is where personality, clarity of thought and the ability to sell themselves is crucial. (Director of Human Resources, St Quintin Chartered Surveyors).

We want people who are flexible and willing to broaden their horizons by working in different areas of the business. This approach allows for continuous professional development as well as leading to corporate effectiveness. (Human Resource Services, Kodak Ltd).

We are looking for high calibre people who are flexible, adaptable and able to drive through change. We require graduates who are resilient, assertive, people-oriented and committed to personal development. (Post Office Group).

Chapter 3

What if...?

It is useful to have a good idea of what you could do or to whom you could turn, should your plans not work out the way you had hoped. However, remember when making your decisions initially, you should not think that there are any right or wrong decisions, only different learning experiences. Believing that any learning – no matter what it is – is never wasted means that you should always find some benefit in past experiences. For example, finding out what you do not like can be just as valuable as discovering what you do like.

Below is advice – in the form of questions and answers – about what to do if your circumstances change or when new possibilities or problems arise.

What if...

- **I change my mind about the subjects or course I have chosen to study once I have started**? First of all, you should think about why you do not like what you are doing. Perhaps it is simply because it is new and you need some time to get used to it. However, if you have given yourself time to adjust and are still unhappy, ask your school teachers or college lecturers whether you can change subjects or course. Think about whether it is the whole course you are unhappy about or just one subject. Ask to see a careers adviser to discuss your options.
- **I decide I do not want to follow the career I thought I did**? Ask yourself what has caused you to change your mind. Have you learnt something new about yourself that may help in any future career decisions? Are there other jobs in the same career area that appeal to you? Ask to see a careers adviser to discuss your options and any new ideas you may have. It is important to ensure that you are studying the appropriate subjects and that you are able to take the relevant route into a future career.

- **I have to change course because my family moves from the area**? Seek advice from your school or college and careers service. The careers service will be able to put you in touch with the one in your new area so you can obtain information about education, training and employment opportunities there.

- **I cannot do the course or subject I want to do**? There may be a number of reasons for this: your circumstances – moving house or changing schools – may have changed; you might not have the grades you need; the course or subject you want to study might not be available in your area; the timetable might not accommodate what you want to study; or you might have an injury or illness. In many cases, it may be possible to consider different courses or subjects or to look at the possibility of studying somewhere else. You could also resit your examinations to improve your grades. Ask for advice from your careers teacher and careers adviser and talk through your options with your family. A change of circumstance may give you the chance to take some time out to rethink your goals and consider other options. Alternatives may include different types of work within the same career area, different routes to a career or a completely different career choice.

- **I cannot cope with the work or the study**? The important thing is to talk to someone (your family, teachers, employer) about this as soon as you can. Once these people know you are having difficulties they can begin to help you. It may be that you need extra tuition or training or that you need to reconsider all your options, including changing courses.

- **I start an arts degree and want to convert to a science degree**? If you decide you want to do a science degree and do not have the necessary A-level subjects you could do one of the many conversion/foundation/introductory science and engineering courses. If it is too late in the year to start a new course immediately and you have to wait until the following academic year you can use this time not only to re-evaluate your career choice but also to travel, earn money in preparation for the years of study or to do voluntary work.

Shelagh

Shelagh had always wanted to work with animals. She spent some time doing work experience in a veterinary practice and took science A-levels as the first step on the road to becoming a veterinary surgeon. However, after completing her A-levels she realised she did not want to carry on studying for a further five to six years. She felt she needed a break from study but still wanted to follow a career with animals. She turned to her careers adviser, who suggested other jobs within the same area: animal technician, veterinary nurse, animal welfare assistant. From her work experience in the veterinary practice she knew what the job of a veterinary nurse entailed but had never really considered it as a career.

She has now been working as a veterinary nurse for over a year: 'I assist the vet in the operating theatre and am even allowed to carry out some minor surgery, which I really enjoy. I am still studying towards my vet nursing exams but only have to go to college one day a week, which suits me. I may one day apply to vet school but I am quite happy doing this job at the moment.'

Fitness for work

Some medical conditions and disabilities may affect a person's ability to carry out some jobs: for example, for certain jobs – ones in which employees come into contact with allergens – people with asthma should seek a medical opinion; and an epileptic experiencing fits should not have a job which involves climbing ladders. However, the Disability Discrimination Act of 1995 places a duty on employers to consider and make adjustments, where reasonable, to the workplace and/or to the employment arrangements to overcome disadvantages encountered by disabled people.

Few conditions prevent people from doing any kind of work at all, and many employers have policies that do not discriminate against people with disabilities. However, some employers consider that the risks involved in employing these people are too great and do not take them on. The Disability Discrimination Act acknowledges the difficulties that people with disabilities face; it places a duty on employers not to discriminate against them without justification and advises employers to have policies covering disability matters.

If you have a disability or medical condition that you think may cause you difficulties in gaining employment, it is important to know the exact physical and intellectual demands of the job. Are you able to carry out the essential tasks? Is there anything ('reasonable adjustment') the employer can do to help you carry out your work? You should also consider any risk to yourself, or to other people, while you are doing the job; for example, is your eyesight adequate for a job that involves driving? Do you have a skin complaint which may be aggravated by certain chemicals (for example, those used in hair-dressing)? If you are concerned, ask for advice from the appropriate professional body for the industry before you decide on subjects, courses and your career.

Further information

Contact your local Employment Service PACT (Placing Assessment and Counselling Team) through your Jobcentre (the Disablement Advisory Service in Northern Ireland).

Refer to the Disability Discrimination Act 1995 (London: The Stationery Office). Basic guidelines can be obtained free of charge from Disability on the Agenda.

Contact the Society of Occupational Medicine.

Part 2

Careers guide

Careers guide

The purpose of the careers guide is to stimulate interest in different career areas and give the reader an idea of what they involve (all the main career areas are dealt with).

How to use the guide

A brief description of the career area is given, together with some sample job titles, opportunities, entry and training details and recommended subjects to study. In addition, a paragraph – 'Other factors to consider' – describes the kind of personal qualities and skills needed for each job. So you can match the type of person you are with a possible career, taking into account your personality, academic strengths, enthusiasms and interests.

If you do not know what you want to do and need some career ideas, use the guide as an 'ideas generator'. The careers are grouped together in broad areas so that you can start by looking at a general field that you think looks appealing. For example, you might know that the financial world interests you but are unsure what the specific jobs are. The 'Finance' section describes accountancy, actuarial work, banking and building society work, insurance and stock broking.

Another way to find out what might interest you is to think about which subjects you are good at and enjoy. Below is a list of the most common school subjects and suggested careers that they lead to. As an example, if you are good at biology you would look it up in the list below and find that you could follow a career in: environmental work, nursing, teaching, healthcare, agriculture, horticulture, medicine, physiotherapy or veterinary science. You can then look up each career in the index to find which career area they come under and then go to the careers guide to find out more about each one.

Many of the subjects need to be combined with others, for example, biology should be studied in conjunction with chemistry for a career in medicine, and mathematics should be studied alongside physics for a career in engineering. For many of the careers listed below you will also need to do additional study and training, and gain experience after you have completed your A-levels or degree.

The subjects listed are also not necessarily an essential requirement for the career suggested but are considered to be useful and relevant.

- **Art**: architecture; advertising; craft work; fashion design; fine art; graphic design; illustration; media; photography; product design; publishing; teaching
- **Biology**: environmental work (preferably with geography and chemistry); nursing; teaching; healthcare; (with chemistry) agriculture, horticulture, medicine, physiotherapy and veterinary science
- **Botany**: agricultural and medical research; the civil service; conservation; forestry, horticulture; pharmaceutical and chemical industries; teaching
- **Chemistry**: biochemistry; chemical industries; the civil service; cosmetics industry; dentistry; food science research and manufacturing; forensic science; medicine; pharmacy; teaching; veterinary science
- **Design and technology**: architecture (with mathematics); engineering (with mathematics and physics); product or 3-D design; teaching
- **Economics**: finance; government; journalism (with politics); planning (town and country); retail management; surveying; teaching. Economics is particularly strong when combined with mathematics
- **English**: advertising; banking and building society work; computing; editing; insurance; journalism; law; library work; marketing; sales; public administration; secretarial work; teaching; writing
- **Geography**: business and commerce; cartography; environmental planning; estate management; geographical research (very limited career options for geographers); geology; landscape architecture; oceanography; surveying; town planning; teaching; travel and tourism

- **History**: archaeology; business and commerce; the civil service; library work; museum work; teaching; and any careers where logical and analytical thinking, sorting and explaining information is required, for example, local government, legal work
- **Home economics**: consumer advice work; food industry; the hospitality industry, nursing; retail (developing new products and recipes); teaching
- **Information technology**: business and commerce; computing; teaching. Computer literacy is essential for almost all jobs
- **Languages**: bilingual secretarial work; business and commerce; the civil service (Diplomatic Service, Foreign and Commonwealth Service, Immigration Service); the hospitality industry; import and export; teaching; translating and interpreting; travel and tourism
- **Mathematics**: architecture; business and commerce; cartography; the civil service; computing; engineering (with physics); finance; psychology; surveying; teaching
- **Music**: music therapy; performing; teaching (particularly primary school teaching)
- **Physics**: the civil service; science (as a physicist); teaching; and if combined with mathematics – engineering, geophysics, medicine, meteorology
- **Politics**: central and local government; journalism; social work
- **Religious studies**: teaching; theology
- **Science**: engineering (physics and mathematics); computing; medicine; pilot (physics with mathematics preferred); psychology (with mathematics); physiotherapy (chemistry, biology); science and technology; teaching
- **Statistics**: business and commerce; the civil service; finance; teaching.

Alternatively, you might have a definite career in mind, in which case, turn to the index first to find which broad area it falls into, then read the whole section. You may find that other careers that you had not previously considered attract your attention.

Reference letter

At the top of each careers section is 'CLCI' with a capital letter after it, for example, the career area 'Animals' has CLCI: W. This is a reference to the Careers Library Classification Index which is used in most school, college and careers service careers libraries. It is given in this book to enable students to find easily more detailed information on their chosen career. Note that this classification system is currently under review and some changes are expected. However, it is likely that the old index will be used in tandem with the new for some time to avoid confusion.

Sample job titles

The sample job titles listed are just a few of the common ones in each area and give a flavour of the range and types of work available and the different existing job titles. Not all the jobs are discussed in detail in the book. All jobs are for both genders unless specified.

Opportunities

This section gives an indication of the prospects of gaining employment and which industries are likely to offer job opportunities.

Other factors to consider

The type of personality, qualities and skills required for the various careers are given in this section.

Entry and training

Entry and training requirements for the different careers are outlined here.

Subjects

The subjects given are those either stipulated, commonly required or preferred at GCSE and/or A-level for the job in question.

Qualifications are usually stated in terms of GCSEs and A-levels for the sake of brevity. It should be understood that GNVQs, BTEC National awards and Scottish qualifications are also generally acceptable. Refer to page 19 for details of GNVQs now available.

Remember that information changes rapidly. Students should check the exact entry requirements with the professional body or institution before committing themselves.

For some jobs no particular academic qualifications are specified, but students who have passed at least some GCSEs often have a better chance of being selected for courses or jobs.

Note that if you find that you have the 'wrong' A-levels for a career, you can usually do a conversion/foundation/introductory course, which will enable you to make your career switch. It is, however, easier and less time-consuming if you study the appropriate subjects in the first place. Read Chapter 2 for help in making your decisions.

Further information

Relevant professional organisations, books and leaflets are listed at the end of each career area. The addresses are listed, along with telephone and fax numbers and email and web site addresses, in the 'Addresses' section at the back of this book.

Administration and office work (CLCI: C)

Administration is the function that supports the core activities of an organisation, so it involves managing resources (people, money, materials and equipment) efficiently. Administrators have to ensure that different tasks are carried out and make decisions, delegate, and organise and plan the management of resources.

Every organisation needs people to deal with the paperwork and administrative side of the business. Duties vary enormously, according to the size of the organisation, the environment and the level of responsibility of the position. For instance, clerks usually do routine work, such as dealing with the post, filing and photocopying; secretaries also do this work but are often, in addition, expected to organise the boss's diary, coordinate travel arrangements and meetings, take dictation and type correspondence and reports (some secretaries may be required to make coffee too); senior secretaries are increasingly responsible for managing entire databases and other information technology (IT) projects.

Secretaries may work either for several people or for just one boss. They can specialise as:

- a bilingual secretary, usually fluent in one or more foreign languages
- a farm secretary, assisting with the accounts and calculating wages. Farm secretaries are often freelance, working for more than one farm manager
- a legal secretary, employed by solicitors or barristers
- a medical secretary, working in hospitals or health centres
- a school secretary.

Personal assistants generally perform all the duties of a senior secretary but work for one boss only.

Office managers are responsible for the smooth running of the office, which means ensuring that tasks are done to the right standard at the right time and that all resources are used and managed efficiently.

Personnel officers are involved in recruiting staff, writing reports and job descriptions, and improving working relationships and organising training. A major part of a personnel officer's job is concerned with the effective use and development of people within the organisation. This means they often become involved with the training of staff. They also work towards getting the best out of people by ensuring that there are opportunities for staff to discuss their future career development or any problems they may have. In this way, working relationships are likely to improve and business needs will be met. However, their role is extremely wide and varied, depending on the size and scope of the organisation in which they work.

Sample job titles

Accounts clerk, administrative assistant/officer, administrator, junior clerk, office manager, personal assistant, personnel assistant, personnel officer, secretary, typist

Opportunities

Because every organisation – whether large or small, in the public or private sector, commercial or non-commercial – requires administration, opportunities for work in this area are enormous. Some of the employers that have large administrative departments are local government (education, social services, housing, planning, finance), civil service (various departments such as Health, Education and Employment, Social Security, Inland Revenue, Trade and Industry), the National Health Service and all kinds of organisations in industry and commerce.

Other factors to consider

Administrative work attracts people who are methodical, organised and who pay attention to detail. Initiative, tact and diplomacy are also valued attributes. Interpersonal skills are important because, depending on the organisation, some office staff will have to deal with members of the public as well as with colleagues. Computer and technological skills are considered essential, as is the willingness to be flexible and learn new skills whenever the technology changes. Clerical and administrative staff have to be happy to take orders from their bosses. A smart appearance is usually required.

Entry and training

Entry can be at all levels. Sixteen-year-old school-leavers can start as accounts clerks, typists and junior office clerks, provided they have some technical skills to offer. Typically, these would include typing, keyboard or word processing skills. Employers often require English and mathematics at GCSE level as a minimum qualification. Eighteen-year-olds with A-levels can also start in junior positions if they have some office skills.

GCSEs (grades A–C) are usually required for entry on to secretarial courses. Graduates wanting to become a secretary or personal assistant take one of a variety of postgraduate courses (which can range in length from three months to a year or more).

For personnel officers, experience and maturity are as important as qualifications. It is therefore not a career that can necessarily be entered straight from school. Professional qualifications are not mandatory, although many employers prefer them. Competition for personnel posts is fierce, so the more qualifications applicants have the better. Personnel management is an option in many business studies degrees and BTEC diplomas. Alternatively, training can be on-the-job, with part-time study towards the Institute of Personnel and Development (IPD) examinations. The Professional Qualification Scheme (PQS), which is the IPD professional qualification programme, is 'open access', which means that candidates need not study a foundation programme in either personnel or training before commencing it. However, the PQS is at degree level, and candidates may therefore have to meet certain educational requirements of the training institution. Certain business studies or similar degrees and a few masters-level qualifications may give exemption from the PQS.

NVQs in administration can be taken at levels 1–4 and in management at levels 4 and 5. NVQs in training and personnel at levels 3–5 are also available.

Subjects

Although employers do not generally specify particular GCSE or A-level subjects, English and mathematics are obvious choices as the work requires writing skills, communication skills and numeracy.

Entry to secretarial or clerical college courses requires a good knowledge of English and an adequate level of numeracy (GCSE level). For someone intending to become a secretary, typing, computer studies, office studies, business studies or IT are relevant subjects at GCSE level. At A-level, business studies, accounting, communication studies and computing are useful.

For personnel work, any A-level subjects are useful for entry to a professional personnel management course, although English, law, business studies and psychology are particularly relevant.

Further information

Association of Medical Secretaries, Practice Administrators and Receptionists Ltd
Institute of Agricultural Secretaries and Administrators
Institute of Health Service Management
Institute of Personnel and Development
Institute of Qualified Private Secretaries

Books and leaflets
Hayward, G. 1995. *Careers in Secretarial and Office Work*. Kogan Page
Working in Local Government. 1997. COIC

Advertising, marketing and PR (CLCI: O)

These areas are concerned with persuading people to buy products or services. They are all inter-related and are to do with different stages of the selling process.

Advertising
Advertising is the promotion of goods and services in order to stimulate demand for them. The most obvious kind of commercial advertising is the familiar display of brands in newspapers, magazines and on television. Advertising also includes the promotion of industrial products through trade magazines, exhibitions, mailings and leaflets, special offers, competitions and all kinds of visual displays, such as posters, shop windows, stickers, and so on; fund-raising; and job

vacancy advertising. Non-commercial advertising or marketing may try to change people's attitudes or give information and includes electoral leaflets and government warnings about smoking, drinking and driving.

Account executives in agencies may be in charge of several accounts, each concerned with a different product, and act as the liaison between the client and the department that is planning and designing the advertisement. Executives spend a lot of time telephoning and seeing clients and suppliers. Account planners and buyers do a similar job but may also have the authority to decide the advertising strategy (i.e. which media to use) and control the budget for the campaign. They or media executives deal with magazines, television, radio and newspapers and buy the advertising space or the airtime.

Other jobs lie within the creative departments; copywriters, designers, art directors (responsible for the visual image) and film technicians (helping to create advertisements for television or cinema) all work to tight deadlines and at high speed. Some large organisations employ all of the above staff in-house, whereas smaller ones might combine the roles or commission freelances to do certain jobs. The job of copywriters is to ensure that the advertising message is put over in a way that will make sense to the customer or to promote the product in an ingenious or mysterious way so as to create interest. They produce headings, text and jingles – the copy – and work closely with art editors.

Marketing

Marketing is a key management discipline and is about getting the right product or service to the customer at the right price, in the right place and at the right time. Marketing staff have to find new markets and customers for their business products or services. Marketing incorporates specialist disciplines, such as market research, product development, marketing planning and control, pricing, distribution, promotion, selling and after-sales service.

Market research is a major area of marketing. Market researchers find out what people want, do not want, and why, using a variety of techniques, such as:

- interviewing people face to face, perhaps in the high street, or in groups

- using postal, telephone or magazine questionnaires
- analysing statistics or records.

They are part of a marketing team and find out the information that will determine the nature of the product and its positioning. They try to discover what customers or clients require/need/would be tempted to buy and what advertising might work. It is a key job in any business because if the researchers get it wrong the company concerned may lose some business. Market researchers also need to be aware of the competition, so they must keep an eye on the market place, shops, stores or wherever the competition is intense.

Marketing managers use the market research to find out what potential customers need and want. Once the product is ready to be launched they carry out the planning and coordination to make it available to customers at the right time and at the right price.

PR

Public relations (PR) is about managing a company's reputation, which can take years to build up and yet be destroyed in only a few hours. PR staff help to shape the organisation and the way it operates and to develop and maintain its corporate identity. The aim is to win long-term public goodwill and support for an organisation's products or services. Through research and evaluation, PR people find out the concerns and expectations of a company's target market and explain these to management. In addition, their work may involve some, or all, of the following:

- **PR programme planning** – analysing problems and opportunities, defining goals, recommending and planning activities and measuring results
- **writing and editing** shareholder reports, annual reports, news releases, film scripts, articles and features, speeches, publicity materials, and so on
- **media relations** – developing and maintaining good relations with the media (local and national newspapers, magazines, radio and television)
- **communications** – liaising with individuals (for example, colleagues, customers, management, designers, photographers, printers, shareholders, suppliers and so on) and groups, speaking at meetings and giving presentations

- **arranging events** such as news conferences, exhibitions, facility celebrations, competitions and award programmes to gain the attention of specific groups of people.

Public relations may be given different titles, depending on the organisation, for example, public information, investor relations, public affairs, corporate communication, marketing or customer relations.

Sample job titles

Advertising: account executive, account planner, copywriter, media executive

Marketing: marketing manager, marketing research executive/interviewer

PR: account executive, communications manager, corporate affairs officer, corporate relations manager, public relations officer, publicity officer

Opportunities

Although advertising is a fiercely competitive business to enter, talented and lucky people can progress far, moving from one company to another fairly quickly, gaining experience and improving career prospects. Some large advertising companies and agencies employ over 400 people, although the majority have between 10 and 50 employees. Copywriters find employment with advertising agencies and in design and media studios which produce designs and copy for clients. Freelance work is also available.

Any organisation in the UK that has a structured approach to product or service development usually has a marketing team. Marketing managers can influence the direction of a business and take a leading role, with excellent opportunities for promotion. Increasingly, marketing has become an integral part of any organisation's business plan; it is no longer limited to fast-moving consumer goods because traditional, non-marketing organisations have also realised the need to market their services. This means that marketing managers can do well in banks, building societies, educational institutions, legal institutions and public service industries.

In addition, over 500 or so market research agencies exist, and these carry out research for companies and organisations, including manufacturing or service companies and government institutions. Some market researchers work for research departments of advertising agencies. Others, once experienced, set up their own agencies.

Direct marketing – targeting specific people directly via telephone or mailshot – is a key growth area.

PR officers working either in independent consultancies or in advertising agencies may represent one or more clients to the media. Others work in the marketing departments or in-house PR departments of large companies and public bodies.

Other factors to consider

People working in these fields all need:

- the ability to get on with all sorts of people – colleagues, clients and members of the public
- communication skills (both written and verbal)
- a persuasive manner
- computer literacy skills
- the ability to work both in a team and alone
- a willingness to be judged on results
- a smart appearance (much of the work involves dealing with members of the public)
- the ability to work under pressure and to meet deadlines
- good organisational skills.

Some work – such as copywriting in advertising and writing and editing in PR work – demands imagination and creativity. Many of the jobs in advertising and marketing are not for people who cannot take criticism of their work.

In addition, some jobs within market research require people who have stamina and who do not mind standing on their feet for long periods at a time.

For PR officers and marketing staff the ability to appreciate and translate people's opinions is often as important as academic qualifications.

Business skills are useful for marketing managers or for those setting up their own market research or advertising agency.

Some jobs can involve a lot of pressure, for example, marketing managers have to 'get it right', and PR officers and copywriters often work to tight deadlines.

Work in advertising involves a lot of stress and long hours. Technical and artistic skills tend to be more important than formal qualifications. People with flair and ability to learn are sought after as are people who are quick to realise creative and commercial opportunities arising from developments in technology.

Entry and training

Although these three areas are grouped together they have different entry and training requirements.

Advertising

No specific entry requirements are necessary for jobs within advertising, although a good all-round education is sought after and A-levels are preferred. Some advertising agencies have trainee schemes for graduates (preferred subjects: economics, languages, business studies, English). An art and design degree is useful for designers. Training is usually on-the-job, supplemented by courses of the Communication, Advertising and Marketing Education Foundation (CAM) and by the Institute of Practitioners in Advertising for those already working in a member agency. The CAM certificate can be studied for part-time at college or by correspondence (A-level entry) and can lead on to study for the diploma.

Marketing

To get into marketing a degree is useful but not essential. It is possible to join a sales team at the age of 16, 18 or as a graduate and learn from experience. However, business studies, economics, marketing or finance graduates/HND students are well sought after. Competition for careers in marketing is fierce. A technological or scientific background is a big advantage (and sometimes required by companies involved in technology), as it helps to understand the technicalities of a product. However, arts graduates often make excellent marketing managers. Specialist marketing degrees and management studies or business studies degrees with a marketing option can also be taken.

Alternatively, post A-level applicants and graduates can take a part-time, two-year college course leading to the qualifying certificate of the Chartered Institute of Marketing, and to NVQs in marketing. These can be followed by the diploma course.

Although it is not essential, a degree is usually required for market research (three-quarters of market researchers are graduates). Any discipline is considered, particularly if followed by a postgraduate course in business studies. Once in employment, they can study towards the diploma of the Market Research Society. Further training is on-the-job.

PR

Entry to PR work is highly competitive: it is the third most popular career choice for graduates. Over 90 per cent of new entrants to the Institute of Public Relations are graduates. There are five full-time undergraduate degree courses which combine theory with practice. Nearly all PR graduates go on to find work in their chosen field.

Subjects

Advertising: A-level English, mathematics, business studies, art and design are all useful. CAM certificate requires two A-levels, with English at GCSE (plus a year's practical experience).

Marketing: at GCSE, mathematics and English are required, and a modern language is useful.

Market research: at GCSE and A-level most subjects are potentially useful, although economics, commerce, mathematics/statistics, psychology, business studies or any other course linked to business are particularly valued. Useful degrees are business, mathematics and statistics. However, arts and science degrees could also be the basis for market research.

PR: useful subjects are English and business studies. Any degree discipline is acceptable.

Further information

Advertising Association
Chartered Institute of Marketing
Communication, Advertising and Marketing Education Foundation
(CAM)

Institute of Practitioners in Advertising
Institute of Public Relations
Market Research Society

Books and leaflets

Grigg, J. and Hird, C. 1996. *Careers in Marketing, Advertising and Public Relations*. Kogan Page
Working in Marketing and Sales. 1997. COIC

Animals (CLCI: W)

Those wanting to work with animals will find opportunities at all levels and in many different areas: breeding, training, protecting and caring for animals (even for those used in experimental work). Work with animals is a popular career choice, and consequently competition for entry is very keen. For example, veterinary science is one of the hardest of all university courses on which to gain a place. The UK has only six veterinary schools (Bristol, Cambridge, Edinburgh, Glasgow, Liverpool and London), offering around 400 places a year. Roughly five candidates apply for every place, and all of them have good A-level grades (AAA or AAB).

Veterinary surgeons (vets) treat animals both medically and surgically and advise on animal healthcare and breeding. Depending on the location of the practice, some vets may deal with farm animals, while others treat only small domestic animals. They may also be involved in research work or developing preventive and curative medicines for manufacturing companies. Most vets, however, work in a veterinary practice, usually in partnership with several colleagues. They may be assisted by veterinary nurses, who feed, nurse and care for the hospitalised animals. Qualified veterinary nurses are registered with the Royal College of Veterinary Surgeons and may now undertake, under the direction of a vet, medical treatment and some minor surgery on pets. Some of the other tasks may involve holding, calming and controlling animals during examination, carrying out simple laboratory tests and assisting in the operating theatre.

Animal technicians are responsible for the care and welfare of animals being bred for or used in research. Some technicians are involved with experimental work. The animals used are generally mice, rats, guinea-pigs, rabbits and hamsters, although some of the work requires the use of other animals such as dogs, cats, monkeys, farm animals, amphibians, fish, insects or even exotic animals. The different requirements of each type of animal and the broad range of experiments lead to a wide variety of working environments, from open fields to hospitals. Much of the work is routine: cleaning out cages, washing and cleaning equipment and rooms, feeding and watering the animals.

Riding instructors not only teach children and adults, both in classes and in private lessons, but are also expected to take on some horse and business management duties, such as training the horses, planning and budgeting or marketing the facilities. Grooms work in stables and may eventually go on to become stable managers, with responsibility for managing horses that hunt, race or are entered for show-jumping, polo and eventing competitions. Both grooms and instructors are generally expected to look after the horses, which involves feeding them, exercising them, and cleaning the tack (saddles and bridles) to keep it in good condition.

Zookeepers care for animals in zoos, feeding them and cleaning out their cages.

Guide dog trainers train young dogs in basic guiding skills so that they can help visually impaired people to achieve more independence.

Sample job titles

Animal technician, animal welfare assistant, guide dog trainer, groom, kennel hand, pet shop assistant, riding instructor, RSPCA inspector, stable manager, veterinary nurse, veterinary surgeon, zookeeper

Opportunities

Those wishing to work with animals can do so in a wide variety of settings and at many different levels: on a farm, for a government department, in local government, in a zoo, dog beauty parlour, kennels/catteries or in their own private veterinary practice. However, competition is stiff, as applicants generally outweigh the number of jobs (at all levels).

About 70 per cent of vets work in private practice. Other opportunities are in research work, drugs firms, feed merchants, central and local government departments, university veterinary schools, animal breeding centres and zoos. Many vets find work overseas, in developing countries and in Europe (where a UK veterinary qualification is valid).

Veterinary nurses usually work in general practice but can also find work in university veterinary schools, animal welfare societies (such as the PDSA or the RSPCA), zoos, safari parks and riding stables or in the Armed Forces. They also work in publishing (advising on publications), pharmaceutical and pet food manufacturing industries.

Prospects for work as kennel hands and assistants/helpers in dog parlours, pet shops or catteries are poor as the number of applicants outstrips the number of jobs. Setting up alone requires business sense and experience as well as premises (well away from residential areas because of the noise from the animals) and a great deal of capital.

The number of opportunities for zookeepers is falling as public interest in zoos declines. Many are employed on a seasonal basis before gaining permanent posts. Employment for guide dog trainers is with Guide Dogs for the Blind at its training centres.

Other factors to consider

Animals need attention 365 days of the year, and people who work with them tend to regard their work as a way of life rather than an ordinary nine-to-five job. The hours are likely to be anti-social and long.

Many young people wish to work with animals because they love being around them. However, those who want to work with animals must be aware of exactly what is involved as it is much harder work than it sounds. Dedication is a prerequisite. The work is not for the sentimental as it can often be tough emotionally, for instance, when an animal has to be put down. It can also be physically demanding work (especially when dealing with large farm animals), dirty and messy. Anyone who is squeamish or who faints at the sight of blood needs to think carefully if considering veterinary surgery. Animal technicians, in particular, need to accept the fact that the animals in their care are being bred for and used for research purposes.

Those working with some animals, such as horses, or on a farm, will probably be outdoors in all weathers. Much of the work can also be routine, such as cleaning and grooming.

Remember that working with animals also often involves working with people, for example, veterinary surgeons and nurses deal with distraught owners of sick pets as well as the animals themselves; although RSPCA inspectors' first concern is the welfare of the animal, they also need to be able to communicate with the owner. Interpersonal and communication skills are as important as a desire to care for animals.

For people who want to work with dogs or cats, jobs in kennels or catteries may be ideal, provided they can put up with the noise, dirt and long hours.

Entry and training

Entry and training vary enormously according to the level and type of job.

The minimum age for entry to veterinary nurse training is 17; students have to obtain full-time employment with a veterinary practice or veterinary hospital approved as a training centre by the Royal College of Veterinary Surgeons. Training is on-the-job for two years, including part-time or block-release study at a technical or agricultural college. Entry requirements are currently four GCSEs (grades A–C) but will increase from September 1998 to five GCSEs (see overleaf for specified subjects). Many entrants have better qualifications, such as A-levels.

The training for veterinary surgeons is long – five years after A-levels at one of the six veterinary schools (except at Cambridge where the course lasts six years). It is essential to have a veterinary degree to be able to practise. All of the veterinary schools require students to have gained a wide variety of experience with a vet before applying for a place at a school; this is because work experience enables students to find out what is expected of them. For those who feel they are unlikely to reach the necessary high A-level grades, it may be worth considering applying for other degree courses as well, such as agriculture, biochemistry or animal physiology, which require the same science A-level subjects as veterinary science (but lower grades).

For people who want to work with horses, training is available in British Horse Society approved riding stables as a working pupil. The terms of work vary according to the establishment, and pupils are often required to pay for board and lodging. The British Horse Society has examinations in stable management and for instructors. Another way of training is to take a full-time higher education course (degree or HND) in equine studies, then look for a job as an instructor, groom or sub-manager. One or two A-levels are required for entry, plus usually a year's experience working with horses. Evidence of riding ability might be asked for.

RSPCA inspectors are aged between 22 and 40 (25 and 45 in Scotland) when they start.

Kennel hands, animal welfare assistants and animal technicians can train after completing GCSEs. Training is on-the-job, sometimes with part-time release for study, for example, towards the Institute of Animal Technology examinations. Animal technology is a practical subject, and much of the training and the learning of necessary skills is undertaken on-the-job. Kennel hands spend up to 12 months working in a kennel or dogs' home. It is usual to stay on the premises because of night and weekend duties.

Zookeepers work towards a City & Guilds qualification in animal management (by correspondence).

Guide dog trainers need to be 18 years old and have a minimum of five passes at GCSE to commence training.

Subjects

Veterinary surgeon: A-levels in chemistry, biology (or zoology) and physics and/or mathematics (grades A–B).

Veterinary nurse: four GCSEs, including English, science or mathematics; from September 1998 – five GCSEs, including English and two sciences, of which one could be mathematics.

Guide dog trainers: GCSEs in English, mathematics and science are essential.

Zookeepers: GCSEs in mathematics, English and biology are preferred.

For most other careers with animals, GCSEs in English, mathematics and science are useful.

Further information

Association of British Riding Schools
British Horse Society
British Veterinary Nursing Association Ltd (BVNA)
Guide Dogs for the Blind Association
Institute of Animal Technology
Royal College of Veterinary Surgeons (RCVS)
RSPCA

Books and leaflets

Shepherd, A. *Careers Working with Animals*. 1997. Kogan Page
Veterinary Science, Degree Course Guide (annual). CRAC/Hobsons
Work with Animals. 1996. COIC
A Career as a Veterinary Nurse. BVNA
Where to Train. British Horse Society (available from riding schools
and the Recreational Riding Office of the BHS)

Architecture, landscape architecture and housing (CLCI: U)

The job of architectural professionals and landscape architects is to
create pleasant and safe surroundings for people to live and work
in. Housing managers are interested in improving people's living
conditions.

Architecture

Architects study traditional and new building methods and materials
to learn about their possibilities and limitations. When designing
buildings they have to take into account many factors, including the
budget, appearance of the building and needs of the users and of
society. Architects spend some of their time in the office and part of
it on site. They carry out initial research to find out what people
want to use the building for. This involves having many meetings
with clients, other professionals, planners and builders. Next they
make sketches, plans and drawings (often using computer-aided
design) until the scheme is designed and contract documents have
been approved. While the building is being constructed the architect
ensures that the contractual obligation is being met by visiting the

site, keeping a close eye on the budget and completion date, checking on materials being used and construction methods. Architects must work closely with engineers in order to design a structurally sound building.

Architectural technologists are part of the architectural team. They are concerned primarily with the technological aspects of building design and construction – from the initial client briefing to completion of the project. They may conduct investigative surveys, which involve gathering, analysing and preparing all the relevant technical information and consulting or negotiating with other people, such as planners and builders. Other responsibilities may include researching and selecting materials and supervising and monitoring development and construction work. A detailed knowledge of relevant legislation and building regulations is essential.

Landscape architecture

Landscape architects are basically designers. They are concerned with the planning, design and construction of the outdoor environment. The scope of the work is wide: in towns and cities it is concerned mainly with the integration of the layout of housing areas, roads, parks and play areas with public and private gardens and with general urban regencration; in the countryside the emphasis is on agricultural, forest and tourist landscapes, roads and industrial buildings, power stations, reservoirs and so on. The aim is to create harmony between the existing and the new, while at the same time causing as little impact to the environment as possible. Their time is split between the office and site visits, checking progress of work. They liaise with many other professionals.

Housing management

Housing management is concerned with meeting people's housing needs. It can be a challenging career. The type of work varies according to the organisation and the location. It usually involves a lot of day-to-day contact with residents, either in their own homes or in the housing office. Much of the work is concerned with solving problems related to repairs, rent and mortgages, and to social issues such as difficulties with neighbours and landlords. It is important that housing managers understand the various welfare benefits when dealing with tenants.

Sample job titles

Architect, architectural technologist, landscape architect, housing officer/manager

Opportunities

Architectural professionals and architectural technologists work for government departments, local authorities, building contractors, large industrial and commercial companies and, occasionally, private house owners. The vast majority work in private architectural practices. Many find work overseas on a contract basis; those with a second language have an advantage. However, jobs in architecture are to some extent dependent on changes in the economy, which affect the availability of funds for the construction of buildings. Some architects study for further professional qualifications and become planners, landscape architects or conservation specialists; others may become writers or journalists, researchers or teachers in schools of architecture.

Although landscape architecture is a small profession, career prospects are good, particularly as environmental awareness is increasing. Jobs are available with central and local government, water authorities, large industrial concerns, design and architectural practices. Many landscape architects become self-employed and some find work overseas.

Housing officers/managers generally work with housing associations, local authorities, private trusts or companies, aid or advice centres.

Other factors to consider

Architectural professionals, landscape architects and housing officers/managers need to be sensitive to individuals' needs as well as to environmental issues. Interpersonal skills and an interest in people are essential because these jobs involve a lot of client liaison and contact with other professionals and the general public.

As architecture training is lengthy and demanding those wishing to embark on it should be sure at the start that it is the right career for them. It may be prudent to visit an architect's office and gain some work experience before making a decision.

Occasionally the work of architectural professionals, landscape architects and housing managers can be stressful because it is often difficult to satisfy people's needs. They may need to compromise and balance the wishes of individuals against what is actually possible.

Artistic skills and the ability to design creatively combined with scientific and technical knowledge are crucial for anyone interested in a career in architecture or landscape architecture. Technical knowledge is also important for housing officer/managers, who need to know about housing law and building technology.

All these jobs require people who are numerate, logical, analytical and who pay attention to detail.

Entry and training

Training to be an architect takes a minimum of seven years after A-levels (five years spent at a school of architecture). Architecture is usually studied full-time for three years at degree level and is followed by a period of practical training in an architect's office. The students then return to a school of architecture (not necessarily the one where the first degree was studied) for study towards a diploma or higher degree. This is followed by another year working in an architect's office before taking the Royal Institute of British Architects (RIBA) professional practice examinations.

To qualify as an architectural technologist, students would normally take a degree in architectural technology or in another built-environment subject with a technology base. Alternatively, it is possible to take a Higher National qualification with the British Institute of Architectural Technologists (BIAT)-specified options. Academic study is followed by a minimum of two years' supervised practical experience and a professional interview. If successful at the interview architectural technologists gain full membership of BIAT. There are other routes to membership for mature candidates and those without standard qualifications. A level-4 NVQ in architectural technology is being developed.

Those wanting to follow a career in landscape architecture need a degree in either landscape architecture/design or a related subject (agriculture, planning, geography, architecture, horticulture). Training is long because a degree in landscape architecture or design takes a minimum of four years and is followed by the professional examination of the Landscape Institute and a minimum period of two years' practical experience before professional status is conferred.

Entry to housing management can be either post A-level or post-degree. It is then possible to work towards the qualifications and membership of the Chartered Institute of Housing on a part-time or distance-learning basis. This can take up to three or four years to complete, depending on whether the person is a graduate or non-graduate. NVQs in housing are also available at levels 2, 3 and 4.

Subjects

Architect: a minimum of two A-levels and five GCSEs (grades A–C) in mathematics, English, physics or chemistry, or double science, or a BTEC National Certificate/Diploma in building studies. Some schools of architecture specify certain combinations of subjects. Contact RIBA for details.

Architectural technologist: four GCSEs (mathematics, science, technology, art and an English-based subject are useful). Some entrants have A-levels (science and technology, or equivalent).

Landscape architect: two A-levels in English, mathematics and/or science. Geography, art, botany, design or biology are also useful; GCSEs – history, geography, or a language.

Housing officer/manager: the minimum qualifications to start training are five GCSEs, including English, and two A-levels.

Further information

Architects and Surveyors Institute
British Institute of Architectural Technologists (BIAT)
Chartered Institute of Housing
Landscape Institute
Royal Incorporation of Architects in Scotland
Royal Institute of British Architects (RIBA)

Books and leaflets

Burston, O. 1997. *Careers in Architecture*. Kogan Page
Working in Geography. 1995. COIC
Working in Environmental Services. 1997. COIC

Armed Forces (CLCI: B)

The Armed Forces comprise the Royal Navy, the Royal Marines, the Army and the Royal Air Force. Their role is to defend and protect Britain's people and overseas interests and responsibilities. Entrants to the Armed Forces must be prepared to fight for their country if war breaks out.

Each force is divided into two levels of trained people: officers and the ranks. The role of officers is managerial, and they are responsible for the men and women in the ranks. They lead by example and must motivate the general workforce they supervise. All ranks have the opportunity to gain academic qualifications within the forces.

Army

The Army is the largest of the forces, with approximately 112,000 serving personnel. Its regiments and corps offer careers in both 'arms' (responsible for combat operations) and 'services' (responsible for support, such as supplies, medical, communications, and so on). Men and women, whether at officer level or in the ranks, develop expertise and experience, which varies depending on which regiment or corps they join. Soldiers (ranks) can add to their skills by learning a trade. They can choose from over 130: from craft level (for example, electrician, carpenter, mechanic, painter) to technician level (for example, electronics or instrument technician, design draughtsman/woman, survey technician).

RAF

The Royal Air Force (RAF) has a small flying force and 18 officer branches as well as support staff, such as engineers, medical staff and caterers. Graduates who wish to become pilots enter as Pilot Officers, usually gaining promotion after six months; non-graduates may enter as Acting Pilot Officers for one year then get promoted. As well as careers in flying, the RAF offers over 50 different specialist jobs on the ground, in a support role for the aircrew. These include engineers, flight controllers, administrators, catering and supply staff.

Royal Navy

The Royal Navy is the smallest branch of the forces and, like the others, has jobs at officer and rank levels (called ratings in the Navy), not all of which are sea-based. Those in the Navy can be: trained for sea warfare; technicians (artificers) and mechanics involved on the engineering support side; administrators, caterers, accountants, and so on, who all make sure the naval bases and ships run smoothly.

The **Royal Marines** are part of the Royal Navy and are a small force of amphibious commandos trained for operations on land and sea. They are among the world's most élite troops.

All forces also have specialist officers, such as doctors, nurses, dentists, lawyers and chaplains. Each Force offers a career in flying, but the RAF provides the widest range of aircraft.

Nurses can join the Queen Alexandra's Royal Army Nursing Corps, the Queen Alexandra's Royal Naval Nursing Service and Princess Mary's RAF Nursing Service, thus combining a nursing and an Armed Forces career.

It is still considered necessary not to allow women to do some jobs within the infantry, Royal Marines, Household Cavalry and Royal Armoured Corps. However, this policy is constantly under review and in reality very few roles now remain closed to women. They are excluded from only one of the RAF trades – RAF Regiment gunner – and they cannot yet serve in submarines or on some smaller warships in the Royal Navy.

Sample job titles

Army officers: Adjutant, Army Air Corps pilot, Commanding Officer, Platoon Commander

Army ranks: Army Air Corps Pilot (this post can be either at officer level or in the ranks), cook, engineer, field survey technician, mechanic, soldier

RAF officers: administrative officer, air traffic controller, engineer, fighter controller, navigator, pilot, supply officer

RAF ranks: aircraft technician, airman/woman, engineering technician, leading aircraftman/woman

Royal Navy officers: engineer, pilot, seaman officer marine

Royal Navy ratings: cook, dental surgery assistant, medical technician, rating

Opportunities

The Armed Forces offers a wide range of opportunities for employment and training. Major world events (for example, the ending of the Cold War, the unification of Germany and the handing over of Hong Kong to China) and cutbacks in the defence budget have led to many changes within the Armed Forces, such as rationalisation, restructuring and the disbandment of some regiments, and an increased commitment to peace-making and the United Nations.

However, the Armed Forces is now facing 'normal exit' rates (end-of-service retirements and end of shorter commissions or engagements) and there is a continuing demand for new recruits in all three forces: for example, the Army looks to recruit about 15,000 personnel a year. The choice of career within each force is wide, as can be seen by the variety of job titles given above. Although regular foreign postings are not as frequent as in the past, the forces often train and exercise overseas. They are also called upon to uphold the peace and respond to crises all over the world.

Other factors to consider

Those who:

- can accept a disciplined and structured lifestyle
- enjoy challenge and variety
- are a good and enthusiastic team worker
- are not worried about being away from home for long periods
- do not mind wearing a uniform

may enjoy a career in the Armed Forces. It is a way of life that can be both physically and mentally challenging. Entrants need to be reliable and to show initiative and common sense as well as a resourcefulness and determination to succeed. Officers need to show they have the potential to lead others.

The Armed Forces trains personnel to be physically fit and to cope in all kinds of weather and circumstances and to react effectively in emergencies. All combat ranks have to be prepared to fight using sophisticated weapons and to keep the peace at home or in war-torn countries abroad.

All candidates must meet the medical standards set by each of the forces. The standards for eyesight, colour perception and hearing vary according to the specific role or career chosen. For instance, pilots and navigators need exceptionally good eyesight and hearing.

Entry and training

The minimum age for entry to the Armed Forces is 16, although most applicants are aged 17-plus. They can start at either rank or officer level; this depends on what qualifications they have and which job they wish to do. Local Armed Forces Careers Offices (address in the telephone book) have a wealth of information on all the different careers offered and the specific entry requirements for each one.

Recruits to the Armed Forces can join up for a specific period (minimum 3–4 years). Ranks have either an 'open engagement' (Royal Navy and Army) or a 'notice engagement' (RAF) term of service, the length and conditions of which differ according to the individual force.

Officers enter on either regular (permanent) or short service commissions: these are the number of years that the recruits commit to serve in the forces.

Initial training is given to all new recruits in each force, followed by a period of professional or specialist trade training, depending on the appointment or chosen specialist field. It is now possible to work towards NVQs in most trades.

Ranks: As well as undergoing intelligence and aptitude tests, applicants have a selection interview and must pass a physical fitness test. No minimum education requirements are necessary for entry at craft/trade level. However, having some GCSEs may well increase the choice of opportunities available. For instance, with a minimum of three GCSEs and the right aptitude and physical fitness, it is possible to be considered for a career as a non-commissioned airman/woman, an air electronics operator or air engineer in the RAF.

A minimum of three GCSEs (grades A–C), including mathematics and science, are required for entry at technician level (called 'artificer' in the Royal Navy).

Promotion is possible through the ranks to officer level for candidates with leadership potential.

Officers: Candidates for officer level entry need a minimum of five GCSEs (grades A–C) and two A-levels. The majority have degrees.

All Army officers follow a 44-week training course (the minimum age for entry is 17 years 9 months) at the Royal Military Academy, Sandhurst.

RAF officers follow Initial Officer Training, a 24-week course at the RAF College, Cranwell, prior to specialist training.

Naval officers begin their training at the Britannia Royal Naval College at Dartmouth. The length of the training depends on entry qualifications and type of entry.

Selection procedures involve intelligence and aptitude tests, practical initiative tests, an interview and a medical, and usually requires candidates to be residential for a period of a few days.

Sponsorships: All the Armed Forces offer potential officers:

- **scholarships** (financial help) to sixth-form students of high academic ability. The RAF also offers a Flying Scholarship which gives 20 hours' free flying training. Contact the Armed Forces Careers Office for details
- **bursaries** (tax-free supplements to grants) for higher-education courses
- **undergraduate cadetships** (salary plus tuition fees) are available for some students with a place at university.

The Army has a residential sixth-form science-based college, Welbeck College, offering a two-year A-level course, which prepares students for officer careers in the technical services branches.

In addition, the Army offers trade apprenticeships to young people aged between 16 and $17\frac{1}{2}$ to train as technicians in the Royal Engineers, Royal Signals and Royal Electrical and Mechanical Engineers and as chefs in the Royal Logistic Corps. Apprenticeships in the Army involve 28 weeks on a foundation course at an Army Apprentices College, followed by further relevant courses and on-the-job experience.

From September 1998 the Army Foundation College will offer a new route for 16-year-olds who wish to enlist in the combat arms. The new residential college will provide a high-quality one-year training programme, leading to nationally recognised qualifications.

Subjects

Army officers: five GCSEs (grades A–C), including English, mathematics plus science or foreign language, plus two A-levels. Mathematics is compulsory, and physics and chemistry at GCSE (grades A–C) are important for entry to the Army's sixth-form college (Welbeck College).

Army ranks: GCSEs in English, mathematics, science plus a practical subject (for example, technology) are useful. In addition, a foreign language is required for specialist communicators and some intelligence operator work.

RAF officers: five GCSEs (grades A–C) including English, mathematics plus a minimum of two A-levels are required (subjects unspecified, except for certain professions, for example, doctor, dentist, engineer).

RAF ranks: GCSEs (grades A–C) including mathematics and science (English useful) for technician level.

Royal Navy officers: three GCSEs (grades A–C), including English and mathematics plus a minimum of two A-levels (subjects unspecified except for engineering – mathematics and physics). Sixty per cent of entrants have a degree; for women a degree is almost essential as competition is so fierce; for the Marines, entry is very competitive; most successful applicants have qualifications above the minimum specified.

Royal Navy ranks (ratings): GCSEs (grades A–C) in English, mathematics and physics are useful; A-levels are required for medical technicians.

Further information

Armed Forces Careers Information Offices (see telephone directory for address of local careers office)

Books and leaflets

Working in the Armed Services. 1996. COIC

Art and design and photography (CLCI: E)

The field of art and design is vast and includes a wide range of specialist areas and skills. Artists generally create work which is valued first and foremost for its aesthetic qualities rather than its practicality and do not usually employ mass-production techniques. They work in a variety of media, such as painting, drawing, sculpture, printmaking, film, video and photography, producing work as a means of self-expression. Designers, on the other hand, generally make products and objects for a practical purpose. Design work can be categorised into:

- industrial 3-D design (cars, televisions, aeroplanes, computers, household products etc.)
- textiles design (fabrics)
- interior design (furniture, houses, offices, shops)
- graphic design and illustration (printed work)
- fashion design (clothes and accessories, see also 'Clothing, fashion and textiles industries', page 102)
- engineering design (this is covered in the section on engineering – see page 136)
- craft design.

Industrial 3-D designers work with a range of materials such as metal, wood, glass or plastics. They usually design the exterior of products for a wide range of industries, while engineers design any moving parts. Their job is to make products functional, attractive and easy to use and maintain.

Textiles designers produce designs for furnishing fabrics, clothes, wallpapers and household linens.

Interior designers are concerned with the effective and attractive use of space and the decoration of all kinds of interiors, including people's homes, shops, offices, theatre sets and exhibitions. They not only produce a design for the space but also advise on materials, furniture, fabrics, fittings and colours.

Graphic designers are responsible for the way the text and pictures are arranged on all printed matter, including magazines, posters and books, plus scientific, medical and technical materials. Many graphic designers are currently finding that their skills are in great demand as people and companies want web sites designed for the Internet.

Illustrators combine the skills of fine art and graphic design in their work, illustrating text with drawings and paintings.

Fashion designers design clothes and accessories for individuals, for mass-production and for the designer ready-to-wear market (clothes sold in fairly small numbers with a designer label). They work closely with sample machinists and pattern cutters or cut the patterns and make up the sample clothes themselves.

Craft designers work on a variety of objects, many of which are mass-produced for industry, such as furniture, ceramics (pottery), silverware and jewellery.

Photography involves taking, developing and printing photographs for a wide variety of social and commercial reasons. Photographers not only use sophisticated cameras to take pictures but also have to be familiar with lighting and video equipment. Photographic technicians are involved in the development and processing side; they may mix chemicals, use various techniques and treatments for printing and check the quality of prints.

Sample job titles

Artist, ceramicist, designer, fashion designer, graphic designer, illustrator, interior designer, painter, photographer, 3-D designer

Opportunities

People with fine art qualifications will find it difficult to make a living from just selling their art; the majority supplement their income by teaching or entering the fringe areas of design, for example, illustration, painting designs on pottery and so on.

A number of designers are self-employed – particularly those in product/craft design (for example, ceramics, glassmaking, jewellery, furniture) and interior design – so they need business skills as well as talent.

Interior designers work in interior design consultancies, for retail chains, hotel groups and individual companies or as freelances.

Over 50 per cent of designers in industry and commerce work in the graphics field, often specialising in advertising, packaging, publishing or in corporate identity (the company image – logos and colours, letterheads). This field is highly competitive.

Very few fashion designers become well-known; the majority work in mass-production, and only a few opt for self-employment.

Textiles designers are employed by manufacturers, often working in design studios alongside the factories where the cloth is produced.

Approximately 50 per cent of professional photographers work in commercial and local photography, based in high-street studios or local newspaper offices. Other opportunities are in advertising, fashion, publicity and printing, industry and commerce (there are also openings in scientific, technical and medical photography). Competition in all these areas is stiff because the number of photographers usually outweighs the number of available jobs, so it is very important for them to be able to sell their skills. Photographic technicians tend to work in photo finishing or professional processing laboratories.

Other factors to consider

Creativity and imagination are essential for art and design careers. Artists and designers must be able to see the whole picture as well as having a good eye for detail. For example, a good interior designer can look at an empty shell of a room and visualise the different ways it could be decorated with furnishings, fittings and use of colour; an illustrator will have a grasp of the whole brochure or book to be illustrated before starting on the first sketch; and a photographer bears in mind the small details that make up the complete photograph. Good eyesight and colour vision are important.

Many of these careers are freelance, which means that business skills such as project management, administration, budgeting, costing, negotiation and time management are as important as the creative skills. It is also vital for designers to be able to talk to their clients and interpret what they want correctly – at the beginning of the project, rather than at the end.

Technical knowledge is necessary for many artistic or design careers. For instance, in the fashion or textiles industry, designers need to understand certain manufacturing processes, such as printing or dyeing; and graphic designers have to be familiar with the technicalities of printing, photography, desktop publishing and colour reproduction. Computer-aided design is used extensively in many fields, including advertising, engineering, publishing, film and television production.

Artists and designers often need a thick skin as not everyone will like the work they produce. They need to be able to accept and deal with criticism and rejection. This is particularly important when trying to get a foot on the ladder at the beginning of a career. It is also important to realise that designers usually work to a brief and frequently have to compromise their own creativity in favour of other factors such as safety, reliability, economics and the client's own requirements.

Freelances and self-employed people must be prepared to work long, and sometimes anti-social, hours if necessary.

Entry and training

Almost everyone starts with formal training and qualifications. Those who are convinced at the age of 16 that they want to pursue a career in art and design could do a preparatory Intermediate GNVQ or a two-year BTEC diploma course in general art and design at a further education college or a specialist art college; these lead on to higher-level specialist courses. Minimum entry qualifications for further education art and design courses are generally four GCSEs (grades A–C), although many students have more. Many of the BTEC and GNVQ courses include work experience and so offer better job prospects.

However, people who wish to keep their options open for longer can do a one-year foundation course at the age of 17, or more typically at 18, after two years in further education or in the sixth-form. Requirements are four GCSEs (grades A–C) and one or more relevant A-levels such as art. Foundation courses are designed to give students a basic understanding of a wide range of techniques and art and design specialisms, such as ceramics, textiles, photography, graphic design etc. They also provide a good opportunity to build up a portfolio of work.

Degree courses are offered by most universities and schools of art and design and specialist colleges. Students usually do a degree after completing a one-year full-time foundation course. Some courses combine fashion and textiles design, and students eventually specialise in one or the other. 3-D design courses can also be called product design or industrial design. Applications for the majority of art and design degree and HND courses – fine art and studio-based – are now made through UCAS and not through the Art and Design Admissions Registry (ADAR), which no longer exists, as these two systems merged in 1996. However, two routes are currently available. Route A follows the normal UCAS timetable, with applicants selecting up to six courses. Forms are sent simultaneously to all the named institutions. Route B has a later deadline, and the candidates choose up to four institutions in order of preference. Forms are sent to institutions sequentially. It is possible to apply for courses using both routes but the maximum number of choices is six, with a maximum of four choices through Route B and the rest from Route A. Candidates are strongly recommended to consult their foundation-course tutors for advice on which route to take.

All artists, photographers and designers generally need to prepare a portfolio, which should contain examples of different kinds of their work – a bit like a record of achievement. It is unlikely that a student would be accepted on to a course unless his or her portfolio had been inspected first. A portfolio is one of the best ways for artists/designers to demonstrate their potential, range and experience to colleges and employers.

Subjects

First-degree art and design course: five GCSEs; or one A-level and four GCSEs; or two A-levels and three GCSEs. Useful subjects are mathematics, technology, art, design, history of art, history and English. Obviously drawing ability is important for most art and design courses.

Ceramics: anyone interested in studying ceramics at degree level should consider taking A-levels in physics, chemistry and mathematics. The BTEC National Certificate in ceramics technology requires at least three GCSEs, including mathematics, English and a science subject.

3-D design: some colleges ask for mathematics, technology or science at GCSE or A-level.

Photography: GCSEs in physics, chemistry and mathematics, with a pass at A-level in one of these subjects, are essential for entry to degree courses in photographic sciences. GCSE and/or A-level photography are useful but not essential.

Further information

Association of Illustrators
British Institute of Professional Photography
Chartered Society of Designers
Institute of Ceramics
Society of Designer Craftsmen

Books and leaflets

Ball, L. and Chapman, N. 1996. *Careers in Art and Design*. Kogan Page

Dixon, B. 1996. *Getting into Art and Design*. Trotman

Art and Design Courses 1997/98. 1996. Trotman

A Guide to Art and Design Courses – On Course for 1998. Trotman and UCAS

Directory of Further Education. CRAC/Hobsons (annual)

Degree Course Guide (Art and Design). CRAC/Hobsons (annual)

Creative Futures: A Guide to Courses and Careers in Art, Craft and Design. 1997.

NSEAD *Working in Art and Design*. 1997. COIC

Beauty therapy and hairdressing (CLCI: IK/IL)

Beauty therapy, massage, image consultancy and hairdressing all come under the umbrella of 'Beauty therapy and hairdressing'. Image consultancy, or colour analysis – where trained consultants help people develop a style of clothing, hair and make-up to suit their image – is a growing area.

Beauty therapy

Beauty therapy is the term used to describe the wide range of treatments for the face and body. Beauty therapists specialise in skin care, which involves treating problems such as bad skin, unwanted hair, blemishes, scars, and psychological factors such as stress and tension. All beauty professionals qualify as a beauty therapist first; they can then choose to specialise further in a particular aspect of beauty therapy, for example, removing hair by electrolysis, giving body massages, manicures and foot treatments or applying and recommending make-up. Some beauty therapists become beauty consultants, which involves helping to sell beauty products by demonstrating them on willing members of the public in department stores and in people's homes.

Make-up artists in the film, television and theatre industries apply make-up to presenters and performers, alter people's features for specific character parts, use make-up to fake injuries and wounds and create different hairstyles.

Masseurs/masseuses knead and rub the body in order to relieve tension or aches and pains.

Hairdressing

Hairdressers cut, wash, style, tint and blow-dry people's hair and may also have to book appointments and deal with money. It is a 'people' job as it involves talking to customers, finding out what they want and ensuring they are happy with the treatment they receive. Junior staff gain hairdressing qualifications by learning theory at a college and through hands-on experience in a salon, learning the basic skills from more senior staff. When they begin working in a salon they spend much of their time shampooing customers' hair and are not allowed to cut and style it until they have had experience. They often have to do the basic jobs in the salon, such as making coffee for customers and staff, sweeping the salon floor and gathering up the used towels. In college they learn about the chemical reactions that take place, for example, when hair is dyed; hair and scalp conditions; cutting and styling methods, and so on.

Sample job titles

Beauty consultant, beauty therapist, electrolysist, hairdresser, make-up artist, masseur/masseuse, nail technician, stylist

Opportunities

Beauty therapists usually work for private salons or run their own practices from home. Some set up a private practice with other therapists. Beauty consultants work almost entirely for perfume and cosmetics manufacturers. They work in department stores, hotels, country clubs and health farms and visit people in their own homes.

Image consultants advise companies and politicians as well as individuals. Some set up a private business, while others work with image consulting organisations, which employ people on a freelance basis.

Those interested in hairdressing and beauty will find plenty of opportunities in a variety of settings: health and sports clubs, health farms, airports, cruise ships, hairdressing and beauty salons, department stores, hotels and country clubs, hospitals and prisons. Many people in this field are also self-employed. Hairdressers and make-up artists can work in the fashion industry, preparing models for the catwalk or a fashion shoot, and in the television and film industry.

People always need haircuts and hair styles and are currently interested in exercise, fitness, health and beauty and so prospects are good for this type of work.

Other factors to consider

Beauty therapy staff need to be able to describe and apply treatments in a courteous and sympathetic manner. They must be well-groomed themselves, be tactful and have common sense.

Hairdressers and beauty therapists are likely to be on their feet all day so they need a lot of stamina. Other useful qualities are artistic flair and patience.

Good communication skills are essential.

Entry and training

The ways into hairdressing and beauty therapy are:

- **via a two- or three-year traineeship** at the age of 16-plus, which is supplemented by training at a college on a day-release basis to gain relevant qualifications and NVQ awards
- **via a full-time two-year course** in hairdressing and beauty therapy at college
- **via a six-month or twelve-month course** at a private hairdressing salon.

Courses often combine hairdressing and beauty therapy and may include massage therapy.

Modern Apprenticeships and national traineeships are also available. Local TECs/LECs or careers offices will provide details of what is available in individual areas.

Beauty consultants are usually expected to be at least 21, with some experience of selling and preferably a qualification in beauty therapy. Training is on-the-job.

Make-up artists usually do a full-time course in hairdressing, beauty therapy or make-up. Most make-up artists do not start their training until they are 21 years of age. Training is both on- and off-the-job.

Image consultants generally do one of the short training courses offered by image consultancy organisations. No formal academic qualifications are required but it is important to have an eye for colour and good communication skills. Experience in beauty therapy, such as the application of make-up, is useful.

Subjects

GCSEs in English, science and mathematics are useful but not essential for beauty therapy; English, science (chemistry, social biology, human biology), mathematics and art are useful and may sometimes be required for hairdressing; English literature, drama and history are preferred for make-up artists in film, television and theatre.

Further information

Beauty Industry Authority
Hairdressing Training Board
International Health and Beauty Council

Books and leaflets

Fitzsimmons, S. 1996. *Careers in Hairdressing and Beauty Therapy.* Kogan Page
Working in Beauty and Hairdressing. 1996. COIC

Clothing, fashion and textiles industries (CLCI: S)

Dramatic changes have occurred within these industries during the late 1980s/1990s, with advances in technology and in manufacturing methods. New, faster and more sophisticated machinery and methods, together with the fact that some clothing manufacturers have relocated abroad, have led to a decrease in the number of people employed.

Clothing and fashion is Britain's fifth largest manufacturing industry, employing about 140,000 people. Clothes are a source of fascination as well as a necessity so fashion design calls for specific skills and originality, although not many people in the fashion industry create original designs. The vast majority adapt or translate other people's ideas to suit a particular market.

Behind the scenes of the couture houses (household designer names) are the workrooms, where designers, cutters, fitters, hand-stitchers and dressmakers work. Out in front are the exhibition organisers, models, financiers and sales staff.

In the ready-to-wear market the most recent fashions are mass-produced, often based on ideas from haute couture but adapted and reproduced, based on careful costings and knowledge of the market.

A tiny proportion of clothes are made individually for customers who buy the cloth and want a personal fit (bespoke). Bespoke tailoring is a very small, highly skilled part of the clothing industry, where tailors produce made-to-measure garments, mainly for men. After measuring each customer tailors help choose the fabric and the style. They then make the pattern and cut out the cloth before sewing the pieces together. The sewing is done both by hand and with machines.

Textile technicians and technologists work in production departments, setting up the machinery, testing materials and supervising the work of the support staff (dyeing, printing and finishing technicians and operatives). Their role is to solve problems relating to the manufacture of materials and to find new ways of using materials and/or improving them. Much of the machinery used is very sophisticated.

Machinists and cutters make the garments. They make the patterns and cut, sew and press the cloth, often using computer-controlled machines to cut out the pattern pieces.

Sample job titles

Dyeing technician, fashion designer, machinist, tailor, textile technologist

Opportunities

A major area of employment in the clothing and fashion industry is ready-to-wear mass-production, with designers, dressmakers, cutters, fitters and support staff making and selling today's fashion before it is overtaken by tomorrow's.

The fashion design world is extremely competitive and there are not many opportunities for employment in the haute couture houses. Very talented and very lucky people make their fortunes early, but the couture houses employ few permanent staff and use freelance or part-time workers instead. They make money by selling designs to the manufacturers for mass-production. Some art and design graduates become self-employed. Often they have little capital and work from home (sometimes alone, sometimes in pairs or in small groups) making new styles of clothes usually for the young. They may eventually set up their own boutiques or make a break-through with a large order from one store.

Together, department stores, boutiques, fashion chains and the dozens of independent or group-owned shops provide by far the largest employment area in the fashion retail industry. A number of positions for managers, sales staff, tailors (for alterations) and cashiers are to be found here.

Most tailors find work in large town centres, especially the West End of London. Opportunities for self-employment are good, with tailors opening their own shops.

Sixteen and eighteen-year-olds and graduates can find openings in manufacturing, design, product development, management and engineering. Many small textile firms require designers, textile technologists, scientists, textile technicians and sales and marketing staff.

Other factors to consider

The clothing, fashion and textile industries need people who have business sense as well as practical training.

Computers are frequently used in these industries so computer literacy is vital.

Tailors need good eyesight and manual dexterity to cope with the minute detail in their work. Numeracy is essential for taking measurements and estimating costs. An eye for colour and design is a prerequisite.

As in most jobs, communication and interpersonal skills are necessary.

Entry and training

Training for jobs in these industries can be gained in several ways. One option is to get a job and to train within a company, studying part-time at college for NVQs and other relevant qualifications. Training can also be company based, as part of a youth training programme. Headstart, a training scheme for young people managed by Kingscourt, part of the CAPITB Trust, the national training organisation for the clothing industry, provides openings for young people in the clothing sector. Trainees work towards various NVQs, such as Manufacturing Sewn Products at levels 1 and 2 and Handcraft Tailoring or Maintenance Engineering: Clothing Machinery at level 3. The clothing industry also offers Modern Apprenticeship and national traineeship programmes. Local careers service companies and TECs/LECs will provide details of what is available in individual areas.

There are also relevant NVQs for the textiles industry, such as Manufacturing Products from Textiles or Manufacturing Textiles at levels 1 and 2, and Textile Technician at level 3.

Another route is via a full-time degree-level textile or clothing course at college or university, providing practical-based technology training together with business/management skills. It is possible to enter management with a degree or HND in clothing technology.

Art colleges and universities offer many courses in fashion design. Applicants need two or three A-levels (at high grades) plus three or four GCSEs, together with a portfolio of work. Drawing ability and an all-round talent in art are required. Given the large numbers of design graduates pursuing too few openings, it may be worth considering combining a fashion course with technology, computing and management skills. Courses that combine these skills with fashion design could lead to practical jobs in an area of demand, particularly if they also include periods of work experience in the industry.

Production workers, machinists and cutters train on-the-job and can study on a day-release basis for relevant qualifications (for example, NVQs in Clothing).

Subjects

Design courses: A-level art is often specified (see 'Art and design and photography', page 94).

Degree-level technical courses: A-levels in mathematics and science; mathematics at GCSE.

Textile technologists: sciences at A-level.

Textile technicians: minimum GCSEs (grades A–C) in mathematics and a science – A-levels often required.

Mathematics and English are useful subjects to pass at GCSE for training at any level in this industry.

Further information

CAPITB Trust
Textile Institute

Books and leaflets

Chapman, N. 1996. *Careers in Fashion*. Kogan Page
Working in Fashion. 1996. COIC

Complementary medicine (CLCI: J)

Complementary medicine embraces a wide range of practices, therapies and techniques that are holistic, which means that the whole person – the body and the mind – is treated and not just the part of the body where there is a problem. Different therapies are available for various conditions, for example, problems with the structure of the body (back pain, bad posture, aching and painful joints) may be dealt with by osteopaths or chiropractors; people with psychological or emotional problems may go to a homeopath, acupuncturist or herbalist. Treatments work to address the underlying causes of the symptoms. Complementary medicine practitioners do not use drugs or surgery in their work.

Most practitioners spend some time, usually longer than a conventional doctor would, discussing the lifestyle and medical history of the client before they begin to discuss possible treatments. Taking the time to gain such information is very important for treating people holistically.

Some of the therapies require considerable knowledge and study of the anatomy and physiology of the body, particularly those that deal with the musculo-skeletal system.

Osteopathy

Osteopaths use manipulative methods of treatment to correct the bone and muscle structures of the body. They deal with bones, joints, ligaments, tendons and muscles. Many people seek treatment for back pain and spinal problems, but osteopaths also treat sports injuries, tension, headaches and respiratory and digestive problems.

Chiropractic

Chiropractic is the third largest primary healthcare profession in the world. Treatment is similar to that in osteopathy in that it involves the use of manipulative methods to relieve pain. However, chiropractors treat mainly spinal disorders. They specialise in the diagnosis, treatment and overall management of conditions which are due to mechanical dysfunction of joints, and their effects on the nervous system.

Acupuncture

Acupuncture is an ancient system of healing developed over thousands of years as part of the traditional medicine of China, Japan and other Eastern countries. The skin is pierced at specific points with fine needles. The points lie on channels of energy called meridians. Acupuncturists treat people with specific symptoms or conditions, such as pain, anxiety, eczema, arthritis, menstrual disorders, intestinal problems and so on. The aim is to treat the whole person and restore balance to stimulate the mind and body's own healing response. It requires an in-depth knowledge of a patient's physical, mental and emotional state prior to treatment.

Homeopathy

Homeopaths use various pills and powders taken from plant, mineral and animal sources in their treatment. They give patients diluted, minute doses of substances (so small that they cannot actually be measured), which activate the body's own natural defences to produce a cure. The theory is to treat 'like with like'. Substances that can produce symptoms of disease in a healthy person if given at toxic levels can cure similar symptoms in a sick person when given in such diluted, minute doses. Two kinds of professionals practise homeopathy: homeopathic doctors, who are medically qualified doctors, and homeopaths, who have not previously trained as a medical doctor.

Reflexology

Reflexologists use pressure points on the feet to diagnose and relieve problems in the whole body. The belief is that each zone of the foot corresponds to a different point in the body, and by applying pressure the healing process is stimulated.

Other therapies include the Alexander Technique (teaching people mind-body coordination to relieve postural-related problems), naturopathy (using psychology and diet to encourage the body to heal itself), Reiki (healing by laying on of hands and distance healing), aromatherapy (using essential oils in massage techniques to stimulate cells in the body) and Bach Flower remedies (using flower essences to treat the personality, mind and emotions).

Sample job titles

Acupuncturist, aromatherapist, chiropractor, herbalist, homeopath, osteopath, reflexologist

Opportunities

Complementary medicine is becoming more acceptable as an adjunct to conventional medicine, opening up more opportunities for qualified and experienced practitioners. Many GPs now advise their patients to consider complementary medicine in addition to conventional medicine and may refer them to practitioners. Some of the complementary therapies, such as homeopathy or osteopathy, may even be available on the NHS in some health authorities. A few chiropractors now have contracts with GP fundholders, although these are still rare.

Most complementary practitioners are self-employed, working in private practice and in health clinics. Although it is possible for some therapists to earn high salaries, the amount of money is dependent on the number of clients they have and the hours they are willing to work. Reflexologists and aromatherapists may be able to set up clinics in health clubs, leisure clubs or beauty salons. Occasionally, therapists set up a practice together in order to share costs and clients.

Other factors to consider

First and foremost, practitioners in any kind of complementary medicine need to be interested in a patient's well-being and have a genuine desire to help. The best practitioners are the ones with good communication skills and who can understand and interpret the concerns of the patient.

Manual dexterity is useful for the 'hands-on' therapies. Some of the manipulative therapies can be physically demanding, so strength and stamina are important qualities to have.

Business skills are an advantage, given the likelihood of self-employment in this area.

An interest in plants is helpful for herbalists.

Some of the therapies take years of study and call for dedication and commitment.

Entry and training

Many people become interested in complementary medicine through their work in other areas of medical and non-medical care or through having treatment themselves.

Training is offered at various private specialist colleges and for some therapies is often lengthy, for example, six years for chiropractic, at least three years for the Alexander Technique, and four years for herbal medicine, osteopathy and naturopathy. Doctors, nurses and other medical staff may be exempt from some examinations as a result of their previous professional qualifications, thus shortening their training. Aromatherapy can be studied full-time (over nine months) or part-time (taking up to two years). Short courses for other therapies, such as reflexology or colour therapy, can be taken at further education colleges.

The Anglo European College of Chiropractic in Bournemouth, Dorset is currently the only place in Europe that offers both a degree and a postgraduate degree in chiropractic. The University of Glamorgan offers a BSc/BSc (Hons) in chiropractic, and the University of Surrey offers a master's degree in chiropractic.

There are two training routes in acupuncture:

- **via colleges accredited by the British Acupuncture Accreditation Board (BAAB)** for students who are non-medically qualified. The length of the training course depends on the individual colleges. However, the recommended training (which provides professional accreditation for acupuncture) is two years full-time or the part-time equivalent. Entry requirements for these courses vary (some colleges ask for two A-levels, while others consider previous experience and commitment to acupuncture as more important than academic qualifications). A minimum age of 21 is sometimes stipulated. Contact the British College of Acupuncture for a list of colleges
- **via a course at the British College of Acupuncture**. The entry requirement is a degree in medicine or a degree or other recognised qualification in naturopathy, osteopathy, physiotherapy, nursing or homeopathy. The training lasts three years for nurses or similarly qualified students and two years, part-time, for doctors.

There are very few grants to assist students, so courses are largely self-funded.

Subjects

Sciences are important for many of these therapies.

Osteopathy: biology and chemistry A-levels and English language at GCSE are preferred.

Acupuncture: science subjects (preferably to a minimum of A-level standard) are useful but not essential for training in most BAAB-accredited colleges and essential for entry to some BAAB-accredited colleges and to degree/diploma courses prior to training at the British College of Acupuncture.

Chiropractic: two A-levels are required, including chemistry and one other science at A-level (preferably biology). English, mathematics and physics at GCSE (grades A–C).

Homeopathy: biology and one other science at A-level are preferred.

Further information

Anglo European College of Chiropractic
British Acupuncture Council
British Chiropractic Association
British College of Acupuncture (will be changing address in 1998 – new details will be available from the British Acupuncture Council)
British College of Naturopathy and Osteopathy
British Homoeopathic Association
British School of Osteopathy
Institute for Complementary Medicine
International College of Oriental Medicine
Society of Teachers of the Alexander Technique

Books and leaflets

Brown, L. 1994. *Working in Complementary and Alternative Medicine.* Kogan Page

Computing (CLCI: C and R)

Computers are used in nearly every kind of job. Even the smallest companies now have at least one computer, and most employees need word processing or keyboard skills. Because of this the choice of jobs is wide. This section covers employment in the supply side of the computing industry.

The computing, or information technology (IT), industry is undergoing constant, rapid change, as developments in technology continue apace. For instance, laptop computers are now common-place, voice-recognition and hand-held computers exist, the Internet – the global Information Superhighway – is becoming available to more and more of us, and computer-aided design and manufacture are revolutionising some industries, especially finance. These developments have opened up new opportunities for careers within the computing industry.

At one end of the computing chain are the hardware and micro-electronics engineers, who research, design and develop the systems and components used in the manufacture and design of computers. Engineers in this area need highly technical skills and good scientific and engineering qualifications to degree/HND level.

Alongside the hardware engineers are the software engineers, applications programmers, or systems designers, who develop and design the software for computer systems. Like the hardware engineers, their technical expertise and knowledge needs to be of a high standard.

In the middle are systems analysts, who identify exactly what an organisation needs in terms of computing equipment and systems for it to be more effective and efficient. They often visit clients to discuss a project brief (exactly what the client wants and why) or the workings of a particular piece of software. As well as technical knowledge of hardware and software, systems analysts have to understand the procedures in an organisation so they can work out which ones would be better performed by computer. The computer system design will be tailored according to this analysis. Systems analysts often work closely with applications programmers, who write computer programs for specific tasks and functions. Sometimes these roles may be combined into one. Applications programmers need to have knowledge of the various computer programming languages and be technically proficient.

At the other end of the computing chain are service technicians or end-user support staff. Service technicians install and maintain computer hardware and software systems. End-user support or helpdesk support is a service that plays a vital role in assisting computer users who have no technical knowledge of the systems they are using. Helpdesk support is often the first rung on the support ladder and could lead to training for more skilled roles, such as employment in the field of development and analysis. Before computers became ubiquitous, demand for computer operators and data-entry clerks was high. However, as the majority of employees possess keyboarding skills today, computer operators and data-entry clerks are not so much in demand. Many people can now operate their own computers without too much prior knowledge and often with little need for technical expertise. Computer networks, however, need support staff as they can often go wrong.

In addition to those listed above other jobs are:

- **in computer sales**. These jobs require a combination of technical knowledge and sales ability. Salespeople may be involved in selling computers to the public in a high-street retail shop or in selling larger systems to industry and commerce
- **as an IT manager**, overseeing the information technology needs – such as what computers to buy, what software to use and so on – of an organisation. This job requires both IT experience and management skills
- **as a network or communications manager**, setting up and maintaining networks of computer systems. This is also often a dual role, combining IT knowledge and management ability.

Sample job titles

Applications programmer, micro-electronics engineer, computer operator, computer programmer, service technician/end-user support, salesperson, software engineer, systems analyst, systems designer, systems programmer

Opportunities

Most organisations have openings for a computer specialist to coordinate, support and maintain the IT function. In addition, skilled and experienced computer technologists are employed and trained in many different roles by software houses, electronics companies, computer manufacturers and computer consultancies. Computer programmers are often freelance. Some big companies employ their own programmers.

Systems analysts and software engineers/systems programmers are in demand because of their highly technical skills and specialist knowledge. They may have the opportunity to work overseas on projects, particularly if employed by large companies with international interests. Some of them also work on a freelance or consultancy basis. There is an increasing trend for companies to use freelance staff.

The computer games market is an ever-expanding one and offers employment opportunities for both software engineers and sales-people.

With the advent of the Internet, the number of openings to create web sites for clients is growing for computer-literate graphic designers, either in-house or on a freelance basis.

Other factors to consider

Many of the jobs require a logical, methodical approach to solve problems and work out customers' requirements. In addition, systems analysts and designers need some creativity and imagination for problem-solving.

It is very important to keep up to date with new developments in this rapidly changing industry – through doing background reading and attending courses.

Teamwork and excellent communication skills are essential for all jobs. It is important to be able to talk to clients to find out what their needs are and to explain clearly and simply any technical information without using jargon. Some jobs may involve travel to and from customers' premises. Some may also involve shift work, as in the case of service technicians, who may need to work on computers out of office hours so that they cause as little disruption for the users as possible. The computer support staff in some companies have to support the computer systems in their overseas offices from the UK. This means that they might have to do shift work (as some of the branches will be in different time zones).

Business sense is desirable, not only for sales jobs and for systems analysis, where there is direct contact with clients, but also for self-employed people.

It is usual to move from company to company fairly frequently to gain a wide range of experience and different skills.

Entry and training

For many jobs in computing, entry is post-degree/HND. Useful degree subjects for the more technical jobs, for example, software engineering and micro-electronics, are electronics, computer studies and software engineering; for systems analysis and sales jobs, business studies is helpful (combined with computer programming experience), although any degree is useful.

Entry to IT support jobs, some applications programming and sales positions may be possible with appropriate A-level qualifications. However, those with lower qualifications may find openings too, as junior helpdesk support operators. As experience and skills develop, it may then be possible to move into desktop (personal computer) or network support roles.

Once employed, training can be on-the-job, in-house, through distance-learning or short courses, for example, those offered by the National Computing Centre. A number of NVQs are available at various levels, for example, in Information Systems and Design, Software Production and Servicing Office Information Technology Equipment and Systems. Employers often value experience more than qualifications.

National traineeships and Modern Apprenticeships may be available, for instance, in computer service technician work or in engineering and IT. Local careers offices and TECs/LECs will provide details.

Subjects

A-levels in mathematics and science-related subjects may be required for some computer-related courses but not all, provided the applicant has GCSE mathematics. A-level computer science may be useful but is not essential.

For anyone interested in computer engineering (electronics) degrees, mathematics and double science (with a strong physics content) is required at GCSE level. A-levels should include mathematics and physics.

Further information

British Computer Society
National Computing Centre Education Services Ltd
National Training Organisation for Information Technology
   (ITNTO)

Books and leaflets
Yardley, D. *Careers in Computing and IT*. 1997. Kogan Page

Working in Information Technology. 1996. COIC
Various computer magazines (from the local public library or news-
agent)

Construction – craft careers (CLCI: U)

Each construction site comprises many people doing a variety of different jobs. Skilled craftspeople do the actual construction work –
helping to repair, refurbish, build, renovate and restore all kinds of
buildings, roads, bridges, tunnels and railways. See 'Construction –
professional and technician careers' for details of other jobs and
careers within this industry.

Sample job titles

Bricklayer, carpenter/joiner, painter and decorator, plasterer, roofer,
tiler

Opportunities

The construction industry employs approximately 10 per cent of the
working population of the UK. Its prospects, however, are closely
tied to the ups and downs of the economy. Craftspeople find work
with general building firms, building contractors, property companies, local authorities and other public organisations.

Many construction craftspeople are now self-employed, working
on a subcontract basis for building contractors.

Other factors to consider

Depending on the type of skilled work, people working in this area
need to have:

- a head for heights
- fitness and strength to climb ladders, lift equipment and materials,
  use various tools
- numeracy skills (for example, to calculate areas and volumes)
- literacy skills (for example, to read technical drawings and plans)
- a strong sense of responsibility (people may rely on and trust them)

- flexibility to cope with changing work patterns and places of work
- manual skills
- a willingness to learn.

Those who do this type of work need to have common sense and an awareness for their own safety and that of others. Some construction workers are outside in all weathers, others work indoors. Good weather can mean working longer hours to get the job finished, especially if bad weather has held it up. Teamwork and interpersonal skills are important as construction often involves working closely with other people, not only on building sites but also in private homes or offices. Good hand-to-eye coordination can be vital. Craftspeople will need to be prepared to travel from site to site to wherever the work is, which may mean working away from home for long periods of time. Business skills are important for those who are self-employed.

Entry and training

Most craftspeople enter the industry straight from school, between the ages of 16 and 18, usually on a training programme or apprenticeship. GCSEs are useful (see below for relevant subjects). The craftspeople learn skills on-the-job but can also work towards qualifications to take them to technician-level jobs. Local TECs/LECs will provide details of the training available in individual areas. Craft construction training combines formal college study with site experience with a building contractor. It can take from two to three years to achieve NVQs level 2/3. Trainees with the potential for NVQ level 3 are considered for transfer to a Modern Apprenticeship.

The Construction Industry Training Board (CITB) and other construction trades training organisations offer aptitude exercises for young people in their last year at school. These help them decide which trade they would be most suited to.

Subjects

GCSEs in mathematics, science, English and technology/practical subjects (woodwork, metalwork) are preferred.

Further information

Construction Industry Training Board (CITB)

Books and leaflets
Working in Construction. 1994. COIC

Construction – professional and technician careers (CLCI: U)

The construction industry employs over one million people in the UK. It needs a variety of people, from those who prefer to work outdoors and are good at managing and supervising people to those whose talents are for research, design or administration. Apart from the craftspeople (see page 116), other kinds of professional and technician-level jobs include managers, designers, surveyors, architects, contractors, civil engineers and technicians. They are all concerned with improving the environment in which people live and work. Some of these careers – design, surveying, architecture – are dealt with in other sections of this book.

Any form of construction requires a team to see the project through from beginning to end. The team combines the talents of the various professionals, technicians and craftspeople. All are dependent on each other's expertise to achieve the desired result. The project team may include some of the following:

- **Architects and landscape architects**, who are also involved at various stages
- **Building control officers**, who ensure buildings meet minimum standards; they work largely within local authorities
- **Building services engineers**, who design, install and maintain the services needed to make buildings comfortable and efficient
- **Civil engineers**, who commission, design and build the necessary infrastructure
- **Construction managers**, who run the site and direct the work of the site engineers
- **Contractors**, who are appointed to convert the design into reality; they employ the different professionals needed for the project

- **Designers, planners and quantity surveyors**, who may meet initially to discuss the way forward, the budget, the costs and the time involved
- **Estimators**, who price the project
- **Planners**, who determine the sequence of the various tasks
- **Project managers**, who head the team of construction professionals; their background is generally within the construction industry, as quantity surveyors, engineers, architects, etc.
- **Site managers**, who are concerned with the progress of the project
- **Structural engineers**, who design the shape and form of various components that give structures strength.

Technicians work on the detail of a project, whereas professionals are more involved in the overall planning and supervision. Technicians can train for one particular job, such as planning, estimating or surveying, but there is usually quite a lot of movement between specialist areas, particularly in smaller firms.

Sample job titles

Architect, builder, building services engineer, builder/technician, buyer, civil/structural engineer, estimator, planner, quantity surveyor, site manager

Opportunities

The construction industry is to a large extent dependent on changes in the economic climate and has struggled in recent years. However, employment prospects are gradually improving.

Opportunities are good with construction companies, such as Wimpey, Taylor Woodrow, Laing and Mowlem, which employ thousands of people and look for young people with management potential. A few technician vacancies are available each year for school-leavers with GCSEs. However, most of the jobs in these companies generally go to people with degrees or HNDs in building.

Civil engineering companies, building/civil engineering contractors, general building firms and local authorities employ many professional, managerial and technician-level staff to carry out construction work.

Young professionals can gain experience on sites in mainland Europe, where UK construction companies have won contracts. These companies are looking for people who are prepared to travel.

Other factors to consider

Professionals and technicians must be able to communicate and develop good working relationships with others in the construction team. It is common in the industry to travel from site to site and occasionally be away from home for long periods of time.

Computers play a big part in the design and planning stages of a project, so computer literacy is important at both levels.

Managers need to be able to motivate people and get the best from them.

Entry and training

Graduates with degrees or diplomas in building and construction, construction management, civil and structural engineering or surveying can join a construction company and learn the business on a construction site. Some of the larger construction companies sponsor students on first-degree courses in relevant subjects. These courses are often four-year sandwich courses.

School-leavers joining companies at age 18 with A-levels can often study by day-release for BTEC National awards in building studies, building, civil engineering and surveying. It is also possible to study part-time for professional or 'higher technician' qualifications, such as those offered by the Chartered Institute of Building.

School-leavers with at least four GCSEs (grades A–C) can study towards NVQs levels 3 and 4 or BTEC National awards on a Modern Apprenticeship.

Preparation for a career as a professional builder or as a building technician involves full- or part-time further education with complementary industrial experience and training. Training to be a technician normally requires a minimum of three GCSEs (grades A–C), although many applicants have higher qualifications.

Subjects

GCSEs in English, mathematics and physics are often requested and are needed for entry to BTEC National awards and for technician training. Some institutions require A-levels in mathematics and physics.

Computer studies or design and technology subjects are also useful.

Further information

Association of Building Engineers
Chartered Institute of Building
Chartered Institute of Building Services Engineers
Construction Industry Training Board (CITB)
Institute of Building Control

Books and leaflets

Introduction to the Construction Industry. CITB
Working in Construction. 1994. COIC

Cultural careers (CLCI: F)

Cultural careers mean those that involve the discovery, study or preservation of historical objects or documents. Anyone interested in this type of work usually has a keen sense of curiosity about both the past and the present – how we come to be as we are today. They may be interested in gathering information about a certain period from objects and materials and in identifying and recording them; in conserving and restoring works of art and objects of historic interest; or in preserving historical records. Some of the jobs in this varied field are described below.

Archaeology is the scientific study of the past, both through looking at material remains and through studying the environment in which communities lived. Modern archaeology is a meticulous scientific discipline, requiring great attention to detail, and it draws on many other traditional areas of study, such as history, geography, religion and so on. Excavation is only one technique used by archaeologists: they can also be skilled in ground and aerial surveying, conservation techniques and the application of scientific techniques as well as underwater archaeology, buildings archaeology and environment archaeology.

Conservators work closely with archaeologists, anthropologists, historians, technologists and chemists. These laboratory-based specialists investigate, treat and restore objects and also design and supervise storage and display areas. They occasionally carry out some fieldwork, excavating particularly fragile or complex objects, and also often work on buildings.

Curatorial staff work in museums and art galleries. They are responsible for the administration, conservation, exhibition, acquisition and circulation of the items in their collections. They also have to identify and record the objects, as well as prepare the museum's publications. The most senior curatorial staff – known as keepers – run the departments of larger museums and are responsible to the head or director of the museum. A keeper or curator might be a specialist in one of many fields, such as art, archaeology, botany, coins, ethnography, geology, natural history, local history and weaponry. Curators in smaller, local authority run museums may be responsible for covering many of these areas and are therefore less likely to be specialists.

Archivists look after documents and other written records of the past, selecting which ones should be kept for posterity. They preserve the records of central and local government, legal documents, and private documents such as diaries, letters, wills, and so on. A major aspect of an archivist's work is to make documents available and more widely known to the public, and archivists often mount exhibitions of archives (records), give talks and prepare publications as well as assisting students, lecturers, teachers and members of the public who wish to study some aspect of local or family history or the law.

Sample job titles

Archaeological consultant, archaeologist, archivist, conservator, keeper, museum curator, museum officer

Opportunities

Opportunities in this area are comparatively limited. Competition for jobs is fierce, even though many positions are poorly paid and insecure. Many people choose these careers for job interest rather than for financial rewards.

Archaeologists will find openings in museums, central and local government, and independent units and trusts, as well as in universities (as lecturers). An increasing number of archaeological consultants (usually graduates with research degrees) are self-employed. They have a wide range of experience and work for archaeological units and museums on a contract basis. Those who cannot find a job in archaeology use their qualifications to find a job in other unrelated areas, such as industry and commerce, education, and IT. Employers like students to have a degree in archaeology as they consider that it teaches them teamwork and leadership skills, and to be good communicators, practical and proactive. Archaeologists also need to have sound analytical skills to bring together many different types of data in one report.

Curatorial staff and conservators of archaeological objects are employed in museums, galleries, in archaeological units and in university departments. However, only a third of conservators work in the public sector; the rest work for private firms, in partnerships or in their own businesses. Conservators may find opportunities for employment overseas. In the museum world, the trend is towards short-term contracts. Career progression is usually dependent on mobility – being willing to move virtually anywhere in the UK. This is true also for archaeologists.

Many museums now use external contractors for many of the jobs, including display and conservation work.

Archivists work in county and city record offices, national libraries and museums, large public libraries, university libraries and in private libraries and institutions. An increasing number of archivists are now involved in managing records and helping with the organisation of current and semi-current records of businesses, both to promote efficiency and to make sure that the right records are kept for the future.

Other factors to consider

Many of the jobs described above need an infinite supply of patience as some of the work is very intricate and can demand extreme concentration and attention to detail. Computer literacy, interpersonal skills and project management are also often required.

In addition, conservators need manual dexterity and excellent colour vision. It helps if field archaeologists are physically fit. They should not mind being outdoors in all weathers.

Archivists should enjoy reading about history and like historical research, which can be a slow, painstaking business. Although they must be prepared to work on their own, listing large archives, they also need to have good interpersonal skills because they come into contact with a wide range of people, including professional colleagues and members of the public. Archivists sometimes have to move heavy and bulky materials.

Teamwork and excellent communication skills are essential in all the above areas.

Entry and training

Those wanting to be archaeologists generally need to have a university degree, either in archaeology as a single subject or combined with a wide range of other subjects such as ancient or medieval history, geography, art or anthropology. The degree can be studied either as a BA or as a BSc depending on the university and the candidate's A-level subjects. Competition for places on courses is fierce, and applicants need three A-levels with high grades. Applicants are also recommended to show evidence of interest in their subject, for example, through membership of an archaeology society and relevant voluntary work.

Some students do a two-year HND in practical archaeology (accredited by Bournemouth University in conjunction with Yeovil College, Somerset) then go on to do a degree afterwards. NVQs in archaeology are now available at levels 2, 3 and 4.

Many conservation courses are available (details from the UKIC – the United Kingdom Institute for Conservation – and Museum Training Institute) and increasingly formal training is a prerequisite. Most candidates have a first degree (science, fine art and art history are all useful) or even a postgraduate qualification. A few apprentice-ships are available in conservation and restoration, mainly in furniture, textiles and stone and wood carving, with opportunities to study part-time towards qualifications.

For a curatorial post a degree is usually required, and it is becoming increasingly necessary to hold a postgraduate vocational qualification. Postgraduate courses offer training in museum studies and related subjects. Details can be obtained from the Museum Training Institute.

A good honours degree is essential for getting a job in archive work. Archivists usually have a degree in either history, Latin or other classical languages, or English. Many posts require postgraduate qualifications in archives administration or studies.

Subjects

Archaeology: A-levels in archaeology, geography and history are useful, although they are not an automatic prerequisite for a degree in archaeology; Latin or Ancient Greek are needed only for classical archaeology. Serious consideration should be given to at least one science subject (preferably biology or chemistry).

Archivist: A-levels in history, Latin or other classical languages, or English are recommended. History degree courses require History A-level plus two other A-levels, all with high grades.

Science-related and conservation courses: science subjects at A-level, particularly chemistry, are often asked for. Useful GCSE subjects include English, mathematics, history, geography and foreign languages.

Science subjects are good for archaeology courses with a scientific emphasis (leading to scientific study of biological remains, geophysical surveys and so on).

Curators: useful subjects at GCSE or A-level include history, fine art, biology, botany and chemistry.

Further information

Council for British Archaeology
Institute of Field Archaeologists
Museums Association

Museum Training Institute
Society of Archivists
United Kingdom Institute for Conservation of Historic and Artistic
   Works (UKIC)

Books and leaflets

Careers in Museums. Museum Training Institute/Museums
   Association
History (with Archaeology), Degree Course Guide (annual). CRAC/
   Hobsons
Working in History. 1997. COIC

Dentistry (CLCI: J)

Dentistry includes the prevention, diagnosis and treatment of diseases
and disorders of the teeth, mouth, jaw and surrounding tissues.

   Dentists treat teeth that are decayed, fractured or badly worn by
putting in fillings, inlays or crowns. They replace missing teeth with
bridges and prostheses (false teeth) and treat dental abnormalities,
diseases and traumatic injuries. Increasingly, preventive measures for
decay and periodontal (gum) disease are being prescribed. Some
dentists specialise in orthodontics work – the study and correction of
mouth irregularities, which are more common in children. Others
are hospital specialists: the dental surgeons who deal with facial
injuries; and the specialists in restorative dentistry, who restore
existing teeth through crown or bridge work and replace teeth with
dentures.

   Dental hygienists work under the direct personal supervision of
the dentist. Their job is to scale, clean and polish teeth and advise on
preventive measures and oral hygiene. In some practices, the dentist
takes on this role too.

   Dental surgery assistants/nurses work closely with dentists. They
prepare and mix fillings, select instruments, process X-rays, keep
patient records and generally look after the welfare of the patients as
well as the professional needs of the dentist.

   Dental therapists provide a support service. They carry out minor
treatment on children's teeth and give oral hygiene instruction both
in the surgery and within the community.

Dental technicians make and repair dentures, plates and bridges according to the prescription given by the dentist. They need in-depth knowledge of the various materials used and their properties for making dentures.

Dentists' receptionists welcome patients, make appointments and keep records. Requirements for this job are as those for any clerical job (see the section on 'Administration and office work'). Experience as a dental surgery assistant or nurse can be useful.

Sample job titles

Dentist, dental surgeon, dental surgery assistant/nurse, dental hygienist, dental technician, dental therapist, orthodontist, receptionist

Opportunities

The majority of dentists set up in general practice, either on their own or more usually with other dentists – they work under contract to the National Health Service but can also treat patients privately; others work in hospitals (in dental departments or in dental hospitals) and community health clinics. Dentists can also be employed in the Armed Forces, in industry, in research and in university and hospital teaching. Dental nurses, hygienists and dentists' receptionists work alongside dentists and so work wherever they work.

Technicians work for the NHS, in clinics, hospitals and dental laboratories. The majority, however, are in commercial laboratories or in laboratories owned by dentists.

Dental therapists are part of a very small profession that works mainly in hospitals and community dental practices. Dental therapists who are also qualified as dental hygienists may work in general practice.

Other factors to consider

All staff need good 'people skills' because patients are often anxious and in pain and need to be put at ease. They should be caring and understand the anxieties that patients have. Dentists need to be able to explain to them in layman's terms what the problem is and what treatment is being prescribed.

Also important are:

- the ability to work in a team
- stamina (to endure long periods standing up)
- manual dexterity
- concentration and attention to detail
- good eyesight.

In addition, dentists working in dental practices need some administrative and business skills as they are self-employed.

Anyone working in dentistry should not be squeamish about blood, diseased gums, decaying teeth and halitosis (bad breath).

Entry and training

It takes a long time to train to be a dentist – five years for a university degree in dentistry/dental surgery (entry with appropriate scientific A-levels) at one of the 14 dental schools in the UK (a list of schools is available from the British Dental Association). Students over the age of $17\frac{1}{2}$ (and under 30) without the right A-levels can opt to do an extra pre-dental year of study. Entry to dental schools and for the pre-dental year is competitive, so good A-levels and GCSEs (see 'Subjects') are required in addition to personal qualities such as a caring attitude, ability to concentrate and to handle stressful situations. Dentists cannot practise until they are registered on the Dentists' Register maintained by the General Dental Council. Qualified dentists entering the NHS general dental services have to spend one year in a general practice as a salaried vocational trainee. They then become an associate dentist before starting up on their own or with other dentists.

Dental nurses need to have a reasonable standard of general education. Training is:

- **via a one- or two-year full-time dental nurse training course at a dental school** (two to four GCSEs are required)
- **on-the-job**, although they sometimes study on a part-time or distance-learning basis towards the National Certificate in Dental Nursing. Many dentists recruit and train their assistants
- through a **one-year full-time course at a college of further education followed by combined work experience and part-time study** for one year.

It is also possible to train as a dental nurse with the Armed Forces.

Dental hygienists need a minimum of two years' experience as a dental nurse as well as a recognised Certificate in Dental Nursing. This means that the majority of entrants are at least 20 years of age. Five GCSEs (grades A–C) are the minimum requirement to do dental hygienist training. Full-time training is via a two-year course that leads to a Diploma in Dental Hygiene at a dental school. Two dental training centres offer a joint diploma in Dental Hygiene and Dental Therapy: the London Hospital Medical College and the Charles Clifford Dental Hospital in Sheffield.

Opportunities for dental therapy training are few and far between. There are currently only three courses: two two-year courses combining dental therapy and dental hygiene (at the dental training centres in London and Sheffield); and one two-year dental therapy diploma course for dental nurses (at the Dental Auxiliary School, University Dental Hospital NHS Trust in Cardiff). Entry requirements are the same as those for the dental hygienist diploma. Qualified dental hygienists with a minimum of one year's employment experience can study part-time for two years at the University of Liverpool School of Dentistry to become a therapist.

Dental technicians need excellent eyesight (with or without spectacles or contact lenses) and good colour vision. Minimum entry qualifications for training are four GCSEs in appropriate subjects (see below). Training is available through:

- a five-year **apprenticeship** in a commercial dental laboratory or dental practice laboratory, as well as part-time study towards a BTEC National Diploma in Science (Dental Technology)
- a three-year **full-time college course** that leads to a BTEC National Diploma
- two years' **study on a part-time basis** towards the BTEC HND. This is done by people who are in employment and who have taken the BTEC National Diploma in Science (Dental Technology)
- a four-year **training programme in a hospital**, leading to the BTEC National Diploma. This is offered by eight hospitals in the UK.

Subjects

Dentist: A-levels (minimum grade B) in chemistry and two others (either mathematics, biology, zoology or physics). The most widely recommended A-level combination for dentistry is chemistry, physics and biology or zoology.

Dental nurse: GCSEs (grades A–C) including English and biology.

Dental hygienist: GCSEs (grades A–C) including English and science (biology). A-levels may also be required by some dental schools.

Dental technician: GCSEs (grades A–C) including mathematics and science. Some hospitals require GCSEs in English, mathematics, physics and biology. Entry requirements for the BTEC First Certificate in Science are generally GCSEs in science, English and mathematics.

Dental therapist: GCSEs (grades A–C) including English and a biology-based subject (botany, human biology, zoology).

Further information

British Association of Dental Nurses
British Dental Association
British Dental Hygienists' Association
Charles Clifford Dental Hospital, Sheffield
Dental Auxiliary School, London Hospital Medical College
Dental Auxiliary School, University Dental Hospital NHS Trust, Cardiff
Dental Technician Education and Training Advisory Board
Dental Therapy Course, Liverpool University School of Dentistry
Local Armed Forces Careers Office

Books and leaflets

Humphries, J. and Brown, L. 1996. *Careers in Medicine, Dentistry and Mental Health*. Kogan Page
Working in Medicine and Dentistry. 1996. COIC

Emergency services (CLCI: M)

The three main emergency services are the ambulance service, the fire service and the police. In addition, there are various search-and-rescue organisations, such as the Coastguard Agency (known also as Her Majesty's Coastguard Service) which is responsible for the search-and-rescue maritime operations, the RAF search-and-rescue wing (helping civilians in distress) and the many voluntary organisations helping in mountain and cave rescues. All staff are highly trained and committed to their job. Emergencies happen at any time and anywhere, and the role of the emergency services is to respond quickly, effectively and efficiently.

Ambulance service

Ambulance crews not only take sick people to and from hospitals, they are also trained to give first aid in emergencies, tending seriously ill and injured people at scenes of accidents or sudden illness. More routine work involves taking infirm or elderly people who cannot use public transport to clinics and hospitals. An ambulance team consists of:

- **ambulance care assistants**, who deal mainly with the routine, non-emergency type of work
- **ambulance technicians**, who are fully qualified and able to respond to 999 calls
- **paramedics**, who are technicians who have undergone intensive extra training to be able to use life-saving equipment
- **control-room staff**, who take the emergency calls from the public and from GPs and allocate the jobs to the ambulance crews and often coordinate the journeys. Shift work is usual.

Fire service

Fire prevention and control are the responsibility of local fire authorities, who are overseen by the Home Office in London and the Scottish Office in Edinburgh. Fire officers not only fight fires but also give advice on how to prevent them. They are also called to road, rail and aircraft accidents and help when there are floods, explosions, chemical discharges and occasional household crises.

Not every hour of a firefighter's day is spent fighting fires; much of it is passed at the fire station, cleaning and maintaining equipment and taking part in training exercises as well as carrying out statutory inspection duties of premises. Periods of relative inactivity are common but can be followed by sudden and dangerous emergencies, such as floods, chemical spillages and explosions, which can often be messy and dirty.

Police

Police forces in England and Wales are the joint responsibility of the Home Secretary, chief constables and police authorities. In Scotland they are the responsibility of the Secretary of State. The main purpose of the police service is the prevention and detection of crime. However, only a third of police activity is connected with crime detection; the great majority of the work is dealing with neighbourhood or family disputes or coping with people under the influence of alcohol or drugs. A few members of the police force have specialist jobs: dog-handlers, river police and road traffic officers, for example. Forensic scientists are mostly chemists and biologists (see section on 'Science and technology').

Each force has its own Criminal Investigation Department, and entry is very competitive, requiring a record of hard work, ability and usually experience on the beat. There are also support staff in police forces; they work as administrative officers, computer specialists, control-room assistants and sometimes as traffic wardens (employed by the police authorities) and Scenes of Crime Officers (SOCOs) – those who gather up the evidence at a scene of crime.

Search-and-rescue organisations

All civil maritime rescue operations around the UK coastline (and for 1,000 miles into the North Atlantic ocean) are the responsibility of coastguards. The Coastguard Agency employs regular (full-time) and auxiliary (part-time) coastguard officers to respond to maritime distress calls. Teams of both paid and volunteer coastguards also rescue people in difficulty offshore and on sea cliffs. They call on and coordinate all available facilities including the Royal National Lifeboat Institution lifeboats, Royal Navy and RAF helicopters, and other aircraft and ships which are placed to offer assistance. As well as their search-and-rescue work, coastguards have other (indoor) duties, such as broadcasting information for navigators and providing weather reports to meteorological offices.

Mountain, hill and cave rescue operations are coordinated by voluntary organisations, staffed by committed fell-walkers, pot-holers, cavers and climbing enthusiasts. The RAF search-and-rescue wing also assists in call-outs to walkers or climbers in distress as well as to fishing vessels in trouble. It liaises closely with mountain rescue teams and the coastguards.

Sample job titles

Ambulance paramedic, ambulance technician, ambulance care assistant, coastguard, control-room assistant, fire fighter, police officer

Opportunities

Self-governing NHS trusts are the main employers of ambulance staff. Openings in private ambulance fleets for NHS-trained staff and abroad with the Armed Forces or with Voluntary Services Overseas are possible.

Local fire authorities, airports, the Ministry of Defence, the Armed Forces and various large companies all have their own fire services.

There are 43 police forces in England and Wales, eight in Scotland and one in Northern Ireland. They all recruit separately. The Metropolitan Police Force in London is the largest of the police forces. Other separate police forces, such as the British Transport Police, the Ministry of Defence Police and the UK Atomic Energy Authority Constabulary, also exist.

Coastguards are employed by the Coastguard Agency. Approximately 480 regular and 3,500 volunteer auxiliary coastguards are based in six search-and-rescue regions throughout the UK: Eastern, South Eastern, South Western England; North and East Scotland, West of Scotland; Northern Ireland.

Other factors to consider

People working in emergency services need the following skills and attributes:

- good verbal and written communication
- ability to stay calm in a crisis

- common sense/responsible attitude
- initiative
- ability to calm and reassure others
- ability to work in a team
- ability to work in a disciplined environment
- willingness to accept working anti-social hours and shifts
- stamina
- physical fitness.

In addition, a smart, conventional appearance is important (for instance, long hair can be a hazard in a fire or accident). Although all emergency services have uniformed staff, some are civilian staff, such as administrators or secretaries and may be non-uniformed. Control room staff may find keyboarding skills an advantage.

In the initial years of training and experience, police officers spend much of their time outdoors, either on the beat or in a car, working long and often anti-social hours. A lot of time is spent on routine work: writing reports, appearing in court and giving evidence.

None of these services is for squeamish people, as accidents and emergencies can involve blood and unpleasant sights.

All services are staffed 24 hours a day so shift work is normal. Regular coastguards must be prepared to work anywhere in the UK and be qualified to drive Group A to E vehicles and hold a valid UK driving licence.

Entry and training

Each emergency service has different entry and training requirements.

Ambulance service

Entry is from age 18 to 21. Candidates must pass a medical examination and have a clean driving licence. Some services have minimum height requirements. Some cadet schemes for 16- to 18-year-olds are available, for which GCSEs are useful. Initial training courses are provided by the ambulance services. Following these, general experience is gained on-the-job at an ambulance station. Ambulance technicians usually take up to 18 months to become qualified. Paramedic training is open to technicians who have undergone extra intensive training to use the sophisticated life-support equipment. Control-room assistants may undertake first-aid courses as part of their induction and will be given training in the use of radio and telecommunication techniques, computers and other related skills. It is possible to do Ambulance Service Institute examinations, which may help in promotion.

Fire service

Entry is from the age of 18. A good general education is necessary, and some services have specific entry requirements. There is no graduate entry; graduates have to work their way up from junior firefighter like anyone else. Promotion is based on ability, not on academic qualifications. Induction training is at a brigade training centre for a short period, followed by further training on-the-job. Modern Apprenticeships may be available. Local TECs/LECs will provide details.

Police

The minimum age is usually $18\frac{1}{2}$ (although some forces prefer older candidates). Applicants need to have a good general education and all have to pass an entrance test. Entry varies from force to force but it is usually from GCSE to graduate level, with an accelerated promotion scheme for graduates (degree in any discipline), who need to pass a more rigorous selection procedure. All candidates have to pass the standard selection procedure. No specific height requirements are set. Eyesight standards vary between the forces. Applicants must be UK or Irish Republic citizens, or Commonwealth citizens with UK residency. Promotion is on merit, experience and initiative.

Only a few forces offer cadet schemes, taking recruits locally from the age of 16. Entry is extremely competitive for the very few places on offer. Cadetship does not guarantee entry into the regular police force. Some forces operate a voluntary (unpaid) cadet scheme.

Training is a combination of two years' on-the-job probation and basic training at a training centre. Post-qualification training is via short courses and attachments to various specialist areas. All support staff training is on-the-job, sometimes supplemented by part-time study.

Search-and-rescue organisations

Coastguards must be British subjects or members of the Commonwealth, aged between 27 and 45, and have a driving licence. They must have good eyesight and hearing as well as the following experience and qualifications:

- a minimum of six years' practical maritime experience or three years' operational search-and-rescue experience (for example, perhaps in a voluntary capacity) *plus*
- three GCSEs (grades A–C), including English and mathematics.

Their initial training takes place in Dorset at the Coastguard Training Centre and lasts just under two months.

The RAF search-and-rescue teams are staffed by RAF personnel, who have to fulfil the normal RAF entry requirements (see 'Armed Forces', page 88) and then after initial training opt for search-and-rescue specialist training.

Subjects

English and mathematics are important subjects for all the services because of the amount of paperwork involved and the communication with the general public and with colleagues.

In addition, science is a useful subject for a firefighter, especially when dealing with dangerous chemicals, and for ambulance service staff. Chemistry would be particularly useful.

Further information

Armed Forces Careers Information Officer (local address in telephone book)
Coastguard and Marine Safety Agency
Fire Services Unit (Home Office)
Local fire services
Local police forces
Local ambulance service

Police – Accelerated Promotion Scheme for Graduates (APSG), Home Office
Police Division, Scottish Home and Health Department
Police Personnel and Training Unit
Scottish Office Home Department, Fire Service and Emergency Planning Division

Books and leaflets
Joss, J. 1994. *Careers in the Police Force*. Kogan Page
Working in Emergency Services. 1991. COIC
Working in Police and Emergency Services. COIC (This is due to be published in autumn 1998.)

Engineering (CLCI: R)

Engineering affects almost every aspect of our lives, from the microchip to the Channel Tunnel, and from sophisticated life-support systems to simple kitchen appliances. Engineers contribute to disciplines as diverse as microbiology, and ship and aerospace technology. They come up with ideas, solve problems, design, construct, maintain and improve products and technology to meet the needs of society.

The main fields are:

- mechanical
- electrical
- electronic
- manufacturing
- civil
- chemical.

Other subsidiary fields of engineering include aeronautical, marine, materials, biomedical and automobile engineering (development, production and maintenance of vehicles and plant machinery and their components). Some of the main disciplines and jobs are explained in more detail below. All branches of engineering offer jobs at all levels.

Mechanical engineering is about designing and making machines. Degree courses include computing as a major element. Mechanical engineers are expected to have an understanding of design, business methods and structures (how machines and equipment are built), the scientific and technological aspects of engineering as well as marketing.

Electrical engineers work in power generation, communications, or computers and automation engineering. They help provide the energy for light and power used in day-to-day life; develop complex information systems using computers and other machines; and design and manufacture electrical equipment, including that used in industry.

Electronic engineers design, make and sell electronic (systems that control equipment electronically) and electrical (power-generated) devices mainly – but not exclusively – within the field of computing. Electrical engineers determine how power is generated and supplied whereas electronic engineers work out the control systems for the power and are concerned with the use and application of energy.

Civil engineering is concerned with civil works (the infrastructure); structural engineering – a specialist branch of civil engineering – is concerned with buildings (the superstructure). Both types of engineer are involved in the planning, design, construction and maintenance of our infrastructure: roads, railways, bridges, tunnels, water supplies, sewage and drainage systems, ports, airports and power stations. They also design the foundations and structural frameworks of buildings.

Chemical engineers are concerned mainly with the design, construction and operation of industrial processing plants. Most work in 'unit operations', converting materials into products via process operations such as chemical reactions, filtration, mixing, distillation and heat transfer. To understand and control what is happening, chemical engineers need to know about gases, liquids and solids. So a good foundation in chemistry and physics (with mathematics) at A-level is required. Knowledge of computers is very useful.

Engineering design is central to all these disciplines. Designers find practical solutions to problems, designing new and improved versions of products, machines, instruments and equipment.

Consulting engineers prepare designs, survey sites, advise on tenders from contractors, check progress and act as troubleshooters, solving any problems that arise.

The maintenance of motor vehicles is part of automobile engineering. Motor mechanics work in garages and other places that sell, repair and carry out maintenance on all kinds of vehicles. The job can vary from working for a small roadside garage, where the mechanic deals directly with customers and is expected to know about different types of vehicle, to working in a large garage which is the agent for a single car manufacturer.

None of the above jobs is carried out in isolation. Engineering is very much about teamwork: no matter what the engineering discipline is, information and cooperation are needed from other professionals in order to complete a project successfully, for example, engineers in research and development work closely with materials specialists, physicists and other colleagues as well as with technicians who support their work.

It is possible to enter the engineering industry at four different levels:

- **craft level**: craftspeople learn practical skills, such as toolmaking or welding, usually working with machinery. They can progress to technician level through further study
- **technician level**: technicians have more technical training than craftspeople and support the work of professional engineers. Again, there is an opportunity to progress to professional level, if particularly able (for example, via higher education)
- **incorporated engineer level**: incorporated engineers are more senior than technicians. They may lead a team of technicians, but their actual work is broadly similar. With further training and study they could go on to chartered engineer level
- **chartered engineer level**: chartered engineers oversee the research, design and planning of engineering projects. Management and interpersonal skills are important, as they must lead teams of engineers and technicians.

Sample job titles

Engineer (aeronautical, agricultural, automobile, biomedical, chemical/processing, civil, electrical/electronic, marine, mechanical, mining, structural), engineering technician, engineering craftsperson, motor mechanic

Opportunities

For qualified people (chartered and incorporated engineers and in some cases technicians), opportunities are not limited to the engineering industry. Engineering is a transferable skill, and with continuing education and training an engineer can often make a very good business executive, an expert on broadcasting and communication systems, a sales and marketing manager or a university or college lecturer. They are employed in almost every sector of industry and commerce, including oil, chemicals, pharmaceuticals, food, brewing, agriculture, banking and insurance.

Telecommunications is an expanding area for engineers. They can be employed by one of the telephone companies or by large manufacturing companies that make, supply and sell telecommunications equipment.

Civil engineers' employment prospects are often dependent on the state of the construction industry, which in turn is dependent on the state of the economy. However, civil engineers can work abroad on projects with British firms of consulting engineers and contractors. In the UK the government and local authorities are the main customers for civil engineering works. Other employers are private and nationalised industries. It is also possible to work in private practice as a consulting engineer or on a freelance basis, selling services to companies.

Motor mechanics (craft and technician level) work for privately-owned garages or for organisations that own fleets of vehicles, such as department stores, delivery firms, the AA, RAC and car-hire firms.

At chartered level, engineers can apply for the title of European Engineer (EurIng), which gives them the chance to work abroad in the European Union (a foreign language is therefore particularly useful).

Other factors to consider

For most of the jobs the following skills and attributes are important:

- analytical skills
- a logical mind
- numeracy

- communication (verbal and written) skills
- the ability to work in a team
- the ability to interpret diagrams and instructions
- practical (good hand-to-eye coordination) skills
- problem solving skills.

Computer literacy is an important skill at all levels, as sophisticated computer technology, computer-aided design and computer-aided manufacture now play a vital role in engineering functions.

Electricians and electrical/electronic engineers need good colour vision.

The environment varies according to the work and discipline: it may be outdoors on site, in laboratories, factories, offices or in work-shops. Quite often travel is involved, from office to site or visiting clients.

Professional engineers need management skills to progress.

Motor mechanics need a strong interest in cars or other vehicles. The working environment can be cold, noisy and dirty.

Entry and training

All branches of engineering have similar entry and training routes:

- **craftsperson**: employers usually set aptitude tests for young people leaving school or college. GCSEs are useful, preferably with mathe-matics and science at grade C or above. Training is on-the-job with part-time study at college
- **technician**: a minimum of four GCSEs (grades A–C) are required. Training is either on-the-job with part-time study at college or via a full-time course, leading to a BTEC National Diploma. GNVQs and NVQs are becoming an increasingly popular way to qualify as an engineering technician. After technician training, it is possible to go on to higher education to do an HND or degree in engineering
- **professional** (chartered or incorporated): entry is with a degree or HND in an engineering subject. There is no one overall degree course but hundreds of degrees in the engineering specialisms. The majority of them are sandwich courses, with work experience as part of the course. Incorporated or Chartered Engineer status can be acquired only by gaining academic qualifications followed by further approved training with a recognised employer.

The Engineering Council has radically revised standards for the education and training of professional engineers. These will be applied in phases from 1999.

The minimum academic qualification for Chartered Engineer (CEng) will be a four-year accredited Master of Engineering (MEng) course or a three-year accredited BEng (Hons) degree plus a further year of additional study. In Scotland most engineering degree courses already last four years. The status of Incorporated Engineer (IEng) will be raised: a three-year accredited IEng degree or a two-year HND plus a further year of additional learning will become the minimum requirement for qualification.

Additional learning can be via full- or part-time postgraduate study, distance tuition and work-based learning.

Modern Apprenticeships and programmes leading to the award of vocational qualifications (GNVQs/NVQs) can provide progression to Engineering Technician registration.

Engineering design can be entered either through a degree or HND in a branch of engineering or by studying art and design (foundation course followed by a three-dimensional industrial/product design course covering engineering principles).

National traineeships, Modern Apprenticeships and traditional apprenticeships are also on offer in many aspects of engineering. The usual route for motor mechanics is via a Modern Apprenticeship or national traineeship. Engineering currently employs a greater proportion of Modern Apprentices than any other sector and accounts for about 25 per cent of all Modern Apprentices. Modern Apprenticeships combine training on-the-job with part-time college study. Another way into engineering is to take a full-time or part-time college course, leading to NVQ qualifications or BTEC awards. This can be followed by further courses to degree level. Many companies offer sponsorship to students on degree courses.

There is still a shortage of women engineers, and this has led to various initiatives to encourage girls to enter engineering training: the WISE (Women Into Science and Engineering) campaign and Insight courses (run by EMTA – the Engineering Marine and Training Authority) for year 12 pupils studying mathematics and science A-levels. The Insight one-week residential courses are held at universities to give female students a taste of engineering.

Ongoing training once in a job is expected, as new skills and knowledge are continually required. Some of the professional engineering institutions expect their members to spend a specified period of time retraining each year.

Subjects

For all levels, GCSEs in mathematics, English and science (physics is preferred, and chemistry is essential for some chemical engineering degree courses) are required. Foreign languages are also useful.

A-levels (for professional engineers): mathematics, physics or related subjects (for example, chemistry for chemical engineers). Anyone with the 'wrong' A-levels can take a one-year conversion foundation course in higher education, which aims to give students the necessary basics in mathematics and physics.

Further information

Engineering Council

Engineering and Marine Training Authority (EMTA), Engineering Careers Information Service

Institution of Chemical Engineers

Institution of Civil Engineers

Institution of Electrical Engineers

Institution of Engineering Designers

Institution of Mechanical Engineers

WISE (Women Into Science and Engineering)

Women's Engineering Society

Books and leaflets

Harris, N. 1995. *Getting into Engineering*. Trotman

The Ivanhoe Guide to the Engineering Profession. 1996. Cambridge Market Intelligence

Hobson's Engineering Casebook. 1997. CRAC/Hobsons

Working in Engineering. 1996. COIC

Environmental services (CLCI: C/Q/W)

The term 'Environmental services' comprises a large number of different areas, from nature conservation, industrial pollution and insecticide research to geology, ecology and oceanography. These all have one thing in common: their purpose is to improve and maintain the environment. Below are examples of jobs that come under the umbrella of environmental services. In addition to the jobs described are posts for finance, administration and legal staff in many environmental organisations.

Water

This diverse area covers river management, flood control, water pollution control, water supply and sewerage. Water pollution officers have to respond to pollution incidents, undertake pollution prevention visits to industry and check water quality. Hydrometric officers monitor the water levels and flows of rivers so that predictions and plans can be made about irrigation, droughts, floods and pollution control. Technicians support the work of the professionals in various areas, including water supply and treatment, laboratory work, sewage treatment, and so on. They generally carry out routine work, such as analysing and testing samples in laboratories.

Waste

Waste management includes recycling, recovery of resources such as scrap metal, waste motor oil, paper, plastics and fabrics and the disposal of waste. Industry, commerce and government are just some of the areas where one or more of the following people may be employed: waste disposal managers handling the collection of waste products; scientists researching methods of waste disposal; recycling officers advising on recycling initiatives; and pollution control officers monitoring pollution. Some organisations may employ environmental managers with a general role ensuring that the company's impact on the environment is minimal.

Public health

Environmental health officers are concerned with public health. Their job is to safeguard people's living and working environments. They inspect any premises where food is prepared, standards of health and safety at work, and accommodation where living conditions are a health threat. Pollution is also one of their growing concerns: they watch out for illicit dumping of waste on land and may liaise with the waste disposal authorities on the safety of official tips, monitor air and noise pollution and enforce the laws designed to reduce the release of waste into the atmosphere. Some environmental health officers specialise in one aspect of the work. Technicians and technical assistants can also work in this area.

Nature conservation

This has become a very popular area of work. At a basic level it is about preserving and sustaining the natural landscape. The openings are at different levels, for example, countryside wardens or rangers, gamekeepers, scientists, managers, administrative and research staff and estate workers. Some jobs, such as countryside management, involve overseeing a conservation area, managing staff, advising the public on environmental issues and solutions, and developing conservation policies and plans. Other jobs, such as estate worker, are more practical and involve protecting the environment through maintenance work (for example, felling trees, digging ditches and mending fences).

Research

Environmental scientists study, monitor and manage the environment as well as formulate environmental policy and control legislation. Other scientists are also concerned with various aspects of the environment, for example, geologists study the earth's crust and the materials that form it; ecologists study how plants and animals interact with their natural surroundings; zoologists study the behaviour and development of animals; and meteorologists observe and chart weather patterns.

Sample job titles

Analytical chemist, conservation officer, countryside warden/ranger, electrical engineer, environmental health officer, environmental scientist, geologist, mechanical engineer, meteorologist, microbiologist, oceanographer, process engineer, public analyst

Opportunities

Many major industrial companies now have environmental departments. Large numbers of consultancies in many different fields recruit environmental scientists to meet the demand for environmental impact assessment work. Public utilities, such as the water authorities, are employers of environmental scientists and water pollution control officers.

In the state sector opportunities are in local and national government and in research establishments. The Environment Agency plays a major role in improving and sustaining the environment as a whole. It has taken over the functions of what used to be the National Rivers Authority, Her Majesty's Inspectorate of Pollution and the local authority run Waste Regulation Authorities. It is also responsible for regulating the disposal of radioactive waste and the management of contaminated land. Many scientists monitor the environment and make policy decisions. They may be employed directly by the Environment Agency or by specialist environmental consultancies which are contracted either by the Environment Agency or by the individual businesses that operate industrial processes which may cause pollution.

Scientists in this field will find opportunities abroad, especially in Third World countries, where the demand for environmental work is increasing as part of aid packages. Other environmental jobs abroad may include management, marketing, fundraising and public relations.

There are openings for nature conservation work in various statutory bodies, such as English Nature, Scottish Natural Heritage, the Countryside Commission, Countryside Council for Wales, national parks and the Forestry Commission. Other jobs are in the private and voluntary sector, which includes Friends of the Earth, Greenpeace, the RSPB, the National Trust and the Wildfowl Trust among others.

Vacancies for estate workers are few and far between. Some jobs are seasonal and temporary, such as those in a wildlife or national park information centre.

Although many organisations are concerned with environmental work, competition is stiff for full-time jobs.

Other factors to consider

Employers in this field look for candidates who are committed to the environment; this can be demonstrated through involvement in local voluntary conservation and environmental activities. They also look for people who have a realistic, practical and objective attitude to environmental issues.

The nature of these jobs means that there is generally a degree of outdoor work. In addition, employees may occasionally have to work in unpleasant conditions (for example, an environmental health officer may have to inspect premises where there are health hazards). A driving licence and car are usually necessary.

Teamwork is important, as are communication skills, both written and verbal. Good public relations are vital in this career area and, depending on the job, it is sometimes necessary to give presentations or talks to the public or the press or to give evidence in court on environmental issues.

Many of the jobs require someone with an analytical, enquiring mind and who enjoys the attention to detail and accuracy that much of this kind of work demands.

Keyboard skills are useful for report writing in all jobs.

Countryside wardens and other staff in wildlife parks or nature reserves open to the public often have to work anti-social hours.

Entry and training

Many jobs in this area require a degree in a related subject. Degrees in environmental science cover the natural environment, and degrees in environmental studies generally deal with the human, built environment. As environmental science and environmental studies courses are becoming increasingly popular, graduates are facing fierce competition for the limited number of jobs. Some environmental courses may be seen to be too general in content for some jobs, and specific technical courses such as engineering or analytical chemistry may be required for some posts. Courses that include work experience in industry are valued by employers. Voluntary work experience is also an advantage.

Most environmental jobs in the water industry involve some training, either on-the-job, via part-time college courses or in-house training. Graduates in research posts may be able to study towards relevant professional qualifications or postgraduate qualifications. NVQs are available in water services operations and distribution.

Environmental health officers need to have a science background – usually a first degree in environmental health, or a science degree followed by postgraduate study. Only graduates who have done an accredited BSc and MSc Environmental Health course can obtain the status of environmental health officer. A list of approved courses is available from the Chartered Institute of Environmental Health. Environmental health technicians or technical assistants usually have A-levels, although some may be graduates.

Nature conservation has openings at various levels, from those requiring no qualifications (for example, estate workers) to those for which a degree is necessary (for instance, conservation rangers, foresters). Senior posts require qualifications in science, agriculture or estate management plus practical experience.

Laboratory technicians need good GCSEs (grades A–C) and A-levels. Some jobs have minimum age restrictions, for example, countryside warden applicants must be at least 21.

Subjects

GCSEs in mathematics, English and science are the most useful. A-levels in sciences are generally required because much of the work has a scientific bias.

For environmental health technician, subjects such as construction, catering and food technology may be useful in addition to science.

Further information

British Ecological Society
British Geological Survey
British Trust for Conservation Volunteers
Chartered Institute of Environmental Health
Countryside Commission
English Nature
Environment Agency
Environment Council
National Trust

Natural Environment Research Council
Scottish Natural Heritage

Books and leaflets

Working in Environmental Services. 1997. COIC
Lamb, R. 1995. *Careers in Environmental Conservation.* Kogan Page

Finance (CLCI: N)

The world of finance is vast, with a huge variety of people employed in many different career areas. The jobs include offering financial advice, selling financial products and services, working behind the scenes and working directly with customers. Some positions are supporting, while others are managerial.

Accountancy

Accountants can choose the type of work they do from three broad areas: private practice; the public sector; and industry and commerce.

About 50 per cent of accountants work in private practice, where privately owned accounting firms comprise either a sole practitioner, two or three people (in a town or country practice), or over 100 partners with portfolios in industrial and international business. In the larger firms, accountants may specialise, for example, in mergers and takeovers, computer systems, corporate finance, VAT and other taxes. However, whatever else they do, all firms audit company accounts, present an analysis of the state of the organisation's finances, and prepare statutory reports such as balance sheets and tax returns. Accountants' roles are also expanding; they are seen as consultants by many of their clients, advising on record-keeping, taxation, investments and other aspects of finance. Audits can be done in a few hours or may take several months, depending on the size and complexity of the business in question. In general, people who gain expertise in one of these fields can build a career in commercial companies and can command high salaries.

Accountants in the public sector act as financial managers for local government, in state-owned industries, such as the NHS, and in central government departments. Their main responsibility is to see that public money (grants, taxes, and so on) is spent properly and used effectively and efficiently. By advising on investments and credit, accountants can help managers and professional staff to keep their departments within their budgets and targets while maximising the value for the company.

In industry and commerce accountants are involved in the day-to-day running of the business, cash flow forecasting, budgeting, investment appraisal and so on. They are either management accountants – assessing the value and contribution to profit of all aspects of the business and making recommendations to improve the company's financial return – or financial accountants, who deal with the day-to-day business of bookkeeping, audits, taxation, VAT payments and wages. Internal audit is an important role within larger commercial and industrial organisations, where the accountants undertake investigative reviews of the operations and internal controls of the whole business.

Accounting technicians work in all sectors of accounting and finance alongside accountants. Jobs vary from accounts clerks to credit control officers to financial managers. Some accounting technicians are self-employed and offer their services to the general public.

Actuarial work

Actuaries make financial sense of the future by assessing the financial impact of tomorrow's uncertain events. They enable financial decisions to be made with more confidence by analysing the past and modelling the future, assessing the risks involved and communicating what the results mean in financial terms. Actuaries carry out vital roles within life assurance companies, advise pension funds, work in general insurance and use their skills in investment, healthcare and risk management. Such work offers management opportunities, often at the highest level, and actuaries have a commercial as well as technical role.

Banking and building society work

In recent years the worlds of banking and building societies have changed dramatically. Competition between the banks and building societies and other financial institutions to attract customers is intense. Just as the building societies are offering banking services, and in many cases even becoming banks, so too are the banks extending their range of services to include house mortgages, Saturday opening (and 24-hour opening in some cases), telephone and computer banking, and are moving into the fields of estate agency, insurance, leasing, merchant banking and pensions. As a result, recruitment is being affected. Restructuring has reduced the number of clerical and management grades. GCSE-level recruits tend to occupy the clerical and back-office positions, A-level entrants go into senior clerk and supervisory jobs, while graduate entrants go into the higher management jobs. At every level promotion is dependent upon performance.

Financial services in our high streets – the banks and building societies – employ people in branches (in personnel, regional head offices and internal audit sections). The work involves providing financial services such as taking deposits, providing loans and overdrafts, financial advice, arranging mortgages, the sale and purchase of houses, stocks and shares and foreign currency. Counter staff are called cashiers, clerks or customer service assistants/executives. Many counter staff hope to move on to supervisory and management posts, although this may take time and depends largely on entry qualifications and abilities.

Merchant/investment banks do not provide services to individuals but advice to companies on all aspects of corporate finance, both in the UK and abroad. They manage the investment of large funds, particularly pension funds. Most of the high-street banks now have merchant/investment banking divisions.

The Bank of England is the central bank of the UK. It is at the heart of UK economic and financial policy-making and sets the level of interest rates. The Bank has an important role to play in ensuring a healthy financial system and promoting efficient and competitive UK financial markets. In addition to graduate careers, the Bank offers a range of clerical and secretarial positions. Most graduates undertake policy-based, analytical work.

Insurance

The UK has over 800 insurance companies, which offer protection against loss or misfortune. Most people need insurance at some point in their lives and are willing to pay regular premiums into a common fund just in case they need access to finance in an emergency. The insurance industry is divided into different sectors. Some companies specialise in just one type of insurance, while others offer a variety of services, such as personal (motor, household, travel) insurance, commercial (fire, liability, goods in transit) insurance, life assurance and marine assurance. The big insurance companies not only sell or supply insurance to individuals and companies but also have employees in branch offices dealing with over-the-counter enquiries and proposals and with customers.

Insurance brokers are independent intermediaries, who provide a service of matching their client's insurance needs with the contracts available from the insurance companies. Clients often ask brokers for advice on how to reduce the risks they are running.

Besides office and sales staff, insurance companies employ:

- **underwriters**, who assess risks; they are experts in insurance and decide on whether or not to insure and on the terms and conditions of acceptance of risk
- **loss adjusters and claim assessors**, who specialise in claims work; loss adjusting is a highly skilled, very small profession, which requires extensive experience
- **investment and pension managers**.

Stockbroking

Stockbrokers are Stock Exchange member firms (trading firms of the London Stock Exchange which may deal in shares on behalf of their clients or on behalf of the firm itself), which advise clients (individuals or institutions) on which stocks and shares to buy and sell and when. They then carry out the transactions, trading through the London Stock Exchange. Trading is now done via the telephone or through the London Stock Exchange new electronic trading system. Computers are used to gain access to up-to-date information on markets. The London Stock Exchange provides central markets for buying and selling stocks and shares on behalf of companies. Stockbroker staff are not employed by the Stock Exchange but by member firms. It is vital that stockbroker staff keep themselves up-to-date with the state of the financial world in order to know which shares are moving. Trainees usually start in the back office carrying out administrative work before moving to the front office to deal directly with clients.

Market makers are Stock Exchange member firms which are required at all times during the dealing day to quote (advertise) two-way prices (i.e. both a price to buy at and a price to sell at) for securities. In this way, they are making a market for these shares. Their staff are highly experienced and knowledgeable about share prices and company performance. They deal with brokers who act on behalf of clients or directly with institutional investors. The companies make a profit by buying shares then selling them at a higher price. They also have special tax exemptions, which makes dealing more financially attractive.

Sample job titles

Accountant, actuary, auditor, bank clerk/manager, broker, building society cashier, insurance clerk, loss adjuster, underwriter

Opportunities

Accountants and accounting technicians not only work in private practice but also for public authorities, in central or local government and in large, medium and small industrial and commercial companies. Accountancy and finance are subjects that are relevant to a wide range of careers in all kinds of businesses, not just accounting firms, so the prospects for students are good. Many accountants move into management or administrative posts as well as other financial careers. However, the field is competitive so good qualifications are particularly important.

Highly motivated and qualified staff can find decent jobs in all the different areas of banking and building society work: in high-street banks and building societies, merchant/investment banks, the Bank of England and overseas institutions.

The majority of actuaries work in insurance companies, while one-third of them work in consultancy, advising companies on their pension arrangements and employee benefit matters. Others are involved in government service, on the Stock Exchange and within the academic world, advising on national insurance schemes, superannuation arrangements and other statistical work. Although it is a small profession, the demand for actuaries is steady, and they can command high salaries.

Most financial institutions have openings for clerical and other support work, such as computer operating, as well as for potential managers.

Many careers in finance afford the opportunity to work abroad, either in overseas branches of UK-based firms or in overseas companies. About one-third of actuaries work overseas, mostly based in Australia, New Zealand, Pakistan, India, South Africa and continental Europe. The UK actuarial qualification is recognised world-wide.

Other factors to consider

Both ability in and often an enthusiasm for mathematics are essential. It is now also impossible to get by in the financial world without being computer-literate as most people will routinely use computers in their work.

People in the financial sector, particularly those at management level in banking, stockbroking, actuarial and insurance work, need to have a well-developed sense of judgement for assessing risks, situations and people.

Management, business and marketing skills are becoming increasingly important as financial institutions compete for business. Staff in stockbroker and market-maker companies also need to be able to think quickly on their feet and manipulate numbers at a fast rate.

Good communication skills are essential as complex financial matters need to be explained clearly to lay people, both in writing and verbally. Banks, insurance companies and building societies, in particular, need people who are customer-friendly.

Languages can be an advantage, particularly for people wanting to work abroad.

Sales skills have always been important in the insurance industry and are becoming increasingly more so in the fields of banking and building society work. Sales techniques, advertising and publicity often win business and convince the public to use a particular insurance company, bank or building society.

Entry and training

For some areas, the training is tough and lengthy (for example, three to five years for accountants and actuaries post-degree), combining practical experience on-the-job with study, either full- or part-time. Eighteen-year-olds wanting to do financial work will need high grades in their GCSEs and A-levels. A degree gives applicants a strong advantage (it is in fact a requirement for the Institute of Chartered Accountants in Scotland) and is increasingly preferred by many employers.

The degree subject for accountancy is not important and in fact the majority of graduate entrants have non-relevant degrees. However, relevant degrees (accountancy, business studies, mathematics) may give applicants credits for some subjects, exempting them from some examinations.

It is possible to train as an accounting technician through studying by day-release, part-time, distance-learning or evening classes. NVQs can be obtained through work-based assessment. The Association of Accounting Technicians is the only professional body accredited to award NVQs in accounting at levels 2–4.

The vast majority of entrants (90 per cent) to actuarial work are graduates, either with an actuarial degree or a numeracy-based degree. Traditionally, mathematics or statistics degrees have been offered by entrants, but increasingly other degrees such as economics, science and business studies, are becoming acceptable (as long as the applicant has mathematics at A-level – usually at grade A or B). Even with a mathematics or statistics degree, mathematics at A-level may still be required.

Four higher education institutions – Heriot-Watt University (Edinburgh), City University (London), London School of Economics and Kent University – offer actuarial science degrees. A good statistics degree (minimum upper second class) may give exemption from the first part of the professional examinations.

Most vacancies in banking, building societies, insurance and stockbroking are at A-level or graduate entry. People with specialist skills and qualifications, such as IT or personnel management, are also recruited. Any degree subject is appropriate, although business studies or accounting and other commercial or mathematical subjects are very useful, as are law and economics. Engineering or some sciences are valuable degrees for an insurance career in specific areas, such as underwriting, surveying or claims inspection in specialist fields. Languages can be an advantage and may lead to work overseas. HNDs are also acceptable. NVQs (levels 2–4) are available in building society services, banking and in insurance. Recruitment at supervisory level in banking is carried out by a bank's head office, whereas lower-grade recruiting is dealt with at regional level.

Although no formal entry requirements are necessary for stockbroking, most entrants are graduates.

Once employed, the majority of people study either full- or part-time for professional examinations during training; these vary according to the chosen financial specialism:

- **accountancy**: The Association of Chartered Certified Accountants (ACCA), The Chartered Institute of Management Accountants (CIMA), The Chartered Institute of Public Finance and Accountancy (CIPFA), The Institute of Chartered Accountants –ICAEW – (in England and Wales), ICAS (in Scotland) and ICAI (in Ireland), The Institute of Financial Accountants (IFA)
- **accounting technician work**: The Association of Accounting Technicians
- **banking / building society work**: Chartered Institute of Bankers
- **actuarial work**: Institute of Actuaries
- **insurance**: Chartered Insurance Institute (CII qualifications are essential for promotion), Chartered Institute of Loss Adjusters
- **stockbroking**: Securities and Futures Authority (Contact the Securities Institute for information.)

Subjects

A knowledge (to at least GCSE level) of mathematics is important for any career in this field. English is also useful, given the degree of communication and interpersonal skills involved. For some degree courses A-level mathematics may be preferred or even specified (actuarial degrees), but generally is not essential, provided GCSE mathematics and English are offered.

English and mathematics GCSEs are essential for almost all professional accounting qualifications, except for that offered by the ICAEW; they are also essential for banking.

A-levels in business studies, accounting, mathematics, statistics, English, law and economics are all recommended.

For an actuary English at GCSE is necessary; Mathematics (grades A/B) and one other subject (grade A–C) at A-level are compulsory.

Any degree discipline is usually considered for careers in finance, although business studies, law, economics and accountancy are obvious choices.

Further information

Association of Accounting Technicians
Association of Chartered Certified Accountants
Bank of England
British Bankers Association
British Insurance and Investment Brokers' Association
Building Societies Association
Chartered Institute of Bankers
Chartered Institute of Banking in Scotland
Chartered Institute of Loss Adjusters
Chartered Institute of Management Accountants
Chartered Institute of Public Finance and Accountancy
Chartered Insurance Institute
Faculty of Actuaries
Institute of Actuaries
Institute of Chartered Accountants in England and Wales (ICAEW)
Institute of Chartered Accountants in Scotland (ICAS)
Institute of Financial Accountants
London Stock Exchange Ltd
Securities Institute

Books and leaflets

Snelgar, D. 1995. *Careers in Banking and Finance.* Trotman
Working in The Money Business. 1995. COIC
Ivanhoe Guides (Chartered Accountants, Actuaries, Insurance). 1996. Cambridge Market Intelligence
Taylor, F. 1996. *Careers in Accountancy.* Kogan Page

Funeral directing (CLCI: IP)

Funeral directors (or undertakers) prepare bodies for burial/cremation and at the request of the family normally make all the arrangements:

- putting notices of the death in newspapers
- setting the time and place of the funeral
- paying the fees
- arranging the flowers
- transporting the coffin and mourners to and from the cemetery or crematorium
- advising people on getting grants from the DSS if they do not have much money.

They may also arrange or carry out embalming; lay the body to rest in a funeral parlour or church prior to the funeral; prepare coffins and bear them at funerals. In addition, they clean and polish the cars.

Funeral directing is not usually a career that attracts young people unless their family is already involved in it.

Sample job titles

Funeral director/undertaker

Opportunities

Funeral directing can be difficult to get into without a family connection as the business is made up mainly of family firms. However, some larger firms have several branches nationwide which may recruit staff.

Other factors to consider

Funeral directors need tact, compassion and understanding. The job can be depressing and distressing as it involves dealing with families who are naturally upset at the death of a loved one. Funeral staff have to present a serious image and tend to wear a uniform of black suit, collar and tie. They have to be prepared to lay out or remove bodies at any time of the day or night.

Funeral directors are often required to drive, so a driving licence is desirable and often essential, as are communications skills.

Entry and training

Entrants study part-time for up to one year for the Diploma in Funeral Directing by registering with the National Association of Funeral Directors (NAFD) and can take up student membership of the British Institute of Funeral Directors (BIFD). Prior to this course, students must take a foundation module and gain at least one year's experience. They must also carry out 25 funerals both under supervision and on their own before being awarded the diploma. Large companies may run their own training schemes.

Subjects

No particular subjects are specified, although English and mathematics at GCSE are useful.

Further information

British Institute of Funeral Directors (BIFD)
National Association of Funeral Directors (NAFD)

Government service (CLCI: C)

Government service covers a variety of careers: in central government (or civil service), working for the different departments; in local government, within a local authority; and in politics, either at a local level or at the heart of government in Parliament. Professional people – from accountants and economists to teachers – and administrative and support staff will find opportunities at all levels in each of these areas.

Central government

The civil service employs over half a million people, who either work as specialists (for example, accountants, actuaries, architects, lawyers, linguists, psychologists, economists, research officers, statisticians, scientists, surveyors, engineers), or take on the role of managers, advisers, clerical officers, typists, secretaries, administrative staff, catering staff, drivers and so on in more than 60 departments and in over 100 executive agencies. The civil service is among the largest employers in the UK. The majority of recruitment is now carried out by the individual departments and agencies rather than centrally. This allows them to recruit to meet their specific needs and also allows applicants to choose where they would most like to work. Fast-stream schemes (aimed at graduates with exceptional ability and potential) are still run centrally by the Recruitment and Assessment Services at Basingstoke.

Each department or agency has its own area of responsibility. Generally, departments are responsible for formulating policy, and agencies are the executive arm of the civil service, concerned chiefly with delivering services to the public. Although people generally stay with the department or agency they first join, it is possible to transfer. An increasing amount of the work has a European flavour, since European Union (EU) regulations affect a growing number of activities from food hygiene to employment legislation. The variety of work is enormous.

Administration Trainees/Higher Executive Officers (Development) have the potential to reach some of the most senior posts within the civil service. Their work may include research, consultation, negotiation, project management and providing support for ministers.

Executive Officers are the backbone of middle and junior management within the civil service. Executive staff are directly involved in the day-to-day running of branches or sections within departments, such as Jobcentres, tax offices and Benefits Agency offices. They work in head offices and regional and local offices around the UK.

Administrative Assistants/Officers are employed in all government departments to carry out support tasks and duties. Their responsibilities include: filing, drafting replies, answering correspondence from members of the public or Departments of State, advising the public (for example, at Jobcentres or Benefits Agency offices), making payments, answering the telephone, checking accounts and preparing statistics. They are generally supervised by an Executive Officer.

Local government

This is one of the largest job areas, employing nine per cent of the working population. Local government also offers a wider range of careers than any other organisation in the UK. The jobs vary enormously and include many professional posts, such as those of accountant, architect, surveyor, teacher, solicitor and town planner. The services provided by local authorities are many – schools, libraries, social services, housing and environmental health provision – and require large administrative teams.

In local government, regulations are devised to protect the interests of the public; each local authority has official guidelines, which are strictly adhered to. Local government officers (middle- to senior-level staff) are directed by elected representatives or councillors, and both the parties and the politicians can change their policies in response to public or government pressure, thus affecting the work of local government officers.

The departments – finance, legal services, education, environment, housing, social services, and so on – employ specialists (for example, countryside rangers, recycling officers, legal executives) who have taken vocational courses or undergone special training, and administrative staff, who are at many different levels and have varying degrees of responsibility.

Politics

Not many people decide to follow a political career while they are still at school or college. Most politicians start by carving out a career in another field and take up politics initially as a part-time interest. They then enter politics full-time if elected Member of Parliament (MP), or if they have a responsible job in local government or as a constituency agent (the party official in an MP's constituency who organises local meetings and acts for the MP in his or her absence). Constituency agents often have long experience of party work in a voluntary capacity. The political parties also have specialist researchers; they are usually graduates recruited to find out about all kinds of subjects, mostly those connected with economics, social topics and finance. Graduates with degrees in these subjects are obviously particularly suitable for research posts. Another category of political staff comprises the secretaries or administrative assistants to MPs: these jobs are advertised in party magazines or national newspapers.

Economics

Economists deal with the organisation, use and distribution of resources. Economics is a very wide and all-embracing subject because it deals with financial and productive resources, both in the UK and internationally. It encompasses politics, social trends and the study of industry. Some economists work as advisers in government departments. Although there are not many of them, their influence is great.

Sample job titles

Administrator, civil servant, local government officer, politician, economist

Opportunities

The civil service is one of the largest recruiters of graduates in the UK. Those taken on have the chance to work overseas, either in a government role or for one of the EU institutions. Foreign languages are an advantage. Posts are usually advertised in the local press or Jobcentre. The Government Economic Service is also the largest employer of economists, who advise ministers and civil servants. Economists are also employed as general recruits into the administrative stream of the civil service.

Local authorities are major employers of many staff. However, careers within local authorities are no longer as secure a career long-term as they used to be. Compulsory competitive tendering has meant that local authority departments have to bid for work contracts alongside private sector companies. This and a recent reorganisation has led to a reduction in permanent staff in some cases; authorities may buy in services when required instead. The reorganisation has also meant many changes in the structure of local authorities.

Local authorities employ a few economics graduates. The rest work in commerce and industry, often moving into general management after further professional training in, for example, accountancy, management or planning.

Politicians usually have another career to fall back on and to support them while they are working their way up the political career ladder. Only a small percentage of politics graduates gain jobs in which they use their degree in the civil service, political parties or parliamentary advisory work. Opportunities do exist for work and travel overseas, particularly as a Member of the European Parliament (MEP). MEPs are elected on the same party lines as British MPs.

There are opportunities to work for the European Commission, the European Parliament, Court of Justice and other institutions of the EU, for anyone with a working knowledge (roughly equivalent to good A-level standard) of at least one EU language other than his or her mother tongue. Staff working in the Foreign and Commonwealth Office are also likely to be able to work abroad. Fast-stream officers (see 'Entry and training', overleaf) spend half their time abroad. If necessary, intensive language training is provided, with the opportunity for some staff to study Chinese or Russian. Competition for the Diplomatic Service is fierce – in 1996 there were 2,200 applicants for 25 places.

Other factors to consider

Many posts in central and local government require good analytical skills, sound judgement, the ability to persuade and work with others and the initiative and determination to solve problems and overcome difficulties. Increasingly, work experience outside the civil service is expected, reflected by the fact that the majority of recruits are aged 25 or over. Some posts require confidentiality.

All fast-stream entrants to the civil service should be prepared to travel during their early years in the post. Although most recruits start in London, there are many other offices around the UK.

Overseas postings can be physically and emotionally demanding, and applicants have to pass a medical test before joining the Diplomatic Service.

All civil servants are required to remain politically impartial. Fast-stream recruits may not take part in national political activities.

A keen interest in politics is a prerequisite for any career in this area, even at the administrative or secretarial level. Some people prepare for a career in politics by joining a political party or by taking a leading role in a college or university political club. Others take up voluntary posts within political parties. MPs need a high degree of political awareness, drive and ambition as well as dedication to the chosen party. Long hours are an accepted way of life for a politician. Family life often suffers as MPs are away from home for part of the week at Westminster and busy with constituency business at weekends. MEPs have a particularly busy and peripatetic lifestyle.

Entry and training

This is at different levels for both central and local government.

Central government

Entry for Administration Trainees/Higher Executive Officers (Development) is highly competitive. A degree in a relevant discipline is required for entry into most of the specialist posts (for example, accountant, lawyer, engineer, and so on). Most graduates enter through departmental and agency recruitment schemes. Only a few applicants (150 out of 20,000 people joining the civil service each year) are recruited to the fast stream. A good honours degree (minimum 2ii) in any subject or relevant discipline – science, engineering, economics or statistics – is required for fast-stream schemes. Fast-stream entry includes an option to pursue a career in one of the EU institutions. The selection process involves written tests, group exercises and assessment and interviews. Almost all fast-stream posts are reserved for UK nationals.

For Executive Officers, two A-levels and five GCSEs (grades A–C) (although this level is now gradually becoming graduate-level entry) are minimum requirements.

Administrative Assistant/Officers require GCSEs (grades A–C), including English. Training includes a mixture of on-the-job development and more formal training to develop relevant skills. Some posts may not require formal qualifications. Check with individual departments and agencies.

Some specialist areas, such as science and engineering, mapping and charting, offer careers to non-graduates. Factsheets are available either from university careers services or from the Civil Service Recruitment and Assessment Services Ltd.

The Inland Revenue operates a separate fast-stream scheme to the ones outlined in the civil service fast-stream development programme. The entry requirements are, however, the same as for the home civil service.

Local government

Entry into local government can be at any level, dependent on experience and training. Many local authorities will allow for training (which often leads to a related qualification) and can provide financial assistance. At officer level, most entrants have a higher-education qualification, usually a degree or HND, and may have postgraduate training and/or experience.

For individual professions, such as engineering, architecture, accountancy or planning, the entrant must take the relevant degree/diploma or other kind of academic or professional course.

For administrative posts, education to A-level standard (or equivalent) is usually desirable. However, graduates apply for many of the posts. It is possible to take a degree in public administration.

For clerical positions, GCSEs are usually required, particularly if entrants want to go on to take more qualifications.

Politics

Students interested in politics can take a degree in politics, political theory or history with options in modern politics. As a degree subject, politics is often linked with economics, history and philosophy. Whatever the course, a substantial part is concerned with political theory, similar to the study of philosophy. However, a degree in politics is not an essential requirement for a political career.

Economists

Economists are graduates, usually with an economics degree, although other related degrees include: agricultural economics (for those wanting to work in the Ministry of Agriculture); economics and social studies; and combined studies courses with an economics option. The training is on-the-job.

Subjects

Mathematics and English at GCSE are highly recommended for any post in local or central government.

A degree in public administration: Mathematics and English at GCSE, plus A-levels (no subjects specified).

Degree in politics: any subject can be taken at A-level.

Economists: A-levels in economics or statistics are very useful; mathematics at A-level is also helpful as economics involves number work and calculations; GCSEs in mathematics, English and economics.

Further information

Application Helpdesk (for fast-stream entry to the civil service), Recruitment and Assessment Services Ltd
Economics and Business Education Association
Graduate and Schools Liaison Branch
Inland Revenue, Human Resources Division – Graduate Recruitment
Local Government Opportunities, Local Government Management Board
Royal Economic Society

Books and leaflets

Degree Course Guides in Economics, Politics (annual). CRAC/Hobson
Working in Local Government. 1997. COIC
CATLOG, Careers and Training Handbook for Local Government. 1996. CRAC/Hobsons

Healthcare professions (CLCI: J)

There are many healthcare professions which are allied to medicine and which are also vitally important for the well-being of many people. People with health problems may go privately or be referred by NHS or private doctors to any of the following: chiropodists, dieticians, occupational therapists, opticians, physiotherapists, speech and language therapists or other professionals who generally work alongside doctors in hospitals and clinics.

Chiropody

Chiropodists (also called podiatrists) diagnose and treat problems of the feet. They deal with minor deformities and cure or treat ailments such as corns, verrucae, ingrowing toenails and other complaints.

They may also recommend treatment and fit any necessary appliances. State-registered chiropodists are able to perform minor surgery under local anaesthetic (removing a toenail, for example).

Dietetics

Dieticians use their skills and knowledge to advise people on how to achieve a balanced diet. They give advice on food, food supplements and additives and the balance of nutrients in special diets and carry out research into what people eat and how different foods affect health.

Occupational therapy

Occupational therapists help people who are temporarily or permanently disabled to lead as independent a life as possible. Clients range from children and adolescents to adults and the elderly. Some clients may have learning disabilities. Occupational therapists use a variety of activities to help people to learn to function properly and to help them overcome any difficult problems. Although occupational therapists work mainly in hospitals or day centres, they also visit people in their own homes. It is possible to work as an occupational therapist helper or technical instructor and work towards full occupational therapist status by part-time study.

Ophthalmics

Opticians (dispensing) supply spectacles, contact lenses and other optical aids. They do not perform eyesight tests or prescribe corrective lenses; this is the role of optometrists. Orthoptists carry out the diagnosis and treatment of visual disorders, supporting medically qualified ophthalmologists (who carry out any necessary surgery).

Physiotherapy

Physiotherapists help people regain their strength and fitness after an injury or illness by using exercise, manipulation, massage, thermal and electrotherapy techniques and education. Anyone interested in physiotherapy could gain useful work experience as a physiotherapy assistant in the NHS. They could then go on to do further training to become a physiotherapist, provided they have the necessary entry qualifications (see 'Entry and Training', page 169).

Radiography

Diagnostic radiographers produce high-quality images of the human body on film and other recording material using ionising radiation (X-rays) and other imaging modalities, such as ultrasound, magnetic resonance and radio-isotopes. These help radiologists (specialist doctors) to diagnose what is wrong with the patient in question. Therapeutic radiographers treat patients using ionising radiation and sometimes drugs. Each form of radiography is a separate profession.

An element of writing – reports or case notes – will be involved in all these jobs.

Speech and language therapy

Speech and language therapists work with people who have difficulty communicating. These difficulties can have physical, mental, social or emotional roots. The therapist will assess the client, then use theoretical knowledge and practical skills to rehabilitate, educate and advise the client and his or her carers. The therapist may use sign language or technological aids to help communication.

Sample job titles

Chiropodist, dietician, occupational therapist, optician, physiotherapist, radiographer, speech therapist

Opportunities

Most of the people in the jobs described above work for the NHS, one of the largest organisations in the UK. Others, such as 50 per cent of chiropodists and the majority of opticians, tend to work in private practice. Some may also work in commercially run clinics. A few chiropodists are employed by companies (for example, large retail organisations).

Occupational therapists may be employed by local authorities, working in day centres or residential homes. They also work in special schools, hospices and prisons, with community groups and in people's own homes. Physiotherapists may find private practice work with sports clubs – helping people with sports injuries – or with some academic institutions.

Orthoptists may work on a part-time basis for the NHS and combine NHS work with private practice or work in other clinics. Some optometrists may enter academic teaching or research posts.

Dieticians work alongside doctors and other medical staff in hospitals and clinics. They also liaise with health visitors, social workers and other healthcare professionals.

Other factors to consider

Communication and interpersonal skills are both very important for relating to colleagues and for listening and talking to patients. Increasingly, people want to know more about their illness or injury and the treatments being advised for them.

Some of the work may be emotional and upsetting, particularly if people seeking treatment are distressed or even depressed. Flexibility, creativity and a willingness to encourage and reassure are significant requirements. Good mental and physical health are essential. Physical fitness, strength and stamina are especially important for physiotherapists, as is manual dexterity for chiropodists.

It is essential for those who work in this area to like what they do – for instance, chiropodists spend much of their time handling people's feet and orthoptists examining defects or disorders in people's eyes – neither occupation suits everyone.

Chiropodists may have to work long and anti-social hours in private practice, as many patients come to see them after normal working hours.

Good communication skills are a prerequisite for dieticians.

Radiographers may be required to work overnight in Accident and Emergency departments. Shift work is also common.

Entry and training

Full-time, three-year training courses are required for entry to most of these jobs.

Chiropodists do three years' study, leading to a degree in podiatry for state registration and entry to the Society of Chiropodists and Podiatrists. A postgraduate programme of training in more advanced foot surgery (operating on bunions, for example) is offered by the society.

Dieticians study for four years, leading to a degree in nutrition or dietetics, or a two-year postgraduate diploma course in dietetics.

Occupational therapists complete a three- or four-year degree in occupational therapy; holders of non-relevant degrees do a two-year postgraduate diploma; and those already employed in an occupational therapy support role do a four-year part-time in-service degree.

Opticians (dispensing) study for two years full-time, then complete a further year's supervised practice before registration, or spend three years in part-time study if recruited as a trainee optician.

Optometrists do a three-year full-time degree course in ophthalmic optics (there are only seven of these in the UK at Aston, Bradford, Cardiff (UWIST), City (London), Manchester (UMIST), Glasgow Caledonian and Ulster universities), followed by a year of supervised practice at the end of which they must pass the qualifying examination of the College of Optometrists.

Orthoptists train for three years full-time towards a degree (courses at Liverpool, Sheffield and Glasgow).

Physiotherapists complete a three- or four-year full-time course leading to a degree; those with appropriate degrees such as a sports science or a biological science can do a postgraduate course at Glasgow Caledonian University. Three A-levels are usually required. Competition for entry to courses is keen.

Speech and language therapists can take a three- or four-year accredited university course, leading to a degree, or a two-year postgraduate course after completing a degree in another subject.

Radiographers do a three-year course (four years in Northern Ireland) leading to a degree in radiography. Radiography is an all-graduate profession.

Subjects

Sciences are important for most of these professions.

Chiropodist: GCSE in English is compulsory, and two science GCSEs are preferable; useful A-levels are sciences, particularly chemistry.

Dietician: GCSEs in mathematics, one which demonstrates a good command of English; A-levels in two sciences, including chemistry and biology are recommended

Occupational therapist: no subjects are specified, but English, science (particularly biology) and/or mathematics at A-level are usual.

Optician (dispensing): GCSEs in mathematics or physics, English and a third science-based subject (for example, general science, biology, human anatomy, chemistry or zoology) are required.

Optometrist: useful A-levels include physics, biology or zoology and another science or mathematics.

Orthoptist: GCSEs in English, mathematics and at least one science preferred. Biology or zoology may be required. A-levels should include at least one science subject.

Physiotherapist: usually GCSEs (grades A–C) in English, mathematics and a spread of sciences are needed; A-levels must include a biological science.

Speech and language therapist: English, foreign languages, mathematics and science subjects are preferred at GCSE and A-level.

Radiographer: English, mathematics or physics and another science subject are required.

Further information

British Dietetic Association
Chartered Society of Physiotherapy
College of Occupational Therapists
College of Radiographers
General Optical Council
Health Service Careers
Royal College of Speech and Language Therapists
Society of Chiropodists and Podiatrists

Books and leaflets

Humphries, J. and Brown, L. 1996. *Careers in Medicine, Dentistry and Mental Health*. Kogan Page

Nazurko, L. 1997. *Careers in Nursing and Related Professions*. Kogan Page

Working in Medicine and Dentistry. 1996. COIC

Working in Hospitals. 1996. COIC

Hospitality industry (CLCI: I)

The hospitality industry is a service industry, providing food, drink and accommodation for customers. It covers a vast range of jobs in a variety of establishments, employs over two million people and is one of the biggest growth industries in the UK. Jobs exist at all levels, from management and supervisory posts to assistant and unskilled work. The many different types of job areas are listed below:

- **food preparation and cookery** – chefs and other catering staff (call-order cooks, kitchen assistants) in hotels, restaurants, contract catering establishments (schools, universities, hospitals, companies), fast-food outlets, pubs and so on
- **food service** – waiters, waitresses, wine waiters/waitresses or bar staff in hotels, pubs, restaurants and canteens. Some jobs may involve food preparation as well as waiting on tables and handling cash
- **housekeeping** – room attendants, supervisors, housekeepers in hotels. Their job is to ensure that customers' accommodation is of a certain standard
- **front office and reception** – receptionists and clerical staff in hotels, and restaurants. They usually have to take bookings for accommodation and meals, deal with enquiries, handle cash and deal with paperwork
- **uniformed staff** – porters, doorkeepers and others, such as valets, pages, butlers, who deal with customers' baggage, car parking, mail and general enquiries, usually in hotels or country clubs.

Job titles and roles vary according to the establishment. In a small country hotel, for instance, the receptionist may also be a waiter/waitress or serve behind the bar, and the manager may be involved in all the day-to-day work; in a large hotel chain, job roles may be more clearly defined, for example, the general manager will primarily oversee the work of other departments, and middle managers and supervisors will be responsible for the more routine aspects. Depending on where they work, catering managers may be involved with the detail of menu planning and food preparation, or may be more concerned with the overall planning, supervision and scheduling of work. Some trainee chefs go on to become catering managers.

There is usually a hierarchy of staff within the kitchen of a large establishment: the mâitre chef de cuisine is the top person, controlling and directing a large staff, planning menus and ordering supplies; a sous chef is his or her assistant, perhaps a specialist in some dishes, perhaps running a section of the kitchen; the chef de partie is responsible for a specific part of the menu, for example, soups, vegetables, roasts, fish, sauces, sweets or pastries; a commis chef is a trainee who is learning the trade on-the-job. Commis chefs spend up to six months in each section of the kitchen learning the different skills.

In the kitchens of fast-food outlets are call-order cooks, who work to demand, answering the instant orders of customers.

Those who enter the industry at a managerial level could be responsible for a particular department, for example, buying food in a hotel, or they could oversee the overall running of an establishment or perhaps even several.

Sample job titles

Catering manager, chef/cook, counter services assistant, food and beverage manager, food services assistant, hotel manager, hotel room attendant, housekeeper, kitchen assistant, porter, receptionist, restaurant manager

Opportunities

The three main types of catering are:

- commercial-sector catering
- contract catering
- catering services.

The commercial sector covers hotels, restaurants, holiday camps, theme parks, leisure centres, public houses, cafés, wine bars, motorway services and fast-food outlets. Fast food is a rapidly expanding industry. According to the British Institute of Innkeeping, pubs employ about half a million people, reflecting the popularity of pub food and the number of staff required to offer this service. Catering in pubs, cinemas and theme parks is expected to account for 40 per cent of the market in 2001, which is a three per cent increase on 1997 figures (Marketpower).

The catering services sector lays on a supply of food for railways, airlines and boat cruises as well as providing for educational and healthcare institutions (where catering operations have not been contracted out) and the Armed Forces. Retail distribution is another aspect of the catering services sector.

Contract catering (feeding people in staff restaurants, schools, hospitals and prisons) is a developing field, covering mainly business and industry, although education and healthcare are growth areas. Privatisation and local authority compulsory competitive tendering has led to many catering operations being contracted out to private-sector contract catering companies.

Opportunities for hospitality staff to work abroad are good, particularly if they have a second language.

Other factors to consider

This is a 'people' career so communication and interpersonal skills are extremely important. The emphasis is on customer service, which means being patient, tolerant, polite and helpful, even when faced with angry, rude or demanding customers. It can be very tough at times. A neat, smart appearance is essential, especially for 'front of house' staff.

Because hotels need to function 24 hours a day and people need catering services at weekends and in the evenings as well as during weekdays, most of the jobs in this industry involve shift work and working long, anti-social hours. However, in contract catering hours are mostly nine to five.

Some of the jobs, especially those in hotels and restaurants, require stamina and fitness to cope with hours standing up and serving customers. The ability to work hard under pressure in a busy, hectic environment is also useful.

Those who handle food must have a high standard of personal hygiene.

Hotel and catering managers usually have to move from one job, and one area of the UK, to another to be promoted. So they must be prepared to be mobile.

Although the hospitality industry is notorious for its low pay levels, management salaries are beginning to increase ahead of those in other sectors.

Managers and supervisors need to have a reasonable level of numeracy and literacy as they have to forecast budgets, keep the books and records and write reports.

Entry and training

The choice of training and qualifications at all levels is wide.

Hotel/restaurant managers generally need an HND/degree in hospitality or hotel and catering management, or the Hotel and Catering International Management (HCIMA) Professional Diploma. The HCIMA Professional Diploma usually takes up to two years, part-time, to complete and can be done by distance-learning. Candidates must be working full-time in the hospitality industry at management level and have successfully completed the HCIMA Professional Certificate or hold equivalent qualifications such as BTEC National awards, or NVQs; the HCIMA Professional Certificate is studied part-time over two years or via distance-learning. Candidates must be working at supervisory level in the hospitality industry with at least two years' previous experience in the industry, and hold four GCSEs (grades A–C) or equivalent. A one-year postgraduate hospitality conversion course can be taken by graduates with degrees in other disciplines at various colleges. Degrees can be a fast route into management, leading on to graduate training programmes, lasting from six months to two years, depending on the organisation.

Other people may start at the bottom and work their way up, gaining experience of the industry on the way.

Many school and college courses lead to qualifications (for example, a GNVQ in Hospitality and Catering) in the various catering and hospitality specialisms, including food preparation and service, reception and housekeeping.

Modern Apprenticeships, national traineeships and NVQs up to levels 3 and 4 can be taken in catering and hospitality. In addition, management trainee schemes, particularly with the large hotel and restaurant chains, provide on-the-job training and experience in various different departments, usually with part-time study towards NVQ, HCIMA or other relevant qualifications.

Subjects

English and mathematics at GCSE are important. Sciences (biology, human biology, social biology, chemistry), business studies and home economics can be useful.

Foreign languages, particularly French, can be an asset in the area of catering.

Further information

Brewers and Licensed Retailers Association
British Institute of Innkeeping
Hospitality Training Foundation
Hotel and Catering International Management (HCIMA)

Books and leaflets

Joseph, R. 1997. *Careers in Catering, Hotel Administration and Management*. Kogan Page
Hospitality Handbook. 1997. GTI Specialist Publishers
Careers Guide 1997, Caterer & Hotelkeeper (available from HCIMA)
Working in Hotels and Catering. 1995. COIC

Land-based industries (CLCI: W)

Land-based industries are key contributors to the national economy and cover a wide variety of closely linked careers. The industry can be roughly divided into: agriculture, horticulture, environmental science, forestry, arboriculture.

Within each area there may be further subdivisions, for example:

- **agriculture** includes farming, fish farming, gamekeeping and food production
- **horticulture** includes amenity horticulture (where facilities are provided for the pleasure of others, for example, parks, sports

fields), commercial horticulture (where profits have to be made, for example in garden centres, nurseries) and food production

- **environmental science** includes work on nature reserves (see 'Environmental Services', page 144)
- **arboriculture** includes tree surgery, landscaping and some amenity work.

Often, and necessarily, these areas overlap, for example, both agriculture and horticulture are concerned with food production; arboriculture and horticulture both include amenity work.

Agriculture

Agriculture has become a highly mechanised industry, and this has led to a decrease in the number of jobs. Farming has changed radically, from being a labour-intensive industry during the first half of the twentieth century to a capital-intensive one. Capital, not workers, is now the major resource, and farms continue to increase in size and decrease in number. Farming comprises various categories of specialist work: arable farming (root crops, cereals and vegetables); dairy farming (milk and cheese production); livestock farming (the raising of cattle, sheep, pigs and poultry); and fish farming (breeding and rearing fish for sport or food). The range of jobs depends on the size and type of farm, and who owns it, but generally includes the following jobs:

- **farm managers**, who are responsible for running the farm or a farm unit, which may be owned by a private individual, company, tenant or commercial organisation. On very big farms the managers will be helped by an assistant or deputy manager. Management involves dealing with personnel, organising and supervising the farm work and making technical decisions about crops, livestock and feed, buildings and equipment. Financial management is also very important. Farm management is a highly popular and competitive career.
- **farm workers**, who are employed on all kinds of farms. The job is demanding and involves working long hours, being outdoors in all weathers and relatively low pay. Some farm workers may specialise in a particular area, while others may do a variety of work. Those on arable farms are trained to drive or operate machinery, such as tractors, cultivating, planting and harvesting machinery and so on. Their busiest time is during harvest, when they have to work very

long hours. Some farm workers may also have to carry out repairs, acting as farm mechanics.

- **stock persons**, who work closely with the animals for which they are responsible on livestock farms. They ensure the animals are reared efficiently within strict animal welfare requirements. They are also likely to use some machinery.
- **farm secretaries**, who carry out the administrative and secretarial work. They either work for one farm, or for several farms via an agency or as a self-employed person. They need to understand the legal and technical aspects of farming in addition to having secretarial skills.

There are other specialist posts in agriculture for advisers, researchers, food scientists, animal feed analysts and nutrition advisers in, for example, agricultural testing and inspecting, teaching, research and advising growers and farmers on production, business methods, and so on. Research work may involve observing animal behaviour, analysing the effects of the climate on crops, studying nutrition, or perhaps specialising in aspects of horticulture, such as plant diseases or plant growth. Many agricultural graduates go into the expanding area of agricultural services, where they give advice and practical help to farmers on a seasonal basis. Agricultural services employ skilled and experienced staff in a variety of posts.

Horticulture

Horticulture is divided into commercial (production), amenity horticulture (cultivation). Commercial horticulture involves growing plants and produce for food or ornamental purposes, including trees and flowers for sale (generally to garden centres, professional growers and wholesalers, although a huge percentage of food crops goes directly to retailers). The work can include planting, harvesting, thinning-out, weeding and transporting plants for sale. Garden centre staff not only cultivate plants but also advise customers about them and are often involved in sales.

Amenity horticulture is the cultivation of plants in private gardens, public parks and leisure areas. Jobs include planting and tending trees, shrubs and flowers and occasionally dealing with customers or visitors.

Sports field provision (green keeping/groundsmanship) is a specialist area within horticulture. Groundsmen/women and green keepers look after the turf, managing and maintaining bowling greens, football pitches, golf courses, tennis courts, and so on. Another group of people, who are sometimes called internal landscapers, have contracts to tend plants in office buildings.

Forestry

Forestry is the management and care of forests and woodlands. It is concerned with the commercial production of trees in an environmentally sensitive way. Those involved produce timber, conserve natural heritage, enhance wildlife conservation and the landscape, arrange recreational activities and carry out scientific research. Forest workers carry out the manual work – fencing, draining, weeding, pruning, felling, and so on – often using highly sophisticated machinery. Foresters or forest officers generally work at supervisory and managerial level, where they oversee the forest workers, plan the work schedules, solve any problems and get involved with the financial and marketing side of forestry.

Arboriculture

Arboriculture is the name given to the planting, cultivation and maintenance of trees mainly for amenity purposes.

Tree surgery is remedial maintenance work to protect and conserve trees. It can be hazardous as tree surgeons often work high up, using potentially dangerous machinery.

Sample job titles

Farmer, farm secretary, farm worker, florist, forester, gamekeeper, garden centre manager, gardener, horticulturist, landscape and garden designer, tree surgeon

Opportunities

The number of farms in the UK is decreasing, and most are larger and employ fewer people than in the past. Many farms are owned and run by companies, as well as by private individuals or tenant farmers. Competition for farm management is stiff, and a significant number of farming people (one-third) have a family background in the industry. Unit or assistant manager posts are more numerous than farm manager posts. Although dairy farming is the largest sector of the farming industry, it is nevertheless in decline. In contrast, deer farming is expanding due to public concern about beef and the desire for alternative types of meat. Organic farming is also becoming more popular as we are becoming more aware of and concerned about what we eat. Fish farming is very specialist and restricted to a few geographical areas. The greatest concentration is in Scotland.

Qualified and skilled workers can find seasonal contract work, mostly on farms at harvest time or for sheep shearing.

Advisers work for ADAS (the Agricultural Development and Advisory Service, although this full title is never used), colleges and commercial companies. Research work may involve working in a government research laboratory or for a commercial company.

Openings in commercial horticulture occur mainly in garden centres, nurseries, market gardens and vegetable or fruit farms; in amenity horticulture, jobs can be found in any large organisation that has gardens, parks, sports facilities or the need for regular flower and plant displays. Horticulturists and gardeners are employed by private contracting firms, large estate or house owners, botanical or tropical gardens, the National Trust and other such bodies; or are self-employed. Others work in zoos, hospitals, theme parks and sports and leisure clubs. Groundsmen/women and green keepers generally work in the leisure industry and for local authorities.

Forestry is a relatively small industry, employing about 32,000 people in the UK. Most jobs are with the Forestry Commission, which manages almost 50 per cent of British forests, or with forest management companies. Other jobs are in land management companies and forest nurseries. The largest forest areas are in Wales and Scotland. In England the main areas are in East Anglia, the New Forest, Northumberland and Cumbria.

Qualified and experienced people can work abroad in many aspects of the land-based industry.

Other factors to consider

The chief attraction of land-based work is a healthy, outdoor life, either working on the land or with animals, or involved in conservation and protection of the countryside and environment. The downsides could be working outdoors in all types of weather, physically hard work and quite often long, anti-social hours. Much of the work, particularly in farming and forestry, may be in remote areas and solitary.

Many of the jobs have a practical element and require manual dexterity, stamina, strength and fitness. Teamwork and good communication skills are also important.

Anyone who works with animals on farms must be unsentimental as many farm animals are bred for the food chain or have to be put down due to illness.

Technology in the form of modern sophisticated equipment is playing an increasing role in the land-based industries so computer skills are an advantage and, in fact, often a necessity.

Business and organisational skills are essential for farm and farm unit managers, and those who are self-employed or in any sales-related jobs such as commercial horticulture.

Some of the jobs (particularly in forestry and farming) can be dangerous, for example, when they involve dealing with hazardous machinery, working at height or at speed. This calls for people who are safety-conscious and highly responsible.

In farming, moving from one farm to another is usually the only way to be promoted.

Entry and training

The range of career entry points and training opportunities in land-based work are varied. In agriculture and commercial horticulture, national traineeships are available and can lead on to full-time education or Modern Apprenticeship programmes (which offer progression to NVQ level 4). There are 14 NVQs in agriculture and commercial horticulture, done via college courses, national traineeships, Modern Apprenticeships, or while in employment: two at level 1 (general agriculture and commercial horticulture); five each at levels 2 and 3 (mixed farming, intensive crop production, extensive crop production, livestock production and poultry production); and two at level 4 (livestock management and crop management). Local TECs/LECs and careers offices will provide details of what is available in individual areas.

Some employers, professional bodies, government or national organisations (mostly science-based industries) offer sponsorships for different types of career. Management training schemes are provided by a number of the larger farming organisations.

Agriculture

One way into farm management is by completing an agricultural HND or degree course at university or specialist agricultural college, preferably combined with or followed by a business/management qualification, Alternatively, a college diploma in farm management could be followed by a postgraduate qualification in farm management, agribusiness or agricultural economics. Agricultural degrees are usually science-based and prepare graduates for scientific or advisory work as well as farm management. As practical farming is generally not included in degree courses, prospective farmers and farm managers should try to gain a year's practical experience before doing the course. Some courses include organic farming as an option.

Farm workers increasingly need some basic qualifications (GCSEs), particularly if they want to progress to more responsible positions.

Horticulture

Qualifications in horticulture can be gained through various full-time and part-time college courses. A minimum of four GCSEs and some previous relevant experience are necessary for ND- or HND-level qualifications, which could lead to managerial/supervisory posts. Degrees in horticulture generally prepare students for careers as advisers and researchers, although an increasing number of growers and managers are also taking this route. Previous practical experience is advisable.

Some horticultural firms take on trainees who have just a few GCSEs. The trainees then work towards NVQs while learning on-the-job. The National Trust offers a few traineeships in Amenity Horticulture, leading to NVQ level 3. Other qualifications are offered by the Royal Horticultural Society (RHS) and the Royal Botanic Gardens at Kew.

Forestry

Forest worker training is on-the-job, sometimes combined with part-time study towards NVQs at levels 1 and 2. Work-based training schemes are available. Foresters/forest officers generally have an ND/HND or degree in forestry. These are offered at only six colleges and seven universities so competition is keen. Previous practical experience is advantageous, and a driving licence is essential.

Arboriculture

Arboriculture can be studied at some agricultural colleges and as an option on the forestry degree course at the University of Aberdeen and at the University of Bangor. The Royal Forestry Society and the Arboricultural Association offer part-time courses which lead to professional qualifications.

Subjects

Modern Apprenticeships: GCSEs in English, mathematics and a science.

Agriculture: GCSEs in English, mathematics and science are always useful and sometimes required by colleges. A-levels in science subjects (preferably chemistry and biology) are necessary for farm management posts. Competition is keen, so A-levels (grades A–C) are required.

Horticulture: useful GCSEs include science (biology), environmental studies, English and mathematics; sciences at A-level (especially for the Royal Botanic Gardens, Kew Diploma and for management, advisory and research level posts).

Forestry and arboriculture: useful GCSEs include sciences, mathematics and English; science A-levels are useful.

Further information

Arboricultural Association
ATB-Landbase
Farming Press
Food and Farming Information Service
Forestry Commission
Institute of Horticulture
Institute of Leisure and Amenity Management
National Association of Agricultural Contractors
National Trust
Royal Forestry Society

Royal Horticultural Society Garden
School of Horticulture, Royal Botanic Gardens, Kew
Soil Association
Timber Growers Association
Willing Workers on Organic Farms
Woodland Trust

Books and leaflets

Directory of Landbased Courses (annual). Farming Press
Working in Agriculture and Horticulture. 1994. COIC

Language-based careers (CLCI: F)

A language degree does not necessarily lead to a career as a linguist. Organisations generally look for other skills as well. The ability to speak and/or read more than one language is, however, of benefit in a wide range of careers and is increasingly requested by employers. The most obvious areas in which it helps are secretarial work, commercial management, sales and purchasing, international marketing, export, industrial training and research, the hospitality industry, travel and tourism, international law and finance, the diplomatic service, librarian and information services, journalism and the public services.

Fluency in one or more foreign languages is a primary requirement in three professions: foreign-language teaching, interpreting and translating. There is a continuing shortage of foreign-language teachers. (The teaching profession is covered in detail in a separate section, see page 267).

Interpreting

Interpreting is the act of oral communication between two parties who do not share a common language. Interpreting is carried out in a wide variety of contexts, which range from informal social or business gatherings to major formal international events. For informal, social conversations, liaison interpreting requires the interpreter to assist individuals or groups who do not speak each other's language to communicate; the interpreter alternates between the two languages. In more formal settings, where rapid, accurate and full rendering of speech is required, interpreters use the techniques of consecutive and simultaneous interpreting. In consecutive interpreting, the speaker pauses to allow the interpreter to communicate what has been said; in simultaneous interpreting the interpreter listens to the speaker and communicates what is being said almost at the same time and continuously. Simultaneous interpreting usually requires sound equipment; the interpreter speaks into a microphone and sits in a soundproof booth. Simultaneous interpreting is tiring; interpreters therefore work in pairs so that they can each have a rest after about half an hour. Interpreting can be divided into three main areas:

- **conference interpreting** Interpreters are employed by a wide variety of international organisations, including the institutions of the European Union and the United Nations to work at international multilingual meetings. Because of the large number of working languages in the EU, interpreters with three languages in addition to their mother tongue are preferred
- **interpreting for business** This is largely concerned with foreign trade and involves, for example, interpreting at business meetings, site visits and accompanying trade delegations
- **community/public services interpreting** This is required whenever non-English speaking members of the public come into contact with the public services, for example, when hospital and other medical attention is required, when witnesses or suspects are interviewed in police stations or appear in court, or when social or welfare services are required.

Translating

Translating also requires a high level of competence in more than one language and in the mother tongue and subject knowledge and specialist vocabulary: for example, for business, engineering, IT, medicine, law or finance. Translators also need to acquire relevant expertise by studying or working in the chosen field. As a result, many translators, like interpreters, start out in other professions.

Openings for literary translators are very limited. Technical translators work in specialist areas and have mastered the concepts and terminology of their particular specialism. For this reason, it can take a long time to become proficient at translating, to build up the skills and the technical knowledge.

A translator should, as a rule, translate only into his or her mother tongue. A knowledge of a non-European language or a less common European language of commercial importance could be a considerable advantage.

Some people are able to do both translating and interpreting work. Many translators and interpreters are bilingual by birth.

Sample job titles

Bilingual secretary, hotel receptionist, interpreter, linguist, teacher, tourist guide, translator

Opportunities

Competition for translating and interpreting is stiff so those who are fluent in more than two foreign languages are at an advantage. People who have a command of less common languages, such as Russian, Japanese, Chinese and Arabic are also sought after. The civil service (Government Communication Headquarters, Immigration Department, Diplomatic Service), international organisations and major companies employ staff translators. Freelance translators can work for translation agencies as technical translators.

Interpreting is a very small and élite profession. The main employers of permanent and freelance conference interpreters are the European Commission, the UN, NATO and international trade organisations. Freelance interpreters are also hired by agencies and are often recruited directly by conference organisers and the other institutions, such as the police and courts, who require their services. Over time, an interpreter can therefore gradually build up his or her own clientèle. However, demand fluctuates and it may be necessary to do other work as well, such as translating or teaching.

Working abroad is an obvious option for anyone with a command of a second language. Careers where languages are useful overseas include journalism, the hospitality industry, the diplomatic service and travel and tourism. However, much of the work abroad in travel and tourism (for example, as tourist guides, couriers, resort representatives, see pages 280–4) tends to be seasonal and not full-time.

Other factors to consider

People who choose a career where they can use a second language must be good at languages and want to communicate well in either written or verbal form in another language. Their command of English as a mother tongue should also be excellent.

Interpreters need to be fluent in both languages but also have the relevant specialist and technical vocabulary, a fast and agile mind and a resilient personality. In addition, they need to be able to deal with stressful circumstances as interpreting is usually carried out at speed and requires accuracy. Interpreters must also be happy to spend time reading long, often technical, documents to gain a good understanding of the subject matter and issues. They must be prepared to travel to conferences and meetings all over the world. Many live and work in the foreign country to gain fluency and awareness of the culture. It can be a very demanding career, with an irregular lifestyle. Interpreters are often required to attend social occasions organised for conference delegates. This is where ability in more than one language is useful.

Freelance translators need persistence and determination to build up a clientèle, either through direct contact or via agencies.

Computer literacy is important. For translation work, it is vital to be able to use a word processor and electronic mail (email).

Entry and training

Ideally, for translating and interpreting, degree-level proficiency in the foreign language should be supplemented by extensive colloquial practice, acquisition of specialist vocabulary and relevant postgraduate training. Most conference interpreters do post-graduate training at university. Language degrees take four years to complete, one of which is spent abroad. For English mother-tongue interpreters, the UN organisations require proficiency in a minimum of two further languages: the institutions of the EU require proficiency in a minimum of three languages other than English unless the interpreter has rare languages for which there is current demand. Applicants for conference interpreting courses with the European Commission must be a native speaker of one of the EU languages and have a thorough understanding, including oral ability, of at least three other EU languages.

Usually a first degree in languages is a good qualification for using languages in other jobs, although graduates must be prepared to undergo further training in a different profession as well, either through a postgraduate course or as a trainee in employment. Many degrees and diplomas, such as business studies, law, engineering or travel and tourism, now offer a language option or are combined with a language.

Languages can be learnt from scratch, post secondary-education, either in further or higher education. This can be done through various short courses, evening classes and distance-learning methods. The Institute of Linguists also offers many examinations at different levels, such as the Diploma in Translation. An NVQ level 5 in translation and interpreting can be taken.

Community/public service interpreting requires ethnic minority languages and languages other than English as mother tongue and good English. The Institute of Linguists' Diploma in Public Service Interpreting (equivalent to first degree language skills level) is the accepted qualification. Many local authorities and some university departments have short training courses for community interpreters.

Subjects

GCSEs (grades A–C) should be in English and the chosen second language(s).
A-levels should be in the chosen second language(s).

Further information

Centre for Information on Language Teaching and Research
Institute of Linguists
Institute of Translation and Interpreting
International Association of Conference Interpreters

Books and leaflets
Ostarhild, E. 1996. *Careers Using Languages.* Kogan Page
Working in Languages. 1993. COIC

The legal profession (CLCI: L)

The legal system in the UK is divided into three: Scotland; England and Wales; and Northern Ireland, although the system in Northern Ireland closely resembles that of England and Wales. Advocates (Scotland) and barristers (England and Wales) do similar work, specialising in advocacy – presenting the client's case to a court or tribunal and advising clients on every aspect of litigation; solicitors in England and Wales advise clients on legal aspects of all kinds, including both civil and criminal court work, private client work, employment law and business law. In Scotland a number of solicitors specialise in conveyancing but, like English solicitors, cover the full spectrum of legal work. Scotland also has procurators-fiscal, who are responsible for the investigation and prosecution of crimes. In England and Wales this is the responsibility of both the police and the Crown Prosecution Service.

Lawyer is the term used to describe solicitors, barristers and legal executives, all of whom have different roles and skills.

Solicitors are the first point of contact for clients and give them advice on different aspects of the law. The work varies according to the client's problem. Solicitors may be general practitioners (dealing with all aspects of law) or, more usually, specialists in one area of the law, including accident claims, criminal law, divorce, tax, conveyancing, making a will, bankruptcy, company and commercial law (and a whole range in between).

Barristers and advocates give specialist advice, usually to an even greater extent than solicitors, in specific areas of the law, such as personal injury, company law, trust, property, conveyancing, criminal law, tax or estate administration. They do not generally have direct contact with clients but are briefed or consulted by solicitors on behalf of clients. Barristers often display theatrical talent as they 'perform' at the Bar (in court), cross-examining witnesses and arguing facts and law. Solicitors also represent clients in courts or tribunals. They have 'rights of audience' (where they represent clients as advocates in court) in magistrates courts, county courts and industrial tribunals. Any solicitor who specialises in criminal work or civil litigation will spend quite a lot of time in court.

Legal executives work for solicitors (only in England and Wales, not in Scotland or Northern Ireland), usually specialising in one aspect of law. As well as doing the day-to-day work in a solicitor's office they manage staff, deal with accounts and provide specialist support on procedural and legal matters and can go on to become solicitors if they are over 25.

Legal secretaries have to be able to understand and use the legal profession's specialist terminology. In addition to routine secretarial work they prepare legal documents.

Justices' clerks assistants support the work of a justices' clerk (a solicitor or a barrister) in an office attached to a magistrates' court.

Sample job titles

Advocate, barrister, barrister's clerk, justices' clerk assistant, legal executive, legal secretary, solicitor

Opportunities

Entry into the legal profession is highly competitive: the number of law students who have completed the Legal Practice Course (LPC) in England and Wales and the Diploma in Legal Practice in Scotland outweighs the number of training contracts (new term for articles) in solicitors' firms. In fact, many students undertaking a law degree either do not wish to pursue a career in the legal profession or find they are unable to. Fortunately, their studies are considered to be good grounding for a variety of other professions. Similarly, not all barristers and advocates find employment at the Bar. Many decide to work instead in industry and commerce or elsewhere after finishing their professional training. The Bar offers about 600 pupillages (similar to apprenticeships) to the 800 to 1,100 (1996 figures) newly qualified barristers. Although some chambers offer paid pupillages, about 200 are unpaid.

Employers are looking not only for extremely well-qualified people, with at least a second-class degree (they prefer 2.is and in England and Wales some – but certainly not all – still like to choose Oxbridge candidates), but also for those who have a broader experience of life. Students who have travelled, held positions of responsibility at school and university and who have some work experience have a greater chance of being recruited than those whose interests are purely academic. Barristers can gain work experience by undertaking mini-pupillages (one-week periods in chambers) during their holidays.

Barristers/advocates need a lot of determination to succeed as it takes a long time to qualify (3–4 years after completing a non-law degree) and to establish a good reputation. It is possible to be practising within two years, having completed the Bar Vocational Course (BVC) and the first six months' pupillage, by earning money while completing the second (practising) six-month pupillage. Barristers are dependent on work passed on to them by solicitors and other professionals, such as accountants, planners and surveyors with direct access to them. The majority of barristers work in the independent Bar, i.e. in private practice, mostly in chambers (some work from home or in rented offices). They are self-employed and do not have a guaranteed income. They work together in a chambers and share the overheads of the building. Consequently, many barristers find it difficult to make a living initially. If they are successful, the rewards can be high although some barristers do have fairly modest-sized practices. Barristers may also work for companies in commerce and industry or for central and local government (the employed Bar).

The majority of solicitors (up to 75 per cent) work in private practice. Others find employment with local authorities, acting as advisers to local government departments on public health, housing, education and other matters. A few become civil servants, advising on and interpreting the law for departments of state. Another area in England and Wales is the Crown Prosecution Service, where solicitors (civil servants) and barristers prosecute offenders on behalf of the state. Some of the larger companies and public bodies have their own legal departments to deal with their interests.

Some firms of solicitors have branches world-wide, advising local clients on English law and international law. The principles of English law form the basis of legal systems in many other countries, and some international agreements and contracts are made under English law and therefore submit to this jurisdiction.

Other factors to consider

Anyone in the legal profession needs to have a good command of the English language, both oral and written. Other languages can be useful. Curiosity and the desire to solve problems are also good qualities to have, in order to research, check and analyse facts and events. Accuracy and close attention to detail are important, and as the work is confidential, absolute discretion is essential. Lawyers spend a great deal of time with clients and in court and therefore need good communication and interpersonal skills. However, a large amount of their time, and the time of the support staff in the office, can also be spent dealing with paperwork, searching through reference books and documents and reading and exploring data on computer files. This requires the ability to digest large amounts of material quickly. Barristers and solicitors need to make sure they have all the facts at their fingertips before they go into court to plead a case.

Lawyers do not always have someone to tell them what to do and when to do it; they are self-motivated people who work on their own initiative with responsibility for others. In addition, barristers in independent practice have to cope with the uncertainty and insecurity of being self-employed in a highly competitive profession.

Computer skills are essential, particularly as many lawyers now wordprocess their own documents and use computer databases for research.

Lawyers need to be logical and have self-confidence too.

Entry and training

Training in the legal profession is lengthy (5–6 years in England and Wales and Northern Ireland and up to 7 years in Scotland) and the standards are high. Although it is not necessary to have a law degree, about 64 per cent of solicitors in England and Wales are law graduates. In Scotland, the alternative is to serve a pre-Diploma traineeship and to pass the Law Society of Scotland's own examinations. Employers view a law degree as providing students with the necessary analytical skills, precise use of language and the ability to present arguments in a well-formed manner. There is, however, no disadvantage in doing a non-law degree and then a one-year full-time or two-year part-time conversion course (the Common Professional Examination) or Diploma in Law prior to the LPC or the BVC.

In England and Wales, students with a law degree who want to be a barrister must:

- complete one year's full-time or two years' part-time training at one of the validated institutions, culminating in the BVC examination
- complete their vocational training with a one-year apprenticeship (called 'pupillage'), which is often unpaid, under the guidance of an experienced barrister in chambers. After the first six months barristers can work on their own cases with guidance
- if they want to work at the Bar they can apply for a tenancy (where a barrister pays rent for a place in chambers), do a third six-month pupillage or stay rent-free in chambers if allowed. The number of people applying outweighs the number of tenancies available.

Students with a non-law degree must complete an intensive one-year full-time or two-year part-time Common Professional Examination (CPE) or an approved postgraduate diploma in law before training for the BVC. Barristers may apply for pupillages via the PACH (Pupillage Applications Clearing House) system, whereby they send their application to PACH on computer disk with a selection of 12 chambers. PACH then sends it on their behalf to the individual chambers. Barristers can also apply direct to chambers without using this system. Pupillage is not funded by LEA grants, although some places are funded by chambers. How much law courses cost depends on the individual institution but CPE can be over £3,000 and LPC over £5,000. It may be possible to get a career development loan and housing benefit while training.

In England and Wales those wishing to become a solicitor must:

- complete either a qualifying law degree or a non-law degree followed by a Diploma in Law or the CPE
- pass the LPC (study lasts for one year full-time or for two years part-time)
- undertake a two-year on-the-job training contract with solicitors, which includes academic study (this training period used to be called articles).

The LPC very rarely attracts any local authority grant so students have to arrange their own funding for studies. Larger firms often provide sponsorship for students.

Qualified legal executives who are over 25 years old and who have worked for a minimum of five years in a solicitor's office can train to be a solicitor by undertaking a further two years' part-time study through the Institute of Legal Executives (ILEX), leading to the LPC. Legal executives are then exempt from the two-year training contracts.

In Scotland students with a law degree from a Scottish university or a non-law degree must complete a one-year full-time postgraduate course at a Scottish university leading to the Diploma in Legal Practice. Trainee solicitors must then obtain a two-year training contract in a solicitor's office. Candidates for admission to the public office of advocate are called intrants and serve a period of training in a solicitor's office of usually 21 months, followed by approximately nine months' training (a period of apprenticeship called 'devilling' or pupillage) before being called to the Bar, when they can practise as an advocate.

Those who wish to qualify as a procurator-fiscal must have a law degree.

Subjects

Check entry requirements carefully. Some courses do not accept some technical or practical subjects, which are considered to be 'non-academic'. English is an important subject to have.

Lawyer/Procurator fiscal: three A-levels (grades A/B) in any academic subjects (no one subject is essential for entry to a law degree).

Legal executive: minimum four GCSEs (grades A–C). Most entrants have A-levels or a degree. Those with A-level law are exempt from taking one of the ILEX examinations.

Justices' clerks' assistant: minimum three GCSEs, grades A–C (most entrants have A-levels or a degree).

Further information

Faculty of Advocates
General Council of the Bar
Inns of Court School of Law
Institute of Legal Executives
Law Society
Law Society of Northern Ireland
Law Society of Scotland

Books and leaflets

The Legal Profession. Ivanhoe Career Guides. 1996. Cambridge Market Intelligence

Working in Law. 1996. COIC

Law, Degree Course Guide (annual). CRAC/Hobsons

Directory of Further Education (annual). CRAC/Hobsons

Library, information and archive work (CLCI: F)

Librarians, information managers and archivists all deal with information in one form or another, but the work in each of the areas is very different.

Library and information work

Library and information work can be divided into four areas:

- public libraries
- education (academic, college and school) libraries
- national libraries
- specialist libraries.

Public libraries provide the widest range of services: the public uses them for leisure reading, independent learning, finding information, doing research, accessing the Internet and listening to music as well as borrowing books, cassettes, CDs, records and videos. Another service offered by most public libraries is the mobile library, which is for those who cannot leave their homes easily or are a long way from a library. Job roles vary according to the level of responsibility and the particular library or information resource, but in general, librarians choose which books and other materials to stock in the library, research information and manage information systems and staff. Some librarians also organise talks and exhibitions both in the library and within the local community, arrange story sessions or other activities for children and organise displays for them.

Librarians in the education sector work in schools, colleges and universities; they manage learning resource centres which combine computing (databases/the Internet) with library services. They have to ensure that the library stocks relevant course materials and may compile bibliographies for course reading lists. They also teach research skills and help students to use the resources.

National libraries provide last-resort research facilities for students and hold valuable, irreplaceable collections.

Librarians or information managers in specialist libraries and information services may work in:

- subject-focused libraries
- libraries of learned and professional bodies
- the voluntary sector
- organisations and government (managing information services)
- the medical and legal professions.

They undertake research, filter and organise information and repackage it for other people in the same organisation. In subject-focused libraries the work may also involve cataloguing and classifying materials; it may require knowledge of the specialist subject or field or similar work experience.

Many library and information jobs are hybrid so they require some archive and records management skills (gained as part of a library and information management professional course).

Library and information assistants – sometimes called paraprofessional assistants – generally work in public libraries or in the education sector, carrying out the day-to-day work such as administration, liaising with suppliers, answering enquiries and issuing books and other materials to the general public. They use computers extensively to find information. Experienced assistants may become professional librarians, as long as they have completed a degree or postgraduate course approved by the Library Association.

The posts with the title 'information officer' in other professions (such as careers guidance and journalism) should not be confused with those in the library and information management profession. People in these posts are often professionals in other fields and are not usually librarians or information managers. Information management may be only part of their role and is often combined with marketing or public relations. Although such people may carry out research and find out information for other people (and even manage small company resource centres), they are usually involved in writing reports, news items, summaries, press releases and so on.

Archive work

Archivists work with historical documents, such as private individuals' diaries, letters, wills, and so on, and legal and government records. They have to make decisions about what to keep and how to preserve it. Archivists also often help individual people (for example, students, teachers, members of the public) to find out more about their family or local history.

Records managers help with the organisation of businesses' current and semi-current records, both to promote efficiency and to make sure that the right records are kept for the future.

Sample job titles

Archivist, information officer/manager, librarian, library and information assistant, records manager

Opportunities

Librarians, information managers and library assistants can work in a wide variety of places including:

- public, prison, school, college, careers service and academic libraries
- libraries and information services in business and industry research organisations
- medical and legal libraries
- government (for example, the House of Commons or a government department or research organisation) and national libraries (for example, the British Library)
- broadcasting and media research (for example BBC and newspapers) libraries. Part-time work is possible in this field.

Information managers work in government and specialist libraries or in information offices or centres, particularly in legal, accountancy and architectural practices, or in the engineering, pharmaceutical, computing and other blue-chip industries. Other job opportunities are in banks, insurance offices and building societies.

Archivists work in county and city record offices, national libraries, large public libraries and in private libraries and institutions. Records managers usually work in industry.

Other factors to consider

Those who are involved with finding, storing, retrieving and exploiting information should:

- enjoy solving problems and doing research using a variety of sources
- be well-organised and methodical
- have a logical mind, an eye for detail and a good memory
- be able to communicate well so that they can relay the information back to the client
- have strong management skills
- be able to promote and market services and give presentations
- be able to understand users' information needs.

In addition, good general knowledge and awareness of current affairs is essential as is the ability to work well in a team.

Anyone working in this field needs to be computer literate and willing to learn (if not already able) to use all kinds of hardware and software and the Internet.

As public and academic libraries are often open in the evenings and at weekends, employees are likely to have to work anti-social hours and do shift work. Some posts are part-time.

Archivists should enjoy doing historical research, which can be a slow, painstaking business, and reading about history. Their working environment may be dusty or even dirty because they occasionally have to deal with very old records. They also need to be accurate in everything they do. Increasingly, computers are being used to classify and record documents so archivists should be computer literate.

Entry and training

Although many of the jobs require graduates, some assistant-level jobs (for example, library and information assistant, information assistant) only need applicants with GCSEs or A-levels.

Library and information work

Professional library and information management jobs are open only to graduates. The two entry routes are:

- **doing a first degree in information studies** (accredited by the Library Association or the Institute of Information Scientists – IIS) *or*
- **taking a degree in any discipline, then doing a Library Association or IIS-accredited postgraduate degree in information studies**.

For some postgraduate courses students need to have up to one year's pre-course experience in information work. It is possible to study towards these qualifications on a part-time or distance-learning basis.

Many of the business libraries do not ask for professional library qualifications. The minimum qualification for library and information assistants is usually five GCSEs (grades A–C). Some posts – for instance those in specialist libraries – may require A-levels. Training is on-the-job, but employees can study towards relevant qualifications, such as the City & Guilds 737 Library and Information Competences Certificate. NVQs in Information and Library Services are available at levels 2–4.

Archive work

Those wishing to do archive work need a first- or upper second-class degree. Archivists usually have a degree in either history, Latin or other classical languages or English. Many posts require postgraduate qualifications in archives administration.

Subjects

GCSE in English is required; a foreign language and science or mathematics are also often asked for. Particular subjects at GCSE or A-level are specified for some degree courses. Contact individual institutions for details.

Further information

Institute of Information Scientists (IIS)
Library Association
Records Management Society of Great Britain
Society of Archivists

The media (CLCI: F/G)

The media industry includes television and radio, film and video, journalism, writing, advertising, PR, publishing and increasingly multimedia education and entertainment. This chapter is concerned with television and radio, film, video and journalism and writing. Publishing, advertising, PR and publicity are covered in separate sections of this book.

Broadcasting and film

The broadcasting and film industry is expanding: cable and digital terrestrial television, new local and commercial radio stations, satellite communication and other existing and impending technological developments (such as home shopping, home banking and Internet access via television) continue to widen its scope. It is also converging rapidly with computers and telecommunications, transforming programme production and transmission. However, despite these growth areas, it is still very difficult to enter this competitive field.

The broadcasting and film industry covers a multitude of jobs, the majority of which are not glamorous. The people who appear on television or in films and videos or who are heard on the radio are the front men and women (the broadcasters/presenters, actors and performers). Behind the scenes are the production and editorial teams (the directors, producers, journalists, writers, editors, researchers and their assistants). They conceive, plan, commission or write the script, engage the actors and oversee the making of the programme. The studio and operational staff – the engineers, technicians, camera operators, production assistants, clerical staff, secretaries, drivers and managers – are all just as essential as the production team in the making of programmes. Their job is to bring the ideas of the production team to life.

The traditional entry-level job in this industry is as a gofer/runner, taking messages, running errands and acting as a general assistant in small independent production companies. In this way, people can learn the basics of the industry. They are then well placed to respond to any internal vacancies for less junior posts that may materialise.

Camera operators and sound technicians work either in studios or on outside broadcasts. In the studio the head of the camera crew is in charge of lighting and camera angles and works closely with the programme director. Assistants load and change films, ensure the correct equipment is in place and is functioning properly, and learn how to operate the camera and lighting equipment. Sound technicians and their assistants rig microphones, track, position and operate sound booms and learn to use a wide range of equipment.

In addition, there is a whole range of essential creative support roles, including graphic design, wardrobe, costume design, make-up and music.

Journalism

Journalists work on the national daily and Sunday newspapers, on regional dailies, local weeklies, free newspapers, magazines and trade journals. They also work for radio and television and news agencies. Most press, television and radio journalists start work as reporters, where they are either given assignments (potential news stories) by editors or chief reporters or generate their own newsworthy copy. They must go out and investigate stories, follow-up leads and gather information about news and other items of interest. They then write articles for publication in the press or for presentation by broadcasters and presenters on television and radio. Programme or newspaper editors may ask a journalist to carry out further research and fact-finding before an article can be published or presented. Some news items may be presented by the reporters themselves, who give background information and interview key people. These reports may be broadcast live or recorded. Not all news stories are about exciting, unique events, many are about everyday events such as meetings, regular sports fixtures, local festivals and courtroom proceedings.

Most journalists begin their careers as reporters on local newspapers. Journalists can progress to become sub-editors who edit the reporters' material and write the bulletins or headlines. Sub-editors check the reporters' copy for accuracy, grammar and spelling, legality and style. They may also reduce the number of words to fit the story into the allocated space.

Other journalists in newspapers or magazines may become feature editors, responsible for generating ideas for stories of general interest, researching them and writing the articles; columnists, writing about topics from their own viewpoint; or even, after much experience, chief editors (of, say, a group of newspapers). Journalists who become leader writers in newspapers are often experienced editors and generally write articles about the major events of the moment, usually giving a subjective, rather than objective, opinion.

Experienced journalists, particularly those who started work as local radio reporters, may go on to become broadcast journalists, working for radio and television companies, reading the news or presenting programmes. Most television or radio newsreaders have a journalistic background.

Writing

Creative writing (fiction) in particular is extremely competitive. Only a few authors, out of the many, many thousands who try, write books that become bestsellers. The market for non-fiction books, on specialised subjects, is slightly less competitive. Technical authors write manuals and user guides, technical reports and documents for various industries that need technical terms, methods and processes explained in a clear and concise manner.

Other professions

The media industry also needs professionally qualified people, such as lawyers, accountants, marketing staff, personnel officers and librarians as well as people to fill the clerical and administrative support roles.

Sample job titles

Author, broadcaster/presenter, cameraman/woman, director, floor manager, gofer/runner, journalist, lighting technician, producer, production assistant, radio producer, researcher, stage manager, technical author

Opportunities

It is common for broadcasters/presenters and all those involved in programme-making to operate on a flexible, contractual rather than permanent, full-time basis. The permanent jobs tend to be in management, clerical work, administration support and sales. Most creative support positions on the production side are now freelance, with many people finding work for only six months or so of a year. The numbers employed by the BBC and ITV companies are 30–40 per cent down on 1987.

The main employers in broadcasting are the BBC, the independent television and radio companies, national/local radio stations, plus educational broadcasting and overseas services and some commercial radio and TV stations. Many jobs are located in London with the TV production companies, recording studios and editing companies. However, most people find first jobs (at a junior level) with small independent production and post-production companies, which are often regionally based, rather than with the large broadcasting companies.

Although film-making is a growth industry, it is still one of the most difficult and competitive industries in which to make a career; it is a small industry and has a high-risk, low success rate profile. Jobs are to be found in large and small independent feature film companies, companies which make feature films for television, and others that concentrate on video recordings, pop 'promos', corporate training films, commercials, documentaries, training and educational programmes.

Other opportunities are in facilities houses, which are small individual companies providing technical staff, studio space, equipment and services (such as editing, animation, computer graphics, sound effects, vision mixing and so on) for hire to production companies.

The main first employer of journalists is the provincial press. More and more newspapers are using freelance journalists.

Many authors start off by writing articles, short stories or regular columns in journals, newspapers and magazines before writing books. Technical authors write for a range of industries such as engineering, software publishing and financial, either as employees or as freelancers.

Other factors to consider

Even when people are qualified and experienced their jobs are not secure because television and radio companies now prefer to offer short-term contracts rather than permanent or long-term ones. As many posts (including many in journalism) are now on a freelance or contract basis, media employees also need business administration and organisational skills, and often another job to go to if media work is not forthcoming. One advantage of being freelance is that it is possible to gain experience in more than one area, for example, in feature films, TV programmes or commercials.

Increasingly, people need to be multi-skilled, either in bi-media (radio and television) or in a range of craft/technician skills (camera operator and sound technician combined).

It is important to be aware of and be confident of using the relevant technology and be willing to learn new skills in this fast-moving industry. Computer literacy is a requirement with most jobs.

Those who want to succeed in any of these posts will need to work hard and have confidence, dedication, determination. The jobs are rarely nine-to-five, and the necessary shift work makes the hours anti-social and often long. Many positions involve working under stress to strict deadlines. Speed, accuracy and teamwork are important.

Although camera operators are directed in what to focus on by producers and directors, the best camera operators still need a degree of creative flair and an interest in the visual arts (especially photography) as well as technical skill.

Journalists do not chase exciting news stories all the time, but can, instead, spend hours inside the studio editing and taping or dealing with technical problems. They need to be skilled at writing clearly and concisely and must have good interpersonal skills in order to persuade people to give information.

An enquiring mind, objectivity and an ability to communicate quickly, clearly and effectively are all useful attributes for a career in the media. It is also important to be aware of current affairs.

Previous experience, such as work on a newspaper, on hospital radio or writing for a school or college magazine will be an advantage. Other paid relevant work, such as in sales, customer service, office work, and so on, may also be useful as it all helps to develop important communication skills. Although a degree is useful, it is just as important that applicants show excellent communication skills and a keen interest in and knowledge of the media industry.

Writers need to be very self-disciplined and motivated as they generally work on their own from home. It is usual for writers to type up their work on a computer.

Entry and training

There are many different entry and training routes for media careers, depending on the part of the industry.

Broadcasting and film

People wanting a career in this area could:

- **become a specialist in a particular field** (for example, journalism, politics, music, writing, computing) and then try to break into broadcasting. Many broadcasters/presenters develop their talents and achieve recognition in other fields before breaking into television (often taking a drop in salary). There is no direct route for joining a television company as a newsreader – many have previous experience in journalism
- **take a 'starter' job in the media** (for example, secretary, technician, in the sales department) and apply for in-company training courses; this route is not as common now as it was in the past
- **enter directly from college or university**, but competition is stiff – only a few people are taken on annually, and entrants have to be particularly talented and enthusiastic to succeed. Practical work or voluntary experience gained while a student are essential. Many training schemes are equal opportunities-led and are targeted towards certain people, such as the unemployed or those from ethnic backgrounds
- **work upwards from a junior position**, for example, gofer/runner, technical assistant, assistant floor manager, assistant/trainee film editor. Enthusiasm, knowledge and skills are important. The majority of people start their careers in small independent production companies as a gofer/runner.

For producers, researchers and broadcasters/presenters, a media studies course at degree level, backed up by experience, might be suitable. Most producers and directors in the BBC start as researchers, assistant producers or production assistants. Directors have previous practical experience in television, film or theatre; useful background experience for producers would be finance, marketing or law. Production assistants require excellent secretarial skills. Many have A-levels, some have degrees, usually in an arts subject or media-related studies.

Once employed in the media industry, training is usually on-the-job, although there are still some traineeships or in-company training schemes. However, these change from year to year and are often directly linked to operational needs, so there is no guarantee as to what will be available at any given time. Currently the BBC offers a Production Training Scheme for trainee producers (graduate entry) and a Regional Broadcast Journalist Trainee Scheme (graduate entry preferred). Scottish Broadcast and Film Training offers a Freelance New Entrants Training Scheme for people based in Scotland (to train assistants). Other organisations, such as ft2 (Film and Television Freelance Training), Cyfle (aimed at fulfilling needs of the Welsh film and television industry), Gaelic Television Training Trust and Channel 4 offer training in selected areas for specific groups, such as unemployed, Welsh-speaking and Gaelic-speaking people or those from ethnic backgrounds, respectively.

Most traineeships are advertised in the national press and specialist press (for example, *Campaign, Broadcast, Screen International, Time Out,* and so on) and competition for entry is extremely tough.

For technical posts in sound, lighting and camera work, a full-time course in electronics, radio or television engineering or telecommunications would be useful. Candidates usually enter with A-levels or a degree. Occasionally, a few traineeships are offered by radio and TV companies, but again they attract vast numbers of applicants for only a few vacancies.

There is no formal system of entry or training for film-makers. People tend to have experience in acting, TV, advertising, writing, entertainment and production fields.

Journalism
The routes into journalism are as follows:

- **studying a pre-entry college or university course** – approved by the National Council for The Training of Journalists (NCTJ) or the National Council for the Training of Broadcast Journalists (NCTBJ) – for one year full-time. The majority of broadcast journalists start out in local radio after completing an NCTBJ-recognised course
- **finding a job as a trainee with a local paper** – about 40 per cent of journalists start this way and train on-the-job as well as pursuing

part-time study. Some newspaper and magazine companies have their own training schemes, accredited by the NCTJ or the Periodicals Training Council

- **taking an HND, degree or postgraduate course in journalism**
- **studying a BBC in-house postgraduate training course for radio and television journalism**. Competition for places is fierce.

Most journalists enter the profession as graduates. First degree courses in communication studies, English, media and business studies, and of course journalism, are particularly useful, but are not a substitute for a pre-entry (practical) training course. Media and communications studies courses have had a bad press. Although they are extremely popular with students, graduates of such courses have not always been successful in gaining employment. Many employers are sceptical of the value of some of the courses. Students should check the destination statistics of graduates of any course they might be interested in, before they commit to it.

For newly employed journalists, training is on-the-job, under the supervision of an experienced reporter, possibly supplemented by part-time study or in-house courses.

Various NVQs either exist or are slowly being developed which are relevant to those already working in the media, for example, Production Research, Camera Assistance, Camera Direction, and Journalism among others.

Writing

There are no formal entry requirements for technical authors, although the majority have previous qualifications and experience in specialist fields. City & Guilds has part-time courses in Technical Information Communication.

There are some writing courses, both creative and technical, although usually writers have a talent and simply begin writing, without any prior training, apart from a good general education.

Subjects

Broadcasting and film: for production and presenter posts, drama, English and communication studies could be useful at GCSE. A-levels in an arts or media-related subject. The majority of entrants have degrees (arts subjects). Technical posts require A-levels in mathematics, physics, electronics.

Journalism: English is the most relevant subject, although any subject using writing skills is also useful, for example, history. Second languages are essential for jobs with international news agencies, such as Reuters, and useful for overseas work. Economics or politics and science are also suggested for those journalists who wish to specialise.

Writing: GCSE in English or a subject where English is used, such as history or religious studies is useful for anyone wanting to write for a living. Keyboard skills are also extremely useful for writing the copy.

Further information

BBC Corporate Recruitment Services
Cyfle
ft2 – Film and Television Freelance Training
Gaelic Television Training Trust, Sabhal Mor Ostaig College
National Council for the Training of Broadcast Journalists (NCTBJ)
National Council for the Training of Journalists (NCTJ)
Periodicals Training Council
Scottish Screen
Scottish Newspaper Publishers' Association
Skillset (National Training Organisation for Broadcast, Film and Video)

Books and leaflets

Ostrov, R. and Hall, H. 1996. *Careers in Film and Video.* Kogan Page
Selby, M. 1997. *Careers in Television and Radio.* Kogan Page
Medina, P. 1996. *Careers in Journalism.* Trotman
A Career in Broadcast, Film and Video. 1996. Skillset – the National Training Organisation for Broadcast, Film and Video
Working in Journalism. 1996. COIC
Working in TV, Film and Radio. 1997. COIC

Medicine and nursing (CLCI: J)

Many different careers come under the umbrella term medicine; they are all concerned with the care of people either in hospitals, in surgeries, at home or in special centres. This section concentrates on doctors, nurses, midwives and healthcare assistants. The many other healthcare professions, for example, physiotherapy, radiography, chiropody, and so on, are covered in a separate section ('Healthcare professions').

Doctors

The work doctors do varies enormously: almost 50 per cent of qualified doctors work in general practice, diagnosing patients' ailments, then either treating the illness or referring the patient to a specialist; some doctors work in hospitals as specialists in one of a wide range of areas, including general surgery, general medicine, paediatrics, geriatrics, obstetrics, gynaecology, pathology, psychiatry, accident and emergency and anaesthetics; others do scientific research, which involves looking into new forms of treatment and drugs; finally, some doctors teach as well as doing clinical or research work.

Doctors choose which area to specialise in within three years of graduation. In hospitals they begin as house officers and may work up through the grades of senior house officer and registrar to consultant. Consultants are the only grade of hospital doctor considered to be fully trained and capable of being personally responsible for the treatments prescribed. They supervise the work of doctors in the other grades.

Nursing and midwifery

Nurses care for people of all ages and deal with a wide range of conditions. Nurses in the 'adult' branch of nursing look after adults (an increasing number of whom are now elderly) with acute and chronic illnesses and disabilities; 'mental health nurses' care for people with mental health problems, either in the community or in hospital; 'learning-disability nurses' work not only with people with learning disabilities but also with their carers, families and the other professionals who are involved, usually in the community; 'children's nurses' care for children from birth to 16 years of age.

Nurses assess patients' needs and work closely with other members of the multi-disciplinary team of medical and healthcare staff. Senior nurses may have a range of managerial responsibilities such as leading a team of qualified nurses, students and care assistants, or overseeing equipment and supplies. Others may choose to develop their career in advanced clinical specialist areas (such as intensive care nursing, theatre and recovery nursing and accident and emergency nursing), research or education.

Midwives care for pregnant women, deliver babies, and educate and support the parents throughout the pregnancy and birth. They need to know about and appreciate the influence of social, political and cultural factors in maternity care provision.

Healthcare assistant

Healthcare assistants have no nursing qualifications. They help trained nurses and other medical staff with the many practical and basic nursing care tasks, such as making beds, taking temperatures, emptying bed pans and bathing patients. They have daily contact with patients.

Sample job titles

Anaesthetist, consultant, doctor, healthcare assistant, midwife, nurse, paediatrician, psychiatrist, sister, surgeon

Opportunities

Medical staff work not only in hospitals (both private and public sector) and in general practice but also in universities, research establishments, industry, the Armed Forces, civil airlines and in local and central government. Some doctors also carry out full-time research. Opportunities to work overseas are possible in theory, particularly within the EU and with overseas development and relief or voluntary organisations. However, in practice, it may be difficult to find employment.

Some nurses devote their working lives to looking after particular kinds of patients, for example, Macmillan nurses look after people with cancer.

Other factors to consider

Anyone interested in training to be a doctor needs the stamina to get through the training – it takes a minimum of five years to complete the initial training, followed by a year as a resident house officer (working in a hospital, admitting and examining patients and taking case histories and so on) before further professional training in a chosen specialist area. Doctors considering a research career take a six-year BSc degree (usually five-year training plus one extra year). Dedication to the profession is essential.

Doctors and nurses need to have compassion, resourcefulness, boundless energy (physical and mental) and perseverance to cope with the stresses and strains of their very demanding jobs. It is not work for the squeamish or fainthearted. Shift work, anti-social and long hours, night duty and working some weekends are the norm, especially for nurses and doctors working in hospitals or in primary care.

Communication skills are important. Patients increasingly want to know about and have a say in the treatment being proposed. Doctors and nurses must be able to explain the options clearly and listen to patients' concerns. Many patients need to be put at their ease and look to the medical and nursing staff for comforting words.

General Practitioners (GPs) in fund-holding practices (where doctors manage their surgery's funds) may find that business skills are an advantage. It is also important to be able to work well with the other people in the practice team: nurses, administrators, the practice manager, receptionists, social workers, and so on. Some GP practices are in partnership with others to share facilities or duty calls.

Midwives need maturity to handle sensitive situations and to make decisions about appropriate care in pregnancy, labour and following the birth.

Healthcare assistants do very basic but necessary jobs, some of which may be less pleasant than others. However, many healthcare assistants enjoy making people more comfortable, no matter what the task. The job also requires people who are practical, caring and sociable.

Entry and training

Requirements are very different for doctors, nurses and midwives.

Doctors

Doctors have to be registered with the General Medical Council (GMC) before they are permitted to practise. Before they can register they need to have completed:

- **five years' full-time study at medical school to gain a medical degree** (a joint Bachelor of Medicine and Bachelor of Surgery)
- **a pre-registration year as a resident junior house officer in a hospital.**

After full registration by the GMC, general professional training takes place in the desired specialist area or in general practice. This is usually followed by a postgraduate qualification, and entry to higher specialist training in the chosen field. It takes a minimum of three years' post-registration training to specialise and eight to nine years' post-registration training to become a consultant. All doctors have continuous professional development throughout their careers.

The standards for entry to medical schools are exacting. High grades are necessary (medical schools usually require three A-levels at A grade). Advanced GNVQ with distinction plus A-/AS-levels may be accepted by some schools but most still prefer all A-levels.

Nurses and midwives

The minimum age on entry to pre-registration nursing and midwifery education is $17\frac{1}{2}$, although it is possible to apply from the age of 16. Both routes to a nursing qualification lead to an academic and a professional qualification.

- The first is via a **three-year diploma programme**. Applications for this path are processed by the Nursing and Midwifery Admissions Service (NMAS). The Diploma of Higher Education in Nursing (DipHE in Nursing) used to be called Project 2000 and is the primary route to obtaining a nursing qualification in England. For details of nursing and midwifery programmes in Northern Ireland, Scotland and Wales, contact the relevant National Boards for Nursing, Midwifery and Health Visiting.
- The second is via a **three- or four-year degree programme**. Applications for this route are processed by UCAS.

Fifty per cent of both programmes consists of supervised nursing practice, which takes place both in hospital and community settings.

Both routes comprise the intensive Common Foundation Programme (CFP) for the first 18 months followed by specialisation in one of the four branch programmes: adult, mental health, learning disability or children's nursing. Selection of a branch programme is usually made at the time of application to enter a pre-registration nursing programme.

After a period of nursing experience, nurses may specialise further, for example, in health visiting, practice nursing or occupational health nursing.

Graduates with a health-related or science degree, for example health psychology, human biology, human physiology, can take an accelerated diploma programme (a minimum of 24 months, including six months for the CFP).

The two routes to becoming a midwife are:

- via a **three-year diploma** to become a registered midwife
- by **becoming a registered nurse (adult nursing) first and then completing further training** (78 weeks) to become a midwife.

As part of their continuous professional development, nurses and midwives are encouraged to undertake further education and training throughout their career.

Subjects

Doctor: GCSE in English language is compulsory and sciences are useful. One chemistry A-level is required plus two others. Many medical schools require chemistry plus one other science or mathematics. General studies is not accepted as a valid A-level for medicine. Although biology A-level is not compulsory, those who have not done it may find parts of the course difficult. Non-science A/AS-level students who wish to study medicine can take a one-year pre-medical course – a first Bachelor of Medicine – in basic science subjects, which is offered in only a very few medical schools. It does not qualify for a mandatory LEA grant.

Nurse: five GCSEs (grades A–C) are required. Chemistry, biology, social biology, human biology, physics, sociology and English are useful.

A-levels in the same subjects plus psychology are valuable. A-levels are necessary for a nursing degree.

Midwives: five GCSEs (grades A–C) are required. These must include English and a science subject.

Further information

British Medical Association
English National Board for Nursing, Midwifery and Health Visiting
    Health Service Careers
National Board for Nursing, Midwifery and Health Visiting for
    Northern Ireland
National Board for Nursing, Midwifery and Health Visiting for
    Scotland
Nursing and Midwifery Admissions Service (NMAS)
Welsh National Board for Nursing, Midwifery and Health Visiting

Books and leaflets

Humphries, J. and Brown, L. 1996. *Careers in Medicine, Dentistry and
    Mental Health*. Kogan Page
Working in Hospitals. 1996. COIC
Working in Medicine and Dentistry. 1996. COIC
Working in Nursing. 1995. COIC

Performing arts (CLCI: G)

To become a performer – actor, musician, dancer or singer – generally requires many years of training, followed by continual practice and performances throughout the artist's life. It is therefore a very demanding profession but one which can bring an enormous amount of pleasure both to the performer and the audience. The glamour and excitement can compensate for the drawbacks associated with this way of life, such as job insecurity and long anti-social working hours.

However, not all jobs in this field involve performing in front of an audience. Many of them are front-of-house (bar staff, those who work in the box office or sell ice creams), backstage, technical and production: these include stage management, costume design, carpentry, wardrobe, set design and make-up.

Arts administration and press/public relations are other areas that may attract people who want to work in the performing arts but who do not want to be performers themselves. People in these jobs promote the activities of their establishment to the media, building up a rapport with the local press, radio and television news teams. In addition, arts administrators are responsible for the day-to-day running of the organisation.

Sample job titles

Actor, comedian, dancer, director, producer, public relations officer, press officer, singer, stage manager, wardrobe assistant

Opportunities

The performing arts is a precarious profession, and competition for any job is extremely stiff.

Actors find work in television, theatre, radio, film, video and commercials. Some team up and start their own companies and may tour the UK with various types of production.

Professional dancers can work for a variety of organisations, including ballet and contemporary dance companies, stage and television dance groups. They may appear in films, on television or perform in commercials, clubs, cabarets and pantomimes.

Orchestras and opera houses in London, the provinces and those run by the BBC employ full-time musicians, although most musicians are freelance. Other opportunities for musicians are in television commercials, films, radio, live concerts, recording sessions and in the Armed Forces' bands.

Openings for backstage and front-of-house staff are few. Vacancies for the jobs in theatres are usually advertised in the press.

Entry to the press/PR work is very competitive.

Arts administrators work for theatres, orchestras and any cultural organisations requiring administration and management. Again, competition is keen for any of these posts.

Other factors to consider

Careers in the performing arts (especially for performers) are only for the determined and dedicated. Talent on its own is not enough.

Many actors, dancers and musicians work in other jobs during the day and perform in the evenings, making it difficult to enjoy a normal social life. The jobs of support, administrative and backstage staff also involve working anti-social hours – evenings and weekends. Performers need time for rehearsals and for practice at home or in the studios and, in the case of actors, for learning lines, making the hours they work long and irregular.

Flexibility, adaptability and determination are necessary attributes for anyone wanting a career in the performing arts. It is also important to be able to get on with other members of the group or team.

Performers are also likely to spend a lot of time away from home, travelling around the UK or even overseas, depending on where the work is.

Auditioning can be exhausting, and soul-destroying if unsuccessful. It is important for performers to present themselves in the best possible way, market themselves and cultivate contacts.

All artists must accept the fact that they will have some periods of time out of work. Many of them have to find alternative ways of earning a living at these times. Some performers teach part-time and perform in their spare time.

There are far fewer parts for women than for men so women face more competition for roles.

Dancers have a relatively short career so it is prudent to keep the option of a second career open and acquire some qualifications as a back-up, particularly in case of injury.

It is usually very difficult to get grants for drama schools (see 'Entry and Training').

Entry and training

Some actors do not attend drama school but gain experience and confidence in amateur roles before auditioning for parts in professional performances. However, most young people undergo formal training.

Drama school diploma courses do not attract mandatory funding from LEAs so performers are advised to check whether they will receive a grant for the course they are considering.

The routes into drama careers are listed below:

- **via drama school** is the main way in for 17- to 25-year-olds; entry is usually by audition or interview. A good general education is preferable, although not required, for diploma courses in acting and technical theatre studies. However, competition for places is keen, and a large number of entrants have A-levels. Many drama schools also offer degree courses in performing arts
- **via a relevant degree course** (for example, drama and theatre arts). This route is more suitable for those interested in teaching drama or in theatre/arts administration than for those wishing to act. Many drama degree students go into directing
- **via the National Youth Theatre or National Youth Music Theatre** which offer practical experience of the theatre to young people who can act, sing or dance, or who are interested in the technical or administrative side of the theatre. Open auditions are held around the UK for the performance roles.

Formal dance training for dancers is essential and usually starts early in life, at least by the age of 16. Some ways into musical and dancing work are:

- **via dance, music or drama school** where entry is usually by audition. A-levels may be necessary for entry to some music colleges, universities and colleges of higher education
- **by direct approach** to clubs, hotels, pubs
- **by using an agent**, who negotiates with the managers of establishments on the artist's behalf.

Entry to a career as a theatre director or floor manager in the television or film worlds is generally via a two- or three-year accredited course at drama school. This involves learning about the theatre, stage management and the technical side, for example, sound and lighting.

Arts administration and public relations posts in the performing arts do not require formal qualifications, although a good general education is preferred.

The Association of British Theatre Technicians advises on technical aspects of the theatre. Theatre technicians usually start with formal qualifications in the relevant technical field. NVQs in theatre/stage craft skills are also available. Some drama schools run accredited courses for stage managers.

Experience at school, college or university can be a huge advantage for any career in performing arts, as can involvement in local amateur dramatics or community theatre.

An advantage of going to drama school is that graduates of accredited courses can obtain their first job without professional experience, which then makes them eligible for an Equity card (a union card which protects the interests of performers). However, at the time of writing, Equity is considering relaxing its rules to allow membership to graduates of accredited courses regardless of whether they have a job, and to background artists who have some experience. The British Actors' Equity Association will provide current details.

Subjects

A-levels in theatre studies/drama and English are recommended. Those intending to teach require GCSEs (grades A–C) in mathematics and English.

Further information

Arts Council
Association of British Theatre Technicians
British Actors' Equity Association
Council for Dance Education and Training UK
Incorporated Society of Musicians
National Council for Drama Training
National Youth Music Theatre
National Youth Theatre

Books and leaflets

Richardson, J. 1995. *Careers in the Theatre*. Kogan Page
Working in Music. 1996. COIC
Working in Performing Arts. 1997. COIC

Post Office (CLCI: Y/C)

The Post Office is one of the UK's largest organisations, employing staff in a wide range of jobs in four separate businesses: the Royal

Mail (delivery of letters); Post Office Counters Ltd (post office services); Subscription Services Ltd (telemarketing and subscription services); and Parcelforce Worldwide (delivery of parcels). All the businesses recruit staff at many different levels.

The majority of staff – 160,000 people – work in the Royal Mail. Most of its employees are involved in collecting, sorting and delivering the 72 million items of mail it handles every working day. There are also other openings in other functions (for example, administrative, clerical, management), which support these activities. Postmen/women may drive vans or deliver mail on foot or by bicycle. Sorting mail is carried out either by hand or, increasingly, by automated machinery.

Post Office Counters Ltd is the UK's largest retailer, with 19,400 retail outlets (more than the six largest banks and building societies put together). The continuing modernisation and development of advanced technology in post offices means that customers are able to use them for a growing range of services, including foreign exchange, travel and health insurance. With the increased automation of the post offices, the need for computer-literate staff is growing. Post office managers and staff deal with the processing of all customer transactions made over the counter, such as selling stamps, television licences, vehicle tax discs and other retail services to the general public. They also provide a service by processing payments for telephone, gas, electricity and water bills. Although computer systems have been introduced into post offices, staff do still have to do some paperwork.

Subscription Services Ltd has its headquarters in Bristol and a number of smaller sites throughout the UK. It recruits people for telephone work (telemarketing) and customer management (handling calls involving database, revenue and subscription management).

Parcelforce is the UK's largest carrier of packages, parcels and small freight. School leavers are recruited for administrative positions. Graduates can take up managerial positions.

Managers have a wide choice of jobs – in finance, information technology (IT) services, retail, operations, marketing and sales, human resources and communications – throughout all four business areas. The range of work varies according to the job.

Sample job titles

Counter clerk, postman/woman, postal assistant, distribution clerk, retail network manager, delivery operations manager

Opportunities

Advertisements for counter clerks, postmen/women positions and administrative positions are placed in local papers.

The Post Office Group recruits about a hundred graduates a year in total (not always in every area of the business). Graduates can become managers in the many different business areas of the Post Office Group and at headquarters. Advertisements for graduates are placed in the national press and in *Prospects Today* (a magazine for graduates, available in higher education institutions). Once employed, with some experience, it is also possible to apply for a position in any other part of the group.

Other factors to consider

Graduates who want to gain a place on the Post Office's management trainee programmes need to have a good degree.

For other positions, such as counter clerks, administrative staff and postmen/women, the emphasis is increasingly on customer service, so patience and a courteous manner are important. In addition, numeracy and literacy are required skills.

Postmen/women must be prepared to work outdoors, although some do work indoors, sorting mail, for example. Some of the work can be very physical, lifting heavy loads of post. Shift work is usual and free uniforms are provided.

Entry and training

The Post Office offers a range of one-, two- and three-year management programmes for graduates. Most of these require graduates to qualify initially in a specialist area, such as finance, retail management, IT, distribution/logistics, sales or marketing, and so on.

Specific entry qualifications are not needed for the positions of postman/woman or parcel handler and sorter, although GCSEs are an advantage (particularly English). Sixteen- or seventeen-year-olds can apply to join the Postal Cadet training programme, which exists at some locations such as larger towns and cities. Selection is by aptitude test and interview.

Training for postmen/women is given on-the-job.

School-leavers enter the Post Office mainly as counter clerks or administrative staff. They do not need formal entry qualifications, although GCSEs are an advantage (particularly mathematics and English). Training may be both on-the-job, and at a Post Office training school.

NVQs in many aspects of Post Office work can be taken.

Subjects

GCSEs in English and mathematics are preferred. The most useful A-levels are mathematics, business studies, computer science, economics and statistics.

Further information

The Personnel Officer at the local Royal Mail, Royal Mail Parcelforce or Post Office Counters office (local address in telephone book) for information about school-leaver posts
Assessment Consultancy for graduate enquiries

Printing and packaging (CLCI: S)

The printing and packaging industries are often grouped together because packaging materials are often printed and sophisticated printing equipment converts plastics, paper, board, foils and other materials into packaging, cartons and labels. However, both are industries in their own right, have separate entry requirements and training and offer quite different careers.

Printing

Although the printing process was once very traditional it is now very technologically advanced. Faster methods of making printing-plates and preparing and running printing presses have been introduced. This development has taken place alongside the advance in

221

technology in publishing: computerised typesetting, desktop publishing (DTP) and electronic scanning.

Printing companies print anything, from postage stamps to encyclopaedias, birthday cards and envelopes to colour magazines and books. Some printers offer a wide range of services (such as printing books, packaging, posters, brochures, stationery, examination papers or greeting cards) while others specialise in just one area.

Printing companies are divided into a number of different departments:

- pre-press
- machine printing
- print finishing
- production control
- estimating and sales.

In the pre-press department, typesetters key or scan copy into the computer and move the text and graphics around to fit the page or layout, using computerised systems such as DTP packages. Page make-up is where the page components are assembled into position prior to plate-making.

In the machine printing department, printing plates for the different colours – usually made from paper or metal – are fitted to the printing press to ensure that the image is transferred exactly on to the paper. The inks are mixed and the paper prepared to ensure it runs smoothly through the press. Once the print run is finished, the machine's rollers are cleaned ready for the next printing job.

Print finishing involves turning the printed pages into a book or magazine by folding, cutting, binding and glueing them. Finishing can be done by machine but for some jobs it is done by hand. The machinery and equipment is very expensive and sophisticated and often controlled by computers. In some printing companies the two processes merge because they have one machine that can do both printing and finishing.

Production controllers oversee the whole production process by ensuring that each task is carried out effectively and efficiently.

Account executives (called estimators in some companies) take the customers' requirements and cost out the job. They work out which machines will produce the job in the most cost-effective way.

In small companies, one person may perform several roles, such as planning and platemaking and DTP. Larger firms may employ several people for each task.

Packaging

Packaging affects almost every aspect of society and every industry and commercial activity; in particular, food, drink and pharmaceuticals. It is used for various purposes: to advertise and promote products; to give information about products; to protect them from being damaged; to enable them to be carried; and to keep them secure. In the UK over 80 per cent of packaging is used to protect, preserve and contain food, drink or tobacco.

Packaging technologists (also known as packaging engineers or packaging technicians) work in all areas of industry and take on a variety of job roles, often working with marketing, sales and production staff as well as with suppliers. Their job is to ensure that every aspect of a product's 'life cycle' is considered when packaging is designed. They need to have a thorough knowledge of a wide range of technical subjects, including materials science (especially glass, metal, plastics, paper and board), printing and labelling technology, production processes, machinery, legal and environmental issues, methods of testing and design, quality assurance and storage, and handling and distribution. Companies spend millions of pounds on packaging so it must be appropriate for its intended use and produced at the lowest cost possible.

Many companies employ just one packaging technologist in a managerial position, who liaises with different departments to ensure that the packaging and the product come together at the right time; that the packaging is being produced at the lowest cost; and that the final packaged product reaches its destination in pristine condition. Other companies may have teams of packaging technologists who work with others (professionals, such as scientists and technicians) to develop new packaging for new products. Their work involves elements of design, materials testing and consideration of legal requirements.

Sample job titles

Accounts executive, estimator, finisher, packaging technologist, packaging engineer, packaging estimator, packaging manager, packaging technician, print manager, production controller

Opportunities

Those wanting to work in the printing industry find employment in large and small printing firms, small specialist print shops and local authorities' printing departments.

Many different companies in various industries need packaging technologists: manufacturers of raw materials that are converted into packaging; companies that carry out the conversion; companies that actually use packaging materials (for example, the food, drink and pharmaceutical industries), design studios, consultancy practices, and specialist suppliers, such as label printers, adhesive manufacturers and companies that make and commission packaging machinery.

Other factors to consider

Computer skills are crucial as both industries use very sophisticated technology.

Teamwork and communication skills are also essential as most jobs involve liaising with a number of people in a variety of different departments and companies.

Good colour vision is essential for most printing jobs.

In some printing firms the presses are run constantly, which means that staff have to work shifts. Deadlines and tight schedules often result in staff having to work long and anti-social hours.

Entry and training

There are various routes into the printing industry:

- **via a college printing course to diploma or first degree level** courses vary from printing technology and graphics technology to print management. Graduates with knowledge of printing technology are sought after

- **via a postgraduate course in printing** first degrees may be in engineering or a science. This route may lead to a junior management or research post. However, any degree discipline could lead to posts such as production, marketing, finance or personnel within printing
- **via a Modern Apprenticeship**, leading to NVQs
- **via an in-house company training scheme** school- or college-leavers with A-levels may be recruited as management trainees.

NVQs can be taken at levels 2–5 in various aspects of printing.

The vast majority of packaging technologists are graduates (with a degree in any discipline) who have joined a company as an engineer, scientist, buyer, designer or in some other capacity, such as marketing, and who are interested in packaging as a career. They then study packaging part time or by distance-learning towards the Institute of Packaging (IOP) Diploma in Packaging Technology, which is the internationally recognised standard qualification.

Other packaging technologists take a postgraduate packaging technology or materials science degree (there are no first degree courses in packaging technology).

Those who enter packaging design usually do so via a graphic and 3-D design degree (for packaging design).

Subjects

GCSEs in English, mathematics and science/technology are useful for skilled printing jobs and for packaging technology. Useful A-levels for printing are science (physics, chemistry), mathematics and/or computing; for packaging/materials science, chemistry and biology are particularly relevant, as are mathematics, physics or physical science.

Further information

British Printing Industries Federation
The Institute of Packaging
Scottish Print Employers Federation

Books and leaflets
Working in Publishing. 1997. COIC

Publishing and bookselling (CLCI: F/O)

Publishing is a broad term encompassing books, magazines, newspapers and journals and the ever-expanding area of multimedia (software, CD-ROM, audio-visual materials and so on). Each of these sectors operates in very different ways. None of them employs huge numbers of people and all are highly competitive.

Publishing

Book publishing is a small industry comprising three main areas: editorial, production and design, and sales and marketing. In larger publishing houses these are separate departments but in smaller ones the various roles may be combined. Some publishing houses specialise in particular types of books (for example, law, medicine, art, educational titles), while others produce books on a wide variety of different subjects. A relatively small number of large publishing houses own most of the leading magazine titles.

The work of editors varies depending on whether they are working on newspapers, magazines or books. However, it is likely that any entry-level editorial job will include copy-editing (checking the text for accuracy and style, completeness, resolving queries with the writer, rewriting and so on) and proofreading. At a more senior level, editors commission articles and books for publication, negotiate contracts, control budgets and schedules, and spend more time than junior editors liaising with other departments, including production and design, to ensure that what is being produced is meeting the requirements of the marketplace. Knowledge of a particular subject can be important for some jobs.

Virtually everyone working in editorial now has to be computer-literate, and many acquire desk-top publishing skills as more and more of what they produce is output electronically.

Sub-editors in newspaper and magazine publishing check journalists' copy, select graphics and headlines and liaise with production staff. Senior editors are responsible for different sections of the publication.

Production staff ensure that the publications go to press on time as well as calculating the costs, print- and paper-buying and progress chasing. Publicity and public relations departments try to get media coverage for publications, while sales and marketing staff control the way in which publications are presented to the market and sold. Sales and marketing jobs will change as developments in electronic publishing provide new ways of publishing, marketing and promoting publications. Sales and marketing jobs are more plentiful than those in editorial and production. Some smaller publishers contract out sales to larger publishers, agencies or freelances.

Many publishing functions, including copy-editing, proofreading, design, indexing, production, publicity and sales, can be carried out by freelances or small, specialist companies outside the publishing house.

Bookselling

While smaller bookshops employ mainly sales assistants, reporting to a manager who may also be the owner, larger ones and the major bookselling chains also have departmental managers, some with buying responsibilities. Bookshop staff have to know their stock and try to match it to the customers they are trying to attract. They have to order new and backlist (already published) titles at the right time, be constantly aware of which titles are selling fastest and may need to be re-ordered, keep the shelves stocked and the books in the right place, deal with the customers, liaise with publishers or wholesalers, issue stock orders and arrange for returns (unsold books) as necessary. In a small outlet, they may also do some simple bookkeeping, and the manager may be responsible for all of the above together with stock control, accounts and managing the staff.

Sample job titles

Publishing: copy-editor, sub-editor, commissioning editor, production controller, production editor, designer, editor, publicity assistant, sales representative, sales manager, marketing assistant

Bookselling: sales assistant, book buyer, branch manager

Opportunities

Book publishers range from the giants that produce hundreds of titles a year to small companies that bring out just a few, but it can be a difficult industry to break into. The magazine industry, a volatile but currently buoyant sector, provides many career opportunities in both large and small companies. New technology has created openings in fields such as software publishing and electronic publishing: storing and retrieving data by electronic means. Growth areas include DTP and multimedia publishing, both of which require technical aptitude.

There is a large number of bookshops in the UK, including several major and many smaller independent shops.

Other factors to consider

A good command of the English language is very important for editorial work, together with an eye for detail. A strong visual sense is also very useful (not just in the editorial and design areas: people in sales and marketing need to be aware of what will appeal to the market in question). For editors, in particular, publication deadlines frequently mean working under pressure, having to chase contributors and colleagues for material, and working long, sometimes antisocial, hours.

Computer literacy is essential for many job functions, as a lot of the editorial and design work is now carried out on screen and many writers now supply their work in electronic form; projects are costed on computer; promotional material is created on computer, and schedules, sales and stock are maintained on computer.

Production staff often work under pressure, trying to get publications printed on time. As well as product knowledge, sales and marketing staff need communication skills, business acumen and confidence.

A good education, willingness to help customers, polite manner and keen business sense are essential for anyone wanting a career in bookselling.

Entry and training

The routes into publishing vary according to the job. Most people – particularly editorial staff – working in publishing houses are graduates, although school and college leavers can take up secretarial, production and sales positions. Some universities run degree-level (and postgraduate) courses in publishing, but a degree in publishing is not necessarily an entrée into a higher-level job. A full-time BTEC national college or university course in, say, business studies (which includes tuition in sales, marketing, bookkeeping and other office skills) can be useful, as can any relevant experience in sales or, for example, as a secretary.

For non-editorial jobs some publishers may require people with specialist knowledge and skills – such as accounting, sales, purchasing, distribution and marketing – in addition to their academic qualifications. Some graduates start in administration, sales and publicity but move on to other jobs in the publishing industry, such as editorial and marketing or selling rights (for example, to book clubs, newspapers or foreign publishers). Art and design graduates (graphic design and typography) are recruited for design work.

Graduates with a technical and specialist background (such as science, law or computing) may be sought after for editorial work with technical publishers, provided they also have some editorial or business knowledge, experience and skills.

The magazine industry offers training schemes designed mainly for graduates, but sometimes for A-level students too. Alternatively, those interested in magazine publishing could study a postgraduate or HND periodical journalism course at university or college.

The majority of editors working in newspaper publishing generally enter as experienced journalists.

Training for publishing can be either in-house, via short courses out-of-house or through distance learning. The Publishing Training Centre (PTC) offers courses in editorial, production, computer, marketing and management skills and electronic publishing. There are many other organisations (such as the Oxford Centre for Publishing Studies, Oxford Publicity Partnership, Publishing and Training, PMA Training, London College of Printing and Distributive Trades, the Scottish Publishers Association) which also offer a range of courses covering various aspects of publishing.

There are no formal entry qualifications for bookselling, although GCSEs and A-levels are the usual preferred minimum. Training tends to be in-house and on-the-job. The Booksellers Association offers a range of one-day courses covering all aspects of bookselling. The PTC also offers courses in marketing, which include 'selling to the book market'.

Subjects

Publishing: a degree in any subject is accepted for editorial, production, sales, marketing and rights jobs, although English and a foreign language are useful for editorial positions. An art and design degree is necessary for anyone wanting a design job in publishing. Keyboard skills are an advantage for any job.

Bookselling: GCSEs in English and mathematics are useful.

Further information

Booksellers Association of Great Britain
London College of Printing and Distributive Trades
Oxford Centre for Publishing Studies
Oxford Publicity Partnership
Periodicals Training Council
PMA Training
Publishers Association
Publishing Training Centre
Scottish Publishers Association
Society of Indexers

Books and leaflets

Lines, J. 1994. *Careers in Publishing and Bookselling.* Kogan Page
Working in Publishing. 1997. COIC

Religious work (CLCI: F)

The ordination of women, secularisation of society and changes in social trends have dramatically altered religious work during the past two decades. Some churches have been facing the major problems of falling attendance and a decrease in interest. However, despite this, the range, scope and impact of religious work are still considerable.

Although the number of different religions throughout the world is large and each religion has its own structure, many of the duties carried out are common to all faiths.

Religious leaders (ministers, priests, rabbis, and so on) play a prominent role in their community by teaching and interpreting the beliefs and doctrines of their particular denomination and by attending to the spiritual and practical needs of church members and other local people. This may involve holding services (for births, marriages and burials), leading acts of worship and preaching sermons, as well as being responsible for pastoral care: visiting the sick or elderly, arranging transport (for those without transport or who are unable to get there without help) to and from the place of worship, comforting the bereaved and being involved in social gatherings and meetings to bring people together. It is also important to be able to delegate tasks, such as arranging transport and administration, to religious workers in the community.

Religious ministers' roles differ according to where they work, for example, in prisons the emphasis may be on the rehabilitation of prisoners, whereas in hospitals the practical and spiritual welfare of patients and staff is the primary consideration. Some Christian ministers combine chaplaincy with teaching.

In the Roman Catholic Church and the Church of England those who wish to commit themselves either to a life of prayer or meditation, or to specific community work (in orphanages, hospices or hostels) can join a religious order or community as a nun or a monk. The orders that are dedicated to prayer are called 'enclosed orders'.

Lay men and women are followers of a faith who are not ordained. They may work in parishes either full- or part-time as preachers, parish workers, teachers or social workers. They come from a variety of backgrounds and professions and bring different experiences to their role.

Other roles within the church are administrative and musical (choir member, conductor, organist, director of music), although these are limited due to funding restrictions. Few of these are well-paid and they are usually on a part-time or voluntary basis.

Sample job titles

Chaplain, clergyman/woman, curate, deacon, dean, lay minister, minister of religion, monk, nun, priest, rabbi, religious leader, vicar

Opportunities

Chaplains work in universities, colleges, church-aided establishments, schools, hospitals, prisons and the Armed Forces. Parish priests, vicars, rectors and religious workers of all religions work within the community in which they live.

It is possible to work overseas in churches and religious orders or with development agencies and missionary organisations.

Other factors to consider

People who do religious work usually feel they have a vocation (a specific calling from God). It is not just work but a way of life for people with a commitment to their faith. The hours may be irregular, and calls for help from individuals may come at any time of the day or night.

Maturity, compassion, a sense of moral responsibility and an active prayer life are essential.

Monks and nuns in the Roman Catholic Church and in the Church of England take a vow of celibacy and promise to renounce financial gain. Life in a religious order is one of self-sacrifice, poverty, chastity and obedience.

The location of the parish may have an impact on the type of work that needs to be done, for example, a rural parish can be very different from one in an inner city. In some denominations housing is provided for the clergy, but they cannot usually choose where it is. Clergy are provided with a house for the duration of their employment but they do then lose it on retirement or when they change jobs. However, the church in most denominations helps with finding and financing retirement housing.

Entry and training

Many people start doing church work after training for another career or as a result of experiences which have led them to rethink their lives. Increasingly, people are entering in their thirties and forties, although it is still possible to enter training from the age of 18. The Church of England has no special preference for older candidates and welcomes young people (aged 18 and over) for professional ministry training. Previous experience such as teaching, nursing or voluntary social work are all useful for a religious vocation.

Entry and training to become a minister varies from religion to religion but can take several years (from two to six or more, depending on the denomination). Ordination is not automatic, and many religions have rigorous selection procedures to assess the suitability and commitment of the candidates.

A minority of candidates have a degree in theology, which may be taken before or after training. However, it is not essential, and vocation and personal qualities are definitely more important than qualifications.

Prison chaplains usually have several years' parish experience before joining the Prison Service. Many are based in local churches and work only part-time in prison.

Degree courses in theology and religious studies can be done at many universities and colleges, and specialist theological colleges or institutes also exist. Those who would like to follow a career in this area should ask for details from the particular church in which they are interested.

Subjects

Useful GCSEs are English, history, religious studies.

Further information

Baptist Union of Great Britain
Catholic Church, Diocesan Vocations Service of England and Wales
Catholic Church, Scottish National Vocations Office
Christians Abroad
Church of England
Church of Ireland
Church of Scotland
Church in Wales
Congregational Federation
Elim Pentecostal Church, Ministerial Training and Selection Board
Jews' College (University of London)
Methodist Church
Office of the Chief Rabbi
United Free Church of Scotland
United Reformed Church in the UK

Retail (CLCI: O)

Retail is a dynamic, changing industry and is one of the largest in the UK, employing over 10 per cent of the working population. It is the link between the wholesaler and the customer, and its aim is to make goods as attractive and accessible to the public as possible. The emphasis is increasingly on customer service. Shops are opening for longer hours and for seven days a week and even 24 hours a day in many cases. The trend has been for retail stores to move out of town centres to retail 'parks' (this accounts for three-quarters of the retail trade now), leading to a decline in town-centre shopping precincts and the 'corner shop', although this now appears to have reached its peak.

Jobs are at all levels, from shopfloor (counter staff, shelf fillers, cashiers, shop assistants) to management. It is possible to work up from shop assistant to senior sales assistant, supervisor and to buyer; from there, promotion to junior or senior management positions within a store is feasible.

Graduates are likely to progress up the retail career ladder more quickly than non-graduates. An increasing number are now entering retail management as a career, attracted by the high salaries, training and rapid promotion prospects. Selling, buying and store management attract the most graduates. Buying is usually a head-office position, particularly in larger chain stores. Buyers have to select stock at the right price, at the right time and in the right quantity. Other head-office specialist jobs include personnel work, finance, accounting, marketing, computing and distribution.

Sales representatives spend much time travelling from customer to customer, selling products. It is vital that they know the product as well as the needs of the customer in order to be able to sell successfully.

Retail display assistants/workers, often called visual merchandisers, use their creative skills in displays to encourage people to buy products. They may work in-store as part of a display team or move from shop to shop within a chain, setting up similar themed displays in-store or in windows. In smaller shops, this may be the job of sales assistants or the manager. Displays can take a great deal of planning, not only in the design but also in the sourcing of materials to use.

The retail trade employs a huge number of part-time staff.

Sample job titles

Buyer/purchasing officer, display person, sales manager, sales representative, store assistant, store demonstrator, store manager, supermarket worker, visual merchandiser

Opportunities

The main retail outlets are hypermarkets, supermarkets, department stores, chain stores, cooperatives and corner-shop independents. However, this last category is declining as rates and price competition from the superstores make retail trade difficult for the small independent trader. Mail-order selling and home-computer-linked shopping are fast-developing businesses. Although computerisation has reduced the shopfloor workforce in the large stores, opportunities and posts for managers are increasing.

Display assistants find work in retail outlets, usually large department stores or high-street chains. Some work for chains of charity shops. Many other companies also have display/merchandising department staff who set up displays in retail outlets or exhibitions. These include perfumery houses, large manufacturers and book publishers. It is also possible to work on a freelance basis. There are opportunities to move into other types of design work.

Other factors to consider

Those wishing to work in retail should:

- be numerate
- be able to work under pressure, particularly at busy times
- be willing to be mobile (for retail managers)
- have business sense (for small shopkeepers, in particular, but also for retail managers)
- be willing to undertake training
- be willing to work at weekends, on bank holidays and in the evenings (and even sometimes at night, for 24-hour shops).

Anti-social and often long hours are generally the norm for many jobs in this field. Sales representatives, in particular, spend many hours on the road driving from client to client. They are usually paid only on commission and need to be able to accept criticism and rejection from customers and pressure from their sales managers to hit the sales targets. The prerequisites for retail management are planning and organising skills, the ability to lead and motivate a team and to make decisions.

Entry and training

Jobs in retail are at all levels. It is possible for a 16-year-old school-leaver to get a job on the shop floor and advance to manager level through experience and part-time study. Personal qualities, such as the ability to communicate and the commitment to service, can be as important as formal qualifications at this level. Many of the larger stores have trainee programmes leading to management positions; these are often open only to graduates or A-level school-leavers. Degree courses in retail management, retail marketing and retail design can be taken, although graduates are recruited from any discipline. Companies are increasingly taking on graduates for retail management and retail buying. Youth training programmes, Modern Apprenticeships and NVQs are also available in retailing.

Sales representatives are often graduates.

Display assistants can start straight from school and do not need academic qualifications, although the majority begin work after a full-time college course in design (display), retail (display), a course with options in display design, or an art and design course; others study part-time once in a job. Further training is in-house and on-the-job. NVQs in interior or exhibition design are offered at some colleges.

Subjects

Recruiters take graduates with a wide variety of subjects, from accounting to zoology. Those with a good knowledge of business studies, management techniques and finance are likely to have a head start. Business studies A-level is useful as are mathematics, English, home economics, biology, economics, fashion and design at GCSE level.

Further information

British Display Society
National Retail Training Council

Books and leaflets
Working in Retail. 1995. COIC

Science and technology (CLCI: Q/J/R)

The range of careers open to those with a knowledge of science and technology is vast. Scientists all have one thing in common: they use scientific knowledge, techniques and principles in their work. Some use their knowledge to solve problems and to develop products and materials; others carry out research into how things work in order to further our knowledge and to improve the world in which we live.

For instance, geneticists may carry out research into the physical and chemical properties of genetic materials and their effects on living organisms; forensic scientists examine evidence found at crime scenes; materials scientists may work in industry or medicine, studying different materials and choosing the best ones or creating new ones for a specific purpose; medically qualified pathologists examine dead bodies and perform autopsies to determine the cause of death; pharmacists work in retail, hospitals or in the pharmaceuticals industry, advising on, researching or selecting appropriate medicines and drugs; pharmacologists carry out research into the preparation, use and effects of drugs; medical laboratory scientific officers (increasingly called biomedical scientists) carry out a variety of medical research – depending on their specialist area – to diagnose and look into the causes and cures of disease; chemists in the civil service deal with a variety of investigations, ranging from environmental safety and pollution control to food preservation or energy research; industrial chemists may make medicines to combat diseases, improve the colour and taste of foods, investigate chemicals in cosmetics or improve the way new materials are used in products such as roller blades and mountain bikes; physicists may work in research, design, development or monitoring and control, applying the theories of physics to practical situations, such as energy supply and management, transport, telecommunications, diagnosis and treatment of injuries and illnesses, developing technology, problem-solving and carrying out experiments. Social anthropology is a social science, where the study of human social development provides an understanding of human behaviour and gives an insight into how people and communities interact with each other.

What scientists actually do depends totally on the field in which they work. Only a few examples are listed above as the choice of career is actually enormous. Which job they decide to do will depend, to a large extent, on which particular sciences they are interested in and which area of work they wish to specialise in, for example, research, industrial (development, production, manufacturing), teaching or consultancy. Scientists are also employed in technical sales and service areas (selling science-based products or providing a technical back-up service) and in the technical writing field. As scientists progress in their careers they are more likely to be involved in managing projects than carrying out the practical work themselves. However, some employers now offer the opportunity for scientists to remain in practical research and still progress through the promotion structure.

Mathematicians and statisticians are similar to scientists in that they apply the principles of mathematics to solve theoretical and practical problems concerned with engineering, economics, marketing, natural and physical sciences, computing and statistics. Statistics are gathered, analysed and used in research mainly to aid decision-makers to come to conclusions based on hard numerical evidence.

Technologists apply scientific and technical principles to technological processes in their given area (baking, brewing, ceramics, chemical, dairy, dental, energy, food science, fuel, glass, instrument and control, leather, plastics, process, rubber, telecommunications, textile, timber, and so on), with a view to designing and developing new products, equipment and processes. Scientists, engineers and technologists tend to work together in teams on design and development, putting ideas or theories into practice and investigating new methods of using technology for a given purpose.

Technicians, technical sales staff, laboratory assistants and many more people work alongside scientists in a support role. Laboratory assistants set up apparatus, carry out tests and analyse and prepare samples, often using sophisticated scientific equipment or computers.

Sample job titles

Bacteriologist, biologist, chemist, food technologist, forensic scientist, laboratory technician, mathematician, medical laboratory scientific officer, pharmacist, physicist, scientist, technologist

Opportunities

Scientists, technologists and technicians can either become involved in research-based work in educational institutions, research institutes, hospitals, industry or government, or they can work in development, production or manufacturing, and testing and quality control within companies. Scientists and technologists can also go into teaching at all levels.

Mathematicians and statisticians are employed by the civil service, in industry and commerce, or carry out work for research institutions. Many others go into actuarial work (see the section on 'Finance') or into teaching. Theoretical physicists and mathematicians can work in City finance houses which need their analytical skills.

Most chemists work in the chemical and pharmaceutical industries in research development or production. Others work in banking, law, publishing, accountancy, teaching and lecturing.

Forensic science is an extremely popular career area but there are very few job opportunities.

Other factors to consider

A strong interest and ability in the sciences and in mathematics is clearly fundamental and usually a motivating factor in entering this kind of work. Scientists, technologists and laboratory staff at all levels need to have a keen interest in scientific study and exploration.

Because of the investigative and analytical nature of much of the work it is vital to pay careful attention to detail and to maintain high standards of accuracy. Good observational and problem-solving skills and an enquiring and logical mind are also important. The ability to work in a team and communicate are also important as increasingly jobs involve working with other people and explaining often complex scientific or technical data verbally or in writing.

People in the field of science and technology need to know how to use computers and other sophisticated electronic testing, data logging and analytical equipment.

It is important to note that in some scientific areas – where there is contact with animals or with chemical substances – people with certain medical conditions, such as asthma or eczema, may have difficulties getting employment. Those considering a career in this area should check with the appropriate professional body before deciding on subjects and courses.

Entry and training

Scientists, including mathematicians and statisticians, generally need to have a degree or HND. A postgraduate qualification is necessary for academic research posts, although it may be possible to join a company after a first degree and study part-time for a research degree.

Degrees are not essential for other scientific or technology-related jobs, such as technologists, technicians and assistant scientific officers (civil service). Entry can be with a minimum of four GCSEs, although preference may be given to candidates with higher qualifications such as A-levels, particularly as they enable them to go on to do further part-time study towards relevant professional qualifications. Technologists can enter at technician level (with GCSEs and/or A-levels) or at professional level (with a degree in the relevant field).

Social anthropology is studied mainly as a first-degree or postgraduate subject.

Subjects

English is useful and usually a requirement at GCSE level for all these career areas.

Chemistry degree: A-levels in chemistry and physics and/or mathematics. However, other combinations are often acceptable, such as chemistry and biological sciences. Advanced GNVQ in science with other A-level or AS-level qualifications may also be acceptable for entry to many higher education institutions.

Physics degree: A-levels in physics and mathematics.

Applied sciences degree: combination of two or three A-levels from physics, biology, chemistry and mathematics.

Biology degree: A-levels in one of the biological sciences plus chemistry, although other combinations may be acceptable.

Mathematics degree: A-levels in pure and applied mathematics are often required.

Statistics degree: A-levels in mathematical subjects (for example, mathematics, statistics, physics) are required.

Anthropology degree: A-levels in sociology and biology are useful. GCSEs in English, mathematics and biology may be necessary.

Food science degree: A-levels in chemistry and one or two other science subjects (biology and mathematics are most useful) are usually required. Other A-level subjects could be social biology, human biology, physics, botany, zoology. Home economics may be considered if it has been studied with science subjects.

Technologist/technician jobs: GCSEs in English, mathematics and two science subjects or double award science are important. A-levels and degree subjects as detailed above. Computer literacy is advantageous.

At technician level GCSEs in a science, or double award science, and mathematics are usually required.

Further information

Chemical Industries Association
Institute of Biology
Institute of Food Science & Technology
Institute of Mathematics and its Applications
Institute of Physics
Royal Society of Chemistry
Royal Statistical Society
Society of Occupational Medicine

Books and leaflets

Degree Course Guide – Chemistry. 1997. CRAC/Hobsons
Degree Course Guide – Biological Sciences. 1996. CRAC/Hobsons
Degree Course Guide – Mathematics and Statistics. 1997. CRAC/
   Hobsons

Working in Mathematics. 1996. COIC
Working in Natural Sciences. 1996. COIC
Working in Physics. 1997. COIC
Science Casebook 98. 1997. CRAC/Hobsons

Security services (CLCI: M/K)

The prison service and the probation service are both concerned with the protection of people and property. Prison officers supervise adults and young offenders in penal institutions, whereas probation officers generally supervise offenders in the community. Both services are the responsibility of the Home Office in England and Wales. The situation is different in Northern Ireland, where all probation officers are appointed by the Probation Board for Northern Ireland. In Scotland the local authority social work departments are responsible for work with offenders and the Scottish Office is responsible for prisons.

As part of a team, which includes prison officers, medical staff, psychologists, welfare officers and instructors, prison officers oversee training and the routine supervision of prisoners, who might work in an institution's laundry, kitchen, gardens, farm or workshops. They are expected to take a part in the pastoral care and rehabilitation of prisoners, by helping them to solve problems, dealing with requests and sorting out disruptive behaviour.

Prison governors are the prison managers. They are ultimately responsible for the prisoners, the staff, resources and the day-to-day running of the penal institution.

Probation officers are responsible for supervising offenders in the community and providing information to the criminal and family courts. Probation staff seconded to prison establishments work alongside prison staff; they undertake direct work with those serving custodial sentences to help rehabilitate offenders and prepare them for release, and to assess whether they pose any risk to the public.

Day-to-day tasks include the preparation of pre-sentence reports about the offender (with proposals for appropriate action to assist the criminal courts in sentencing decisions) and liaison with social workers and other agencies. Much of a probation officer's day is spent working on a one-to-one basis with people under supervision, for example, those serving probation orders, on bail, newly released from prison or on Community Service Orders.

Specialist probation officers, known as family court welfare officers, do not work with offenders, but with families where parents are separating or divorcing and there is a dispute about the children's future. The role of probation officers here is to assess the situation, provide detailed information to the courts, mediate and perhaps help the parents and court to reach a decision that is in the best interests of the children.

Most probation officers spend at least one day a week presenting information in court.

The challenge and satisfaction of both jobs come from forming positive relationships with those who have been before the courts or who are in prison, in order to reduce the risk of them offending again. The primary purpose of prison and probation officers' jobs is the protection of the public: they work with offenders but never for them.

Sample job titles

Assistant governor/governor (the Prison Service), family court welfare officer, prison officer, probation officer

Opportunities

Prison officers can be asked to serve in any one of the different kinds of penal institution:

- remand centres (where people are awaiting trial or sentence)
- local prisons
- training prisons ('open', 'closed' or maximum security)
- young offender institutions (for 16- to 21-year-olds).

There are about 16,000 probation service staff in England and Wales, of whom just under half are probation officers. Each of the 54 local probation services employs its own staff and is supervised by a probation committee. Promotion to senior grade is dependent on ability and relevant experience. In Northern Ireland officers are appointed by the Probation Board for Northern Ireland; in Scotland the local authority social work departments are responsible for work with offenders.

Other factors to consider

Although prison and probation work can be rewarding it can also be depressing, unpleasant and dangerous; not only can prisoners and probationers be difficult and uncooperative, but their behaviour can range from hostile and resentful to violent and abusive towards the people supervising them. Both groups of officers have to be able to build working relationships with these people. Patience, assertiveness and a caring approach are all important.

Conditions in prisons vary enormously; some are unpleasant because the prisons are overcrowded, and others – 'open' prisons or where the facilities are good – are better. Governors and assistant governors must be prepared to move around from prison to prison if they want to reach the most senior posts.

Hours can be anti-social and long (prisons have to be staffed 24 hours a day, and probation officers' clients are often available only in the evenings or at weekends). A shift-work system is operated in the prison service.

Entry and training

Officer is the lowest position on the promotion ladder in the prison service, followed by senior officer, then principal officer at the top. Above that are five governor grades (1 to 5, with 1 being the highest). Governing governors are all grade 1, 2 or 3. Promotion is dependent on annual reviews of an officer's suitability for the next grade. Promotion to the lowest grade of governor takes a minimum of five years to achieve. However, graduates and prison officers with potential can take part in the accelerated promotion scheme. Almost any degree is suitable but psychology, sociology or criminology are preferred.

The minimum educational requirement is five GCSEs (grades A–C), including English and mathematics. In addition, applicants need to pass an aptitude test prior to interview. There is also a minimum eyesight requirement, although contact lenses and glasses are allowed. The age range for entry is 20 to 49.

Training is on-the-job or through in-house or residential training schemes. NVQs are available.

New arrangements for the recruitment and qualifying training of probation officers were announced by the Home Office in July 1997 and will be introduced in late 1998. The arrangements include a flexible approach to training, making it easier for people with wider experience and talents to join. Previous paid or voluntary work experience with offenders or closely related work is an advantage. Probation services will select and recruit trainees who will be required to study for a new Diploma in Probation Studies, which will be linked to an NVQ. The training will involve a mixture of academic work and work-based supervised practice. The name of the probation service and its officers is currently under review.

Subjects

Prison service: GCSEs must include English and mathematics.
Probation service: none is likely to be specified for the probation service, although English and mathematics at GCSE would be useful. Related subjects such as criminology and psychology might also help with the Diploma in Probation Studies.

Further information

Prison Service, Directorate of Personnel, The Home Office
Probation Board for Northern Ireland
Probation Unit, Home Office

Books and leaflets

Atkinson, E. 1997. *Careers in Social Work*. Kogan Page
Working in Social Work. 1995. COIC

Social and related work (CLCI: K)

This is a very large career area, covering a vast range of jobs, all with different responsibilities and roles. The one thing they all have in common is that the work involves providing people with social or pastoral care or some form of counselling, guidance or help.

Social work

Social workers help individuals, families or groups of people to cope with or overcome a wide range of problems that may arise from family, social or environmental circumstances. They can choose to work with children and families, young people or adults. In their work they may cover a wide variety of areas or specialise in particular issues, such as:

- child welfare and protection
- fostering and adoption
- physical or learning disabilities
- mental health problems
- youth and criminal justice
- homelessness
- alcohol and drug misuse.

Social work and care in adult services (known formerly as field social work) provides help and support to adults in their own homes, within healthcare settings (such as hospitals, clinics, GP practices and hospices) and in residential and day-care establishments.

Social work and care with children and young people includes residential social work, working in children's homes and supporting children in need or at risk in the community. Some social workers also specialise in working with young offenders. Others work in hospitals to support the parents of seriously ill or dying children.

Social workers often liaise closely with professionals such as doctors and teachers to evaluate which is the best way to care for their clients. They spend some of their time in the office, writing reports or meeting clients, and a proportion of it out and about, visiting clients in their homes, day centres, residential (or group) homes or hostels, hospitals, schools or prisons.

In Northern Ireland qualified social workers work as probation officers and in Scotland they provide criminal justice services (supervising offenders within the community).

Home carers provide personal care (dressing, bathing and supervising any medication) and emotional and practical support to people in their own homes. These people may be elderly, have physical disabilities, HIV or AIDS or have mental health problems.

Home-care organisers (social work assistants in Northern Ireland) assess a person's need for care and their ability to pay for it. They organise home care or purchase the care from an outside agency. Home-care organisers work in teams, sometimes with social workers and care managers.

Care managers coordinate and develop 'packages' of care for individuals, for example, they might assess the needs of a physically disabled person and organise a package of care which may include two days of home care, five days' attendance at a day centre, six days of meals on wheels, and so on.

Careers work

Careers advisers (sometimes known as careers officers or careers consultants) generally advise school and college students on job opportunities, training and courses, and place young people in jobs and on training schemes. Many careers service companies also provide an information and guidance service for adults who may be thinking about changing a career or who may be coming back to work after a period of time out of work.

Much of a careers adviser's time is spent interviewing people, advising and giving them information. Sometimes computer-based tests may be used to find out people's interests or aptitudes for certain careers. Time is also spent talking with parents, liaising with teachers, visiting employers and training providers or organising special careers events such as careers fairs or conventions. Careers advisers also carry out administrative work in the office.

It is possible to specialise in particular areas of careers work, such as work with sixth-form or college students or people with special needs, or information work ensuring careers advisers have the information they need – this may mean buying in resources or writing them. Some companies offer routes to management posts.

As well as advising students on job opportunities, advisers in college or university careers services spend their time liaising with graduate recruiters and arranging interviews and work experience for students.

Careers service companies employ many other staff, such as information officers, employment assistants, careers assistants and customer advisers, who receive clients, provide information services and help place clients with employers or training providers.

Psychology

Psychology is defined as the scientific study of human behaviour, thoughts and feelings in either their normal or abnormal states. Its study is based upon observing what people do and what they say. It is a social science as it studies people in their social settings. Some psychologists apply their knowledge to help people through crises in their lives. Most specialise after graduation, for instance, in educational psychology (working with pupils and students in educational establishments), clinical psychology (working with people with a learning disability or psychological problems in hospitals or clinics), forensic psychology (working with prisoners or others within the penal system) or occupational psychology (investigating how people perform and behave at work and in training and how organisations function). Other branches of psychology include health, sports, counselling and research.

Nursery nursing

Nursery nurses are not nurses in the true sense of the word as they generally deal with healthy children (although some may specialise in caring for children with special needs). The job involves more than just physical care: young children learn and develop through play, communicating with adults and other children and responding to all kinds of stimuli. It is the job of the nursery nurse to provide and organise these activities and an environment in which a child can develop. Nursery nurses work with children under the age of eight years. Qualified nursery nurses work alone as well as in partnership with other professional staff such as teachers, health visitors, social workers, therapists, doctors, education advisers and so on.

Youth and community work

Youth work supports the personal and social development of young people. Some workers work in a youth centre setting, but many operate away from youth centres, reaching those who choose not to use them. Detached workers meet young people in places where they congregate – city centres, pubs, cafés and amusement arcades. Others are based in schools, colleges or work in advice and information centres or on young volunteer projects or health promotion initiatives. Youth workers offer young people a chance to pursue activities and interests as part of a wider developmental process in which they learn about themselves and the society in which they live.

Sample job titles

Careers adviser, counsellor, educational psychologist, nursery nurse, social worker, psychologist, youth worker

Opportunities

The main employers of social workers are local authority social services departments (England and Wales), local authorities (Scotland), and area health and social services boards, NHS trusts, the Probation Board and education and library boards (Northern Ireland). Social workers are also employed in voluntary organisations and in private agencies.

Careers advisers are employed by careers service companies, higher and further education colleges and universities, adult guidance units and private careers or vocational guidance companies. Some public schools also employ their own careers advisers.

Psychologists work in higher education or in government carrying out research; educational psychologists are generally employed by local authorities in child guidance clinics or in the school psychological service; clinical psychologists work mainly for the NHS; and occupational psychologists work in local government or organisational consultancies, for industry and commerce, and in teaching or research posts. Forensic psychologists (or criminological and legal psychologists) work in penal establishments or the NHS. Those who work in special hospitals and regional secure units in the health service have usually qualified first as clinical psychologists. Prison psychologists work in prisons, youth custody centres and remand centres.

Nursery nurses work in nursery classes in day schools, infant schools, special schools, day nurseries, family centres, hospitals, private homes (as a nanny), private nurseries and crèches (for example, in holiday resorts, on cruise liners, in large companies, in town or country locations).

Youth workers are employed in voluntary organisations and in local authority youth services (sometimes called youth and community services, or in Scotland especially, community education services). Their skills are also increasingly sought after by other organisations such as those involved in health promotion services and housing projects.

Other factors to consider

People in this area need to have a caring attitude towards their clients and a desire to help people. Communication skills and the ability to build good relationships with people are especially important.

It must be remembered that many of the clients come to these professionals for help with problems or issues in their lives. Some areas of work, such as social work, youth work or psychology, may be distressing or depressing at times. Staff may have to work anti-social hours in order to fit in with the clients' spare time.

Social workers have a great deal of responsibility. They may have to make unpopular decisions, for example, about whether to remove children from their families or to admit someone for psychiatric treatment. They must be able to stand back and view situations dispassionately and objectively.

Social workers have to be understanding and able to communicate with people from all backgrounds. The work requires maturity and the ability to cope with long hours, often in stressful circumstances.

Most residential social workers work shifts, including weekends, and spend some nights sleeping in residence.

Patience is a vital attribute for nursery nurses, especially when dealing with unruly or upset children. The work can be very demanding. Nursery nurses need to like children and to enjoy being with them. Creativity and imagination to think up new and different activities are very useful attributes to have.

Youth workers need to understand young people and be sensitive to their needs. Evening and weekend work is expected in most posts.

Entry and training

Entry and training varies according to the area of work.

Social work

The professional qualification for social workers and care managers is the Diploma in Social Work (DipSW). The main routes towards this are:

- **taking a three- or four-year university or college course** which combines a degree, usually in social sciences, with professional training for the DipSW

- **via a two-year postgraduate route**, completing a Master's degree in a related topic combined with the DipSW

- **via a three- to four-year undergraduate route**, taking first degree in a related topic combined with the DipSW

- **via a two-year non-graduate route**, studying for a Diploma in Higher Education (DipHE), combined with the DipSW. Most of these courses are for candidates over 21 years of age.

All courses require evidence of relevant social work experience, either in a paid or voluntary capacity. Distance- and open-learning routes are also available. The majority of applicants to DipSW programmes are over 25 years old. The diploma cannot be awarded to students under the age of 22. Alternative qualifications for care managers are: an NVQ in care; a nursing qualification; or an occupational therapy qualification.

The DipSW is an essential qualification for heads of residential children's homes and for most residential child care staff in Northern Ireland.

Home carers need knowledge and experience of working with people in a care setting. An NVQ in care is a suitable qualification. Training is on-the-job, and the work is supervised by a home-care organiser. Home carers can go on to become home-care organisers, social work or occupational therapy assistants or can study for the DipSW.

Home-care organisers need relevant experience in care or management. Either an NVQ in care or management or a diploma in domiciliary care management or a certificate/diploma in management studies is also desirable.

Careers work

The various routes into careers advisory work are as follows:

- **via a one-year, full-time or two-year, part-time Diploma in Careers Guidance (DipCG) course**, which is usually a postgraduate course (it does not matter what the first degree is). However, applicants over the age of 25 may offer relevant work experience, for example, in industry or teaching in lieu of a degree. Having successfully completed the initial part of the DipCG, both graduates and non-graduates can apply for the same jobs to undergo the probationary year and become fully qualified careers advisers

- **via an open learning DipCG course offered by the College of Guidance Studies**, where the majority of applicants are graduates, and those who are not must successfully complete a written assignment prior to entry
- those already employed in careers service companies can take **NVQs in guidance at levels 2 to 4**. NVQ level 4 is considered to be an alternative route to the DipCG for training as a guidance practitioner. This route is available for non-graduate staff
- **a Modern Apprenticeship in guidance for students or existing staff aged between 16 and 25**, which is available for non-graduate staff.

Following the DipCG course, careers advisers undergo a probationary year in employment. Some careers service companies take on trainees as employees and sponsor them through the DipCG course.

Not all careers advisers in university or college careers services, in adult guidance companies or in private agencies have the DipCG qualification. Other qualifications in counselling or related work may be acceptable. A psychology background can be useful.

Psychology

In order to become a chartered psychologist, a first degree accredited by the British Psychological Society (BPS) is needed in addition to professional training and experience.

Educational psychologists have both psychology and teaching qualifications (first degrees and postgraduate qualifications) plus teaching experience. The average age for entry to the profession is the late thirties.

Clinical psychologists need to take a full-time three-year accredited postgraduate training course in clinical psychology, following a first degree (honours) in psychology.

To become a chartered forensic psychologist, it is necessary to complete a BPS accredited postgraduate course in forensic/criminologist psychology, followed by at least two years' supervised training.

The main route to becoming an occupational psychologist is via a BPS-accredited first degree in psychology, which gives 'Graduate Basis for Registration' as a chartered psychologist, followed by a postgraduate master's degree in occupational psychology plus a minimum of two years' supervised training. If the first degree in psychology is not a BPS-approved course (i.e. it does not give 'Graduate Basis for Registration'), it is necessary to do a postgraduate conversion qualification (one year full-time) before doing the master's degree and the supervised training.

Nursery nursing

The two routes into child-care work are:

- **via the one-year Certificate in Child Care and Education**, in which candidates must be aged 16 or over. No formal entry requirements are needed. This qualification could be used as a route towards the Council for Awards in Children's Care and Education (CACHE) Diploma in Nursery Nursing (NNEB). Nursery nurses who complete only the certificate enter work which is closely supervised
- **via the two-year full-time CACHE NNEB**. It is also possible to study this part time. This is the main qualification for anyone wishing to work with children. There are no formal entry requirements but in practice, because competition for places is so keen, colleges ask for several GCSEs (grades A–C). Nursery nurses who complete the diploma enter work which is largely unsupervised.

NVQs are available in Early Years Care and Education (for work with young children), and in Playwork and Playwork Development (for work with children aged from 5 to 15).

Nursery nurses who have completed NVQ level 3 in Early Years Care and Education or the CACHE NNEB can build on these qualifications by taking the CACHE Advanced Diploma in Child Care and Education (ADCE).

Youth work

Youth and community work qualifications can be achieved through a variety of courses and qualifications approved by the National Youth Agency. Entry requirements vary considerably. Previous experience as a volunteer youth worker or in paid relevant employment is an advantage, and maturity is important (some courses have a minimum entry age of 21, and the average age of students on courses is 27).

Subjects

Psychology A-level is not necessary for entry to a psychology degree course. GCSEs in English and mathematics are useful for all the jobs specified. A-levels in sociology, communication studies, psychology, law, business studies, history, social biology and human biology are all helpful for jobs of this type.

Further information

Advice, Guidance, Counselling and Psychotherapy Lead Body
British Psychological Society
Central Council for Education and Training in Social Work (CCETSW) Information Service (England)
CCETSW Information Service (Scotland)
CCETSW Information Service (Wales)
CCETSW Information Service (Northern Ireland)
Council for Awards in Children's Care and Education (CACHE)
Institute of Careers Guidance
National Youth Agency
Royal Anthropological Institute of Great Britain and Ireland

Books and leaflets

Atkinson, E. 1997. *Careers in Social Work*. Kogan Page
CRAC Degree Course Guide to Psychology. 1997. CRAC/Hobsons
Working in Social Work. 1995. COIC
Free information leaflets are available from the British Psychological Society.

Sport and leisure (CLCI: G)

In the UK we spend an enormous amount of money and time on sport and leisure activities. Improved medical care and healthier life-styles have contributed to longer life expectancy. In addition, working lives are shorter than they used to be, with many people retiring at an earlier age. As a result, an increasing number of people have more time (and perhaps money) to spend on sport and leisure.

The leisure industry is vast, covering sports, games, indoor and outdoor pursuits and events and many other cultural and social activities, such as theatre, cinema, carnivals, concerts and festivals. The private sector – the big leisure companies – as well as local authorities provide a range of leisure facilities, from bowling alleys and bingo halls to night-clubs and holiday villages. The jobs are varied, with posts for managers, administrative staff, catering and technical staff, and coaches in the various activities.

Managers are usually responsible for the staff and for the administrative and financial organisation of the enterprise.

Administrative staff may either have specific roles and duties or be expected to turn their hand to any task to ensure the smooth running of an organisation. For instance, they may have to deal with customer enquiries, do some receptionist work, help behind the bar or even do some cleaning. The important point is to ensure that the customer's needs are taken into account.

People who want a career in sport need to decide which aspect of it appeals to them:

- playing
- organising/administration
- coaching/training/teaching
- researching (as a sports scientist).

To be a player, talent is essential. In some sports – such as snooker – there are very few professionals, while in others – tennis, golf and horse racing, rugby, football and cricket, for example – the number is quite large.

Some instructors have skills that are specific to just one sport or activity, while others have a number of skills which they use in a variety of sports and fitness activities, for example, at a sports club. Coaches, trainers and teachers are usually very talented in their chosen field. Many amateur coaches may not get paid but work in a voluntary capacity. Full-time coaching jobs often include a degree of administrative work, organising matches and liaising with customers. Some coaches offer other services – such as racket restringing or equipment repair – to supplement their income.

Recreation assistants (sometimes called leisure-centre assistants or similar) have a variety of duties, depending very much on where they work. However, they may include some or all of the following: lifeguarding, cleaning, teaching, reception work, undertaking the organising, promotion and supervision of events and activities.

The field of personal fitness is expanding. Instructors devise suitable exercise programmes for individuals and work with them to help them to achieve a desired level of fitness.

Outdoor pursuits, adventure centres and ropes courses (using ropes, wires, poles and trees for challenging activities) are becoming more popular, not only for the individual wanting outdoor adventure but also for companies wanting corporate entertainment for their clients and/or management training for their staff. Some outdoor centres, ropes-course centres and outward-bound schools now offer a range of specialist training programmes such as character development, teambuilding and leadership skills. The use of the outdoor facilities forms the main part of the training; by using such facilities and working as a team or individually, people take on challenges and learn to trust others and push themselves to their chosen limit.

Sports scientists apply the knowledge of science to sports. They are interested in research into the effects of sport and exercise on the human body and, conversely, how personality, mood and other factors affect sports performance. A small number are employed by professional sportspeople to help improve their performance and achieve their full potential. They analyse what the sportsperson does by using sophisticated techniques and equipment. Others work for research institutions or pharmaceutical companies, where they may carry out research into the effects of certain drugs on the body.

Sample job titles

Coach, leisure centre manager, outdoor pursuits leader, personal fitness trainer, sports assistant, sports scientist

Opportunities

Leisure managers and other leisure industry staff work in sports centres, parks, holiday camps, outward-bound schools, theatre and arts centres, historic houses, and centres with nature trails, fishing and camping facilities. It is a growth industry.

Opportunities are available for personal fitness instructors, coaches/trainers, lifeguards and recreation assistants in sports clubs, health clubs, educational institutions and in the Armed Forces. Many positions are part-time on a self-employed basis. It is also usual for such people to work in a variety of different clubs on a contract basis. Some national and professional coaches are employed by the governing bodies of particular sports, professional football clubs, golf clubs, local authorities, and so on.

Sports science is a relatively small profession. Many scientists do not apply their science in practice but instead are involved in academic research for higher education institutions or privately funded research organisations. Only a small percentage are employed by individual sportspeople.

Other factors to consider

Key qualities for most leisure careers are flexibility and adaptability, as well as a keen interest in people and a willingness to work when other people are enjoying themselves.

Much of the work in sport and leisure is part-time and not very well paid, particularly fitness teaching, coaching or training. The emphasis is on customer service, and anyone who cannot cope with working long and anti-social hours should not consider a job in this industry.

Sportspeople need dedication to their sport as well as talent and ability. Many, many hours are spent in training, which can sometimes interfere with school work or with a young person's social life. It is also common practice to travel around the UK and sometimes abroad, too, taking part in competitions, tournaments and matches. Professional sport is extremely competitive, and very few people actually make a living from it. Many have to work full-time to earn a living, and train and compete in their spare time.

It is important to have a second career to turn to (or at least have the qualifications to do another job) because injuries can put an end to a promising sports career at any time. Sports careers tend to be short anyway as a result of age or a decline in talent.

It may not always be fun to coach, train or teach if the weather is cold or wet or if you are nursing an injury. Coaching can also be very tiring mentally as well as physically, as coaches and trainers try to build up confidence in their clients, who may take time to learn to do something correctly. The majority of coaches work part-time in a voluntary capacity, usually unpaid.

Entry and training

The most direct training route for leisure and recreation management is through a degree or HND. Some courses are specifically related, such as leisure studies, sports studies and recreation management. The Institute of Sport and Recreation Management (ISRM) provides training and the opportunity to gain qualifications at various levels (up to NVQ level 4), from assistant to supervisor to manager. The Institute of Leisure and Amenity Management (ILAM) also offers a range of qualifications for managers already working in the industry.

Potential professional sportspeople's talents are usually discovered at an early age. Many of them play sport for their school or at local or county level before becoming professional at a later age. It is important for them to gain qualifications at this stage so that they can earn some money while training or start another career after the sports one has ended.

Apprenticeships or traineeships are available for some sports. Local TECs/LECs or careers service can provide more information on what is available.

Every sport has its own governing body, which sets coaching requirements. No specific academic qualifications are stipulated, but coaches need to have qualifications relevant to their particular sport or activity as well as ability. Various short courses are on offer for coaches, aerobics and dance teachers. Information is available from the National Coaching Foundation.

Recreation assistants either enter with teaching or coaching awards or work towards them, perhaps as part of a Modern Apprenticeship or other training programme.

Those wishing to be sports teachers in schools need a teaching qualification (see the 'Teaching' section for details of entry and training) as well as an ability and experience in sport. One way of achieving this experience is to take coaching qualifications alongside a degree in, for instance, sports studies. The teaching qualification would then be studied at postgraduate level. Alternatively, any degree subject could be taken, and the coaching qualifications studied for in spare time, followed by the postgraduate certificate in education.

NVQs in sport and recreation are available at various levels for those already working in the industry who wish to have more work-related qualifications.

A growing number of institutions offer sports science degrees as well as other related degrees, for example, in human movement studies.

In addition to National Diplomas and Certificates in outdoor education, there are various short courses run by governing bodies in outdoor pursuits. A practical skills qualification is important as is the ability to teach or coach people. Teachers who are also qualified in outdoor pursuits are welcomed as outward-bound instructors.

Modern Apprenticeships are available in various aspects of sport and recreation. Local TECs/LECs or careers service can provide more details.

Subjects

Sport and leisure management: GCSEs in English and mathematics are useful.
Sports science: A-levels in science or mathematics are preferred but not essential; GCSEs should include at least two science subjects.
Coach or outward-bound instructor: no specific subjects are required. English at GCSE is useful for communication.

Further information

English Sports Council
Institute of Leisure and Amenity Management
Institute of Professional Sport
Institute of Sport and Recreation Management
National Coaching Foundation
Scottish Sports Council
Sports Council for Northern Ireland
Sports Council for Wales
UK Outdoor Institute

UK Sports Council
Women's Sport Foundation

Books and leaflets
Fyfe, L. 1996. *Careers in Sport*. Kogan Page
*Guide to Careers in Outdoor Education, Development Training and
    Recreation*. 1997. National Association for Outdoor
    Education. (Available from the UK Outdoor Institute)
Working in Sport and Fitness. 1996. COIC
Working in Leisure. 1995. COIC

Surveying and planning (CLCI: U)

The surveying and planning professions incorporate many disciplines
involved in developing and shaping property and the environment.
Valuation, auctioneering and estate agency work come under the
umbrella term of surveying and are functions carried out by surveyors, but they also have separate professional bodies. Because of
this they are described separately in more detail below. Although
some surveyors specialise in planning and development, there is also
a discrete profession of town planning, described under 'Planning'.

Surveying

Surveying embraces nearly every aspect of the numerous uses of
property and land, so the skills required are very diverse. Surveyors measure, manage, develop and value property and land.
Experienced surveyors are as likely to sit at a boardroom table
planning major investments as they are to visit a farm to discuss
crop rotation or even attend an arbitration hearing with judicial
authority.

Surveyors are all members of one profession but normally specialise in only one area, such as:

- **general practice** (agency, valuation and management), where they
  act as estate agents; value all types of land and property, including
  fine art, plant and machinery; specialise in auctioneering; are
  involved in housing management
- **rural practice / agriculture**, where they advise landowners, farmers
  and others with an interest in the countryside on the use, manage-

ment, development, marketing and valuation of all rural property, including country estates, farms and livestock

- **land and hydrographic**, where they measure and map the natural and built environment
- **quantity**, where they manage the finances of building projects, both before and during construction
- **building**, where they advise on the construction of new buildings and the maintenance and repair of existing ones
- **planning and development**, where they plan, supervise and manage buildings, the use of land and the environment
- **minerals surveying**, where they measure, manage and extract mineral resources.

Other specialist areas include historic building conservation and civil engineering. It is sometimes possible to change areas at a later stage, particularly if they are in similar fields, such as building and quantity surveying, for example. The type of work varies enormously, depending on the specialism. Generally, however, a surveyor's time is divided between the office, meeting clients, dealing with other professionals, and field or site work.

Valuers examine properties to assess their value in terms of location, condition, age, character, site and building costs. They work in four main areas:

- **in general practice**, where they undertake the sale, purchase, lease and valuation of all types of land and property. They also conduct the sale of property by public auction, carry out structural surveys, values for rating, purchase, rental valuation and mortgage advances, negotiate compensation in respect of compulsory purchase, manage property and advise clients on development. The majority of valuers work in this area
- **in agricultural practice**, where they deal with agricultural land and buildings. The work includes farm management, agricultural law, tenant rights, construction and repair of farm buildings, live and dead stock, property and cattle auctions, markets, agricultural machinery and equipment
- **in fine arts and chattels**, where they assess values for the sale of antiques, works of art, furniture and all types of personal property. This type of work also includes valuation for insurance purposes, inheritance tax and probate and sale by auction

- **in plant and machinery**, where they assess industrial and commercial equipment and property for all purposes including purchase, sale, investment, insurance, balance sheets and mortgages.

Surveyors and estate agents may undertake auctioneering as part of their jobs.

Some auctioneers specialise in the sale of land and commercial, industrial and residential properties, while others deal with works of art, furniture, motor vehicles, plants and machinery. The famous art auction houses, mostly based in London, are staffed by specialists who advise on the value of an item and who auction goods as part of their job. Outside London are firms which operate livestock markets. They may also be called upon to auction the contents of houses. Others specialise in the sale by auction of the equipment and stock of bankrupt or liquidated companies.

Auctioneers do not just sell goods at auction, they also have to know a lot about the value of goods and property, compile inventories and catalogues, arrange for the insurance and security of goods and negotiate with dealers and customers.

Estate agents are involved in the sale of residential property, shops, factories or farm and building land, and with the lease of all types of buildings on behalf of their owners. In rural areas the work of an estate agent is closely allied to that of the agricultural surveyor. Estate agents split their time between office and outdoor activities, visiting clients, inspecting properties and negotiating between buyers and sellers. Some estate agency staff are negotiators, others are valuers or surveyors.

Planning

Planning and development surveyors and town and country planners are involved in the overall shaping of the urban and rural environment. Planners working for local government are involved in the setting up and implementation of policies regarding the development of urban and rural areas. This is done by compiling data on a local level of industrial needs: transport, roads, housing, education and social and leisure facilities. This information, with regard to national policy, is then translated into a development plan (guide to development), which should address the needs of both community and industry. The work of a town planner could involve anything from passing plans for an extension to a local resident's house to agreeing to the development of a new town. Planners can also work for private consultancies and in-house for large companies.

Throughout their work, planners liaise with other professionals, such as architects, surveyors, landscape designers and barristers. They also need to have some knowledge and general understanding of an enormous number of different subjects, such as architecture, design, geography, geology, economics, politics, law and social studies.

Technicians are employed in all branches of surveying and planning to support the work of the professionals by collecting, interpreting, collating and analysing information. Their work may include cartographical draughtsmanship (charting and mapping), design, surveying, preparation of plans and using information and computer systems.

Sample job titles

Auctioneer, estate agent, land surveyor, planning and development surveyor, quantity surveyor, rural surveyor, surveyor, town planner, valuer

Opportunities

Surveyors, valuers and technicians can find employment with local authorities, government departments, estate departments or nationalised industries, banks and large companies, and in private practice either with estate agents, building and construction companies, auction houses or independent firms.

Auctioneers work in rural practice surveying firms, estate agencies, auctioneering firms and art auction houses, and a few are employed as art experts in art salesrooms.

Most town planners work in local government, although some work in central government, large companies, nationalised industries and in private practice.

Overseas work is possible.

Other factors to consider

All surveyors and surveying technicians need to have an aptitude for mathematics because much of their work involves taking exact measurements and making complex calculations. Accuracy and attention to detail are therefore very important.

All of the jobs described above involve dealing with people: clients, other professionals, members of the work team or members of the public. So good communication skills, both verbal and written (for example, for report writing and presentation of data) and the ability to deal with people from a variety of backgrounds are essential, as is the ability to understand a wide range of related areas, for example, environmental and conservation issues for agricultural surveyors or town planners, farming for rural practice surveyors, the antiques market for auctioneers working in this field, and so on.

Sound business sense, negotiating skills and the ability to influence others are useful for most of the professional jobs.

Auctioneers and valuers need to be thorough and accurate and have an eye for detail.

Estate agents must have a full driving licence and enjoy meeting people. Those involved in residential estate agency are likely to work in the evenings and at weekends occasionally, when clients are free. The work may often be paid on a commission-basis.

Town planners need to sympathise with the needs of others, while at the same time retaining a sense of realism and being aware of any environmental or financial constraints. They need to have imagination to visualise the shape and implications of various developments. Effective public speaking is also required.

Entry and training

The entry and training varies for each profession.

Surveying

Most surveyors enter the profession with an accredited degree in a surveying specialism or other relevant subject, although some have HNDs. A list of accredited courses is available from the Royal Institution of Chartered Surveyors (RICS) or the ISVA (Professional Society for Valuers and Auctioneers). NVQs have recently been developed in valuation, building control, property management and spatial data management.

Those wishing to qualify as a surveyor have to complete professional training and become a member of one of the relevant professional bodies (see 'Further information'). To qualify, a surveyor must either pass or be exempt from the exams of the chosen professional body and pass the professional assessment, which consists of two years' approved training/practical experience.

Valuers can either become surveyors or study for professional qualifications awarded by the Institute of Revenues, Rating and Valuation (IRRV) and ISVA. Entry for IRRV and ISVA qualifications is usually post A-level.

For estate agency work, professional qualifications in surveying or valuation are advantageous but not essential. NVQs levels 2 and 4 can be taken in Residential Estate Agency and level 3 in Selling Residential Property.

Auctioneers may be trained surveyors, estate agents or valuers, with professional qualifications awarded by RICS, IRRV or ISVA.

Surveying technicians can train in one of two ways:

- most **find a job first and then take part-time day-release college courses**, leading to BTEC National awards in surveying. Training schemes, such as Modern Apprenticeships for young people, offer college-based training as well as practical experience. Local careers offices or Jobcentres will have more information
- other entrants take **full-time courses before finding work**, for example, relevant full-time/part-time BTEC National awards in surveying. Some entrants go on to study for Higher National awards, which allow associate membership of the Society of Surveying Technicians (SST). Full membership of the SST also requires completion of the Joint Test of Competence (jointly administered by the SST and RICS).

Planning

Planners can qualify as chartered surveyors through the routes described above or become chartered town planners – members of the Royal Town Planning Institute (RTPI). The two main methods of qualifying as a chartered town planner are:

- **via a degree/diploma course accredited by the RTPI**
- **via a related degree** (for example, architecture, geography, economics, geology, statistics) followed by a postgraduate planning qualification accredited by the RTPI.

All planners then undergo two years' practical training. They are then eligible to apply for chartered planner status.

Planning technicians are recruited with four GCSEs (grades A–C), including mathematics and English. Training is on-the-job but is combined with college study on a day-release basis, towards a National Certificate in Town and Country Planning or a Higher National Certificate in Land Use or Land Administration (Planning).

Subjects

Most of the jobs require GCSEs in mathematics and English.

Estate agency: GCSEs in mathematics and English are helpful.

Surveying technician work: GCSEs should include English, science and mathematics.

Rural practice/agricultural: GCSEs in geography and science are useful.

Land and hydrographic surveying: GCSEs in mathematics, science or geography are preferred; A-levels in geography, mathematics, economics or physical science, or equivalent.

Planning and development and valuation: GCSEs in English and mathematics.

Town planning: GCSEs in English, mathematics, physical science, economics or geography are preferred.

Minerals surveying: GCSEs, including mathematics, English and a science; A-levels in mathematics, physics or engineering science are preferred.

Further information

Architects and Surveyors Institute
British Cartographic Society
Institution of Civil Engineering Surveyors
Institute of Revenues, Rating and Valuation (IRRV)
ISVA (the Professional Society for Valuers and Auctioneers)
National Association of Estate Agents
Royal Institution of Chartered Surveyors (RICS)
Royal Town Planning Institute (RTPI)
Society of Surveying Technicians (SST)
Society of Town Planning Technicians

Books and leaflets
Working in Buildings and Property. 1997. COIC

Teaching and lecturing (CLCI: F)

The teaching and lecturing profession has undergone a transformation since 1988, as changes in the education system and the financing of education have affected how schools, colleges and universities are managed, and – in schools – what pupils are taught. The government is still in the process of making changes so the profession will remain in a state of flux in the foreseeable future.

The three areas of education are primary, secondary and tertiary, and broadly speaking, the institutions in which teachers work are:

- **nursery and primary schools** (pupils aged 3– or 5–11)
- **middle schools** (pupils aged 8–12 or 9–13)
- **secondary schools** (pupils aged 11–16/18 or 13–18)
- **sixth-form colleges** (pupils aged 16–18-plus)
- **tertiary colleges**, incorporating sixth-form work and further education courses (students aged 16-plus)
- **independent schools**, which can be primary (pupils aged 5–9/11), preparatory (pupils aged 7–13) and secondary (pupils aged 13–18-plus)
- **special schools** for children with special educational needs.

All teachers and lecturers have two roles: academic and inspirational. The academic role involves teaching pupils the subjects; the inspirational role is concerned with stimulating children and preparing them for future learning and achievement.

Primary teachers must understand the National Curriculum and the place and scope of the primary core and foundation subjects and religious education. Primary school teaching covers nursery, infant and junior schools. Nursery and infant school teaching is usually for children aged from 3 to 7 years, and junior from 8 to 11, although provision does vary across the UK, with schools providing for different age ranges. Secondary teaching is for pupils from the age of 11 or 13 upwards, depending on the school.

Some teaching posts carry extra responsibilities, for which there is extra remuneration, such as special needs coordination, careers education or being head of a department or year. Most primary school teachers are expected to hold some managerial responsibility, for example, curriculum development, for a curricular area. In addition, all teachers (but primary teachers in particular) play an important part in the development of children's social skills. Secondary school teachers specialise in one or more academic subjects.

Deputy head teachers or head teachers are responsible for curriculum development, managing budgets and staff, overseeing the day-to-day running of the school and liaising with governors, parents and the LEA.

Lecturers teach students in one or more subjects from the age of 16 or 17 (in sixth-form or further education colleges) and from the age of 18 (in higher education institutions) through to mature students (those who are 20 years of age or over at the start of the course). The subject range is wide, covering both the academic and vocational (work-related) curriculum. In higher education, they may also be expected to carry out research and to assist in management tasks required by their college or university. Lecturers not only impart knowledge to students but also help them develop their critical and analytical abilities, and research and writing skills. Promotion in the further and higher education sectors is dependent on experience and ability. In higher education, lecturers at all levels need to publish their own work regularly in order to be considered for promotion.

Sample job titles

Teacher, deputy head teacher, head of department, head teacher, lecturer, primary school teacher, professor, senior teacher

Opportunities

Further education colleges vary greatly in size and numbers of staff. Some are generalist, teaching a wide range of subjects and qualifications; others are specialist, for example, art and design, the hospitality industry, printing, and so on. Opportunities are available for full-time and part-time work.

Competition is fierce for higher education lecturing posts and candidates are usually aged at least 24. As well as full-time posts, there are some part-time opportunities and short-term contract work.

Lecturing posts are advertised in the national press and in the *Times Educational Supplement*.

Some teachers become educational advisers, inspectors, examiners or officers within the education departments of local authorities; others are promoted to be senior teachers, deputies or head teachers. Teachers also find that many of their skills are transferable to other careers, such as publishing, broadcasting or commerce and industry.

Mathematics, science and modern language teachers are constantly in demand.

Other factors to consider

People enter teaching and lecturing for many reasons. They want to:

- play an active part in shaping and developing the lives of children
- work with all kinds of different young people
- pass their knowledge of and enthusiasm for their particular subject on to others.

In addition, all good teachers and lecturers like children and students and enjoy working with them.

As well as having decent academic qualifications, teachers and lecturers need to be good communicators and able administrators (to deal with paperwork and planning lessons and so on). Creativity, energy, enthusiasm and a sense of humour are vital.

Teachers need to be flexible so that they can use a wide range of suitable teaching techniques to get the information across to all kinds of pupils. Managing and controlling classes requires skill, as does stimulating pupils' minds and keeping them motivated.

Because of the constant flux in the teaching profession, teachers need to keep themselves up-to-date with current curricular and educational developments, such as new vocational qualifications, technological advances, the evolution of the National Curriculum, target-setting and teacher assessment (procedures for assessing and recording students' progress).

The work of lecturers, like that of teachers, does not end when term ends, as there are always courses to prepare and administration duties: lecturers in higher education have to carry out their research work in vacations, in the evenings or at weekends. Lecturers in further education are often expected to do some evening teaching.

Entry and training

Teachers who wish to teach in state-maintained schools must have Qualified Teacher Status (QTS), which is awarded after successful completion of an Initial Teacher Training (ITT) course. Teachers in independent schools do not need QTS, but will need it should they wish to transfer to state schools.

Although most teachers are graduates, there are various ways to achieve QTS. These are listed below.

The undergraduate routes are:

- via a **full-time three- or four-year Bachelor of Education (BEd) degree course**, offered by some ITT and higher education institutions. The range of subjects offered by ITT institutions is limited in these courses. This route suits those students who know before starting higher education that they want to be a teacher. It is the most popular way to gain QTS for primary school teaching and offers practical teaching experience
- via **a full-time two-year BEd course** for students (aged 21 years and over) who have already done a higher education course for a year and whose knowledge of the subject they wish to teach is of a suitable standard. This is usually for secondary school teacher training, although primary school teachers can take it too
- via a **BA or BSc degree course combined with teacher training**. The full-time three- or four-year course is similar to the BEd. The shortened full-time two-year course is often taken by those aged 21 and over who have successfully completed one or two years of full-time higher education. Places are usually for secondary teacher training, although, again, primary school teachers can follow this route.

The postgraduate routes are:

- via **a first degree course followed by a one-year full-time Postgraduate Certificate in Education (PGCE)**, with the first degree in a subject relevant to the National Curriculum (see pages 14–17 for details of National Curriculum subjects). Other subjects might be accepted at the discretion of the training-course or programme provider. The PGCE course combines some further subject and professional studies with practical teaching experience. This is the most popular route by which to achieve QTS for secondary school teaching, although it is also possible to become a primary school teacher through this route

- via **a full-time two-year PGCE conversion course for subject shortage areas at secondary school level** (such as science, mathematics and modern foreign languages) for those who want to teach a subject that they did not study for their first degree. Usually candidates must have completed at least a year of full-time higher education in the subject they want to teach

- via a **part-time, two-year PGCE course** which is offered by some ITT institutions (mainly for secondary level teaching)

- via a **distance-learning PGCE**, offered by the Open University for both primary and secondary school level. Maryvale Institute offers a part-time distance-learning PGCE in religious education at secondary school level

- via a **full-time one-year postgraduate School-Centred Initial Teacher Training (SCITT) course**. This combines theory and practical teaching experience, and students are based at a consortium of designated schools responsible for the delivery of the ITT. Most courses usually lead to a PGCE qualification as well as QTS.

Employment-based routes are:

- via a **one-year full-time Graduate Teacher Programme (GTP)** for graduates with a degree relevant to the subject they wish to teach

- via the **Registered Teacher Programme (RTP)** for non-graduates who have successfully completed a minimum of two years in higher education. Trainees study for a degree as well as QTS. QTS is awarded only once the student has successfully completed the degree studies. The programme usually takes two years.

The above routes are all for applicants who are aged 24-plus and who are employed at a school that is willing to support them (by giving them a placement, experience and a mentor) through the programme. They became effective as of 1 December 1997 and replaced the old Licensed Teacher and Overseas Trained Teacher schemes.

There are shorter programmes for candidates with substantial teaching experience, for example, in the independent or further education sectors or for those who have trained overseas.

Students who wish to work in schools with children who have special educational needs should acquire QTS first and then gain some experience in a mainstream school. Specialist training is usually via in-service education and training.

All teachers are given the opportunity to have continuous in-service education and training – short courses to gain additional expertise and qualifications.

Provisions are being made for:

- professional standards for teachers nationally
- fast-track routes into the profession and promotion for high calibre-candidates
- 'advanced skills' teacher status for the very best teachers who will be given extra responsibilities and pay
- a new compulsory National Professional Qualification for those teachers hoping to become head teachers.

As the above is currently being developed, some of the names of the routes and qualifications may change.

Lecturers in further education are usually expected to have a teaching qualification (particularly for academic subjects), although this is not essential. The Certificate in Education (Further Education) can be taken as a one-year full-time course or on a part-time and day-release basis. There is also a part-time City & Guilds Further and Adult Education Teachers Certificate course. Relevant work experience and/or professional qualifications are often required for lecturers in vocational subjects, as is teaching experience for lecturers in academic subjects.

For higher education posts, lecturers need good first degrees (a first or an upper second), plus a higher degree. Applicants (usual minimum age 24) may be expected to have teaching experience, evidence of further study and possibly of research too. Some lecturers may come from an industrial or commercial background.

Subjects

Primary and secondary school teaching: GCSEs (grades A–C) must include English and mathematics. From 1998, science is also mandatory for those applying for primary teaching courses and encouraged for secondary school teaching courses for those born on or after 1 September 1979.

Further and higher education lecturers: the subject choice is dependent on what the individual wants to teach. However, for teaching qualifications, the advice for primary and secondary school teaching should be followed.

Further information

Bench Marque Ltd
Department for Education in Northern Ireland
Graduate Teacher Training Registry (GTTR)
Maryvale Institute
National Association of Teachers of Further and Higher Education (NATFHE)
Teacher Education Admissions Clearing House (TEACH)
Teacher Training Agency Communication Centre
Teaching Information Line
UCAS

Books and leaflets

Taylor, F. 1997. *Careers in Teaching*. Kogan Page
Handbook of Initial Teacher Training in England and Wales (annual). NATFHE
Teaching – A guide to becoming a teacher. 1997. Teacher Training Agency
Working in Teaching. 1997. COIC

Transport (CLCI: Y)

Transport is important to us all. We rely on it to get to work, to the shops or to a holiday destination; and industry needs it to distribute and receive all kinds of consumer goods, animals and industrial raw materials. The main areas of the transport industry are discussed below.

Air transport

Airlines and airports employ people in the following departments:

- customer services
- engineering
- finance
- marketing
- operations
- environment
- personnel.

Operations is probably the most specialist sector and includes air traffic control, fire fighting, marshalling and safety. Air traffic control officers control and monitor the aircraft taking off, landing and approaching airfields by means of radar and radio communication with pilots.

Customer services may involve working on the ground at ticket desks, as sales and reservations agents or in transfer services and helping passengers arriving on delayed flights. Air cabin crew welcome the passengers on board the aircraft, serve meals and attend to customer needs.

Pilots fly fixed-wing aircraft and helicopters. They handle sophisticated navigational and communications equipment.

Air brokers act as agents for airlines in the import/export business, matching cargos to aircraft. The job is very similar to that of ship-brokers (see overleaf).

Rail

Jobs in the rail industry are at many levels: train drivers, guards, signallers, railmen/women, technicians and management staff. The railways transport freight as well as passengers. The organisation and operation of the railways has undergone considerable change in recent years (see 'Opportunities').

Road

Road transport involves handling and transporting freight and passengers throughout the UK and overseas. It includes heavy goods traffic, passenger bus services and general haulage work, both local and national. Posts include drivers (lorry, bus, taxi, car) and their instructors; planners who deal with contracts and orders and plan routes, and so on; technical staff (engineers, mechanics, electricians); and road transport managers, who coordinate the schedules, administer safety policies and investigate complaints among their many other tasks.

Sea

The Royal Fleet Auxiliary (RFA) operates a fleet of merchant ships for the support of the NATO Armed Forces, most notably the Royal Navy (providing essential supplies) and the British Army (transporting personnel, vehicles and stores). It is one of the largest employers in British shipping. Cadetships in deck and engineering are available for those who want to become deck or engineering officers. Deck officers develop various skills, including navigation, cargo handling, ship manoeuvring; engineering officers are responsible for the running and maintenance of a ship's propulsion machinery.

The Merchant Navy consists of many different shipping companies (including the RFA), which operate a range of passenger and cruise liners, container ships, oil tankers, ferries, and so on. These companies recruit a wide variety of staff, including deck and engineering officers.

Shipbrokers and freight forwarders work for importers and exporters, organising the movement of cargo between countries. Shipbrokers act as agents for ship owners or merchant firms, matching cargos to vessels, negotiating terms and dealing with customs.

Sample job titles

Cabin crew, driver, driving instructor, Merchant Navy deck officer, motor mechanic, pilot, road transport manager, shipbroker, train driver

Opportunities

Airlines and airports employ people in various air transport roles. The National Air Traffic Services Ltd (NATS) is responsible for the provision of air traffic control in the UK and is owned by the Civil Aviation Authority (CAA). Pilots are employed by civil airlines, air-taxi companies, freight services, aerial surveying, photography and crop-spraying firms and private individuals who need a pilot.

Railtrack is now the national infrastructure operator on the main-line rail network, providing the routes, equipment and signalling for train operators. Many different separate companies now carry out the functions that British Rail used to operate. Job opportunities are therefore with these individual train-operating companies and with Railtrack, as well as with the London Underground. Light rail developments are in London's Docklands, Manchester and Sheffield, and more are planned, which means many more jobs will become available.

Among the employers in road transport are large bus, freight and transport companies and operators plus thousands of smaller firms operating bus services or haulage contracts. It is also possible to work in transport sections of huge industrial companies, in the Armed Forces and with motoring organisations.

The Royal Fleet Auxiliary and the Merchant Navy are the main employers of people involved in sea transport. Brokers work mainly in London, which is the international centre for the chartering of ships.

Opportunities for working overseas are good in all of these areas, and, indeed, many employers require staff who are willing to relocate if necessary.

Other factors to consider

Jobs in transport often involve long and anti-social hours, sometimes with shift work. A foreign language is often an advantage in many careers in this area.

Communication and IT skills are important for most jobs. Transport operations rely heavily on computerised systems.

Promotion is often dependent on experience gained by working in other areas of the UK.

In the areas where the safety of others is dependent on the skills and competence of just one person, or perhaps a few people – for example, pilot, ship captain, air traffic controller – the job can be immensely stressful. It requires a calmness of mind and a high sense of responsibility.

In many jobs – for example, for air traffic control, air cabin crew, drivers, pilots – certain medical requirements need to be met, such as good eyesight and colour vision; in addition, anyone with asthma, hay fever or other respiratory problems will find it extremely difficult to pass pilot training. Pilots need a high level of fitness. Air cabin crew and personnel at sea need to be able to swim.

Entry and training

Entry and training requirements vary according to the job and the transport area.

Air

Specialist safety staff from an aviation or safety background and fire-fighters from a local authority fire service background are needed in airports. Most engineers and managers are educated to degree level and have considerable experience. The minimum age requirement for customer services staff varies but is usually 18. The minimum age for entry to air cabin crew is usually 20. A good standard of education (often a minimum of four GCSEs, including mathematics and English) is required, with a second spoken language or sign language desirable, and there may be minimum height and weight requirements, depending on the airline. Good colour vision is often specified.

NATS runs a one-and-a-half-year training scheme for air traffic control officers aged 18 to 27, with courses at the College of Air Traffic Control at Bournemouth Airport and practical training at a designated operational unit. Entry is very competitive.

Pilots must have a Commercial Pilot's Licence and Instrument Rating or the Airline Transport Pilot's Licence issued by the CAA. A licence can be obtained in three ways:

- **via a full-time course**, which is very expensive – about £60,000 – unless sponsored by an airline
- **through courses at approved flying schools/clubs** (cheaper but still very expensive) to gain a Private Pilot's Licence. After 700 hours' flying experience, a short course is undertaken to become a commercial pilot. This route is likely to cease from July 1998
- **via an Armed Forces pilot career** Ex-RAF/Royal Navy pilots can transfer to civil aviation with appropriate training.

Training in airbroking is gained through practical experience in aviation or in freight forwarding. There are no formal entry requirements or professional examinations in airbroking.

Rail

The minimum age of entry for drivers and conductors is 18. Some companies offer special training schemes for young people. Although no minimum educational requirements are needed for railway jobs, candidates must sit an aptitude test. NVQs can be taken in various aspects of rail transport.

Road

Drivers of taxis, trucks and lorries must be at least 21 (preferably 25) and hold a Passenger Carrying Vehicle (PCV) or Large Goods Vehicle licence. Taxi drivers need a local licence and have to pass a special driving test. Black cab drivers also have to pass a test of knowledge of the area concerned. Driving instructors must have held a full and clean driver's licence for four of the preceding six years, have no criminal convictions, be able to read a car number plate at 90 feet and must pass the Driving Standards Agency driving instructor's examination.

EC regulations stipulate that all road transport managers must now have a certificate of professional competence, which is gained either by passing a written test or as part of a relevant professional qualification, such as that awarded by the Chartered Institute of Transport or the Institute of Road Transport Engineers.

Motor mechanics usually need some GCSEs and have to pass an aptitude test.

Sea

The RFA and Merchant Navy recruit 16- to 20/21-year-old cadets with GCSEs or A-levels. Training consists of a sandwich course (approximately 3–4 years) at nautical college and at sea working towards relevant qualifications (certificates of competency in seamanship, chart work, meteorology, for example); successful completion leads to officer-level status.

Shipbroking can be entered from the age of 16 to 17 as a chartering clerk. A good general education, preferably including knowledge of a foreign language is important.

Both school-leavers and graduates can apply for jobs in freight forwarding. NVQs levels 2–4 are available.

Management jobs

Often any degree is acceptable for managerial jobs. Relevant degrees are, however, required for the professions, such as accountancy or engineering. Degrees and HNDs in transport studies can also be taken.

Many companies run management or graduate training schemes and in-house courses for their employees or allow them to study part-time for the examinations for membership of the appropriate professional body.

Many NVQs are already available in various aspects of the transport industry and still more are being developed. There are also Modern Apprenticeships on offer in some transport sectors. Local TECs/LECs or careers offices hold more information.

Subjects

Air transport: English and mathematics are useful. One or more foreign languages can be an advantage, particularly for those working in companies with links outside the UK and for air cabin crew.

Air traffic control officers: GCSEs in mathematics and English; A-levels unspecified.

Pilots: GCSEs in English, mathematics, science; A-levels in mathematics and physics preferred. Many pilots have a degree (sciences preferred).

Motor mechanics: GCSEs in mathematics and a science preferred.

Sea transport: deck and engineering officers: GCSEs in mathematics, English and science (with physics content); A-levels in mathematics and physics.

Further information

Chartered Institute of Transport
Civil Aviation Authority (Air-traffic control)
Institute of Chartered Shipbrokers
Institute of Road Transport Engineers
Merchant Navy Careers, The Chamber of Shipping
National Air Traffic Services Ltd (NATS)
Office of the Commodore, Royal Fleet Auxiliary Flotilla

Books and leaflets

Careers on the Move. The Chartered Institute of Transport
Working in Transport and Distribution. 1997. COIC

Travel and tourism (CLCI: G)

Travel and tourism are areas of considerable employment growth. About 1.5 million people are currently employed in the travel and tourism industry, which has the potential to become the UK's largest by the year 2000. The industry consists of a wide range of different sectors, all providing facilities and services for tourists and travellers. These sectors include accommodation, catering and transport as well as tour operators and travel agents and the national, regional and area tourist organisations or boards, which may be described as the 'official' face of tourism. The hospitality industry is covered in another section (see page 172).

The tourist industry also includes those services that cater for tourists' leisure activities and interests. These are in the form of recreation and entertainment facilities, such as sports centres, country parks, theatres and cinemas, and tourist attractions such as museums, historic properties, zoos and theme parks.

Tour operators provide package holidays. In a large company, product managers plan and cost the holidays, decide which resorts to use and negotiate hotel and flight prices. Contractors are often employed to visit new resorts and find appropriate hotels. Product managers may also become involved in deciding the content and design of the holiday brochures. In smaller companies, staff may carry out a range of duties including bookings, administration, planning itineraries, designing brochures, negotiating prices and arranging insurance.

The main bulk of travel agents' work is selling package holidays to the public, although it may also include planning individual holiday or travel itineraries, advising on visas, foreign currency and necessary injections, and making hotel or flight bookings for business people or holiday makers, with the use of computerised reservations systems.

Holiday or resort representatives and couriers may work in the UK and overseas, looking after holiday makers. A foreign language is an asset for overseas work. Many tour operators recruit staff for these jobs on a seasonal basis, often taking on students who want holiday jobs. Duties may include meeting holiday makers at the airport or port, escorting them to the resort, and holding welcome parties on a regular basis. The jobs involve a great deal of customer contact, and local knowledge is essential.

Tourist guides spend time conducting groups of visitors on tours of cities, either on foot, on coaches or by boat. They have to provide commentaries about various sights and monuments and must be prepared to answer questions.

The role of local authority tourism managers is to increase the number of visitors to their area in order to support and improve the local economy. At the same time, they have to ensure that the residents' quality of life is not adversely affected by an influx of too many visitors. Their duties may include coordinating events and exhibitions, visiting accommodation and the various local tourist attractions and conference centres to encourage marketing and development activities by each of the companies.

The English Tourist Board and regional tourist boards are responsible for the network of Tourist Information Centres (TICs), which give out information on accommodation and local and regional attractions and facilities. Some TICs may also provide tour guides and book hotel and guesthouse accommodation for visitors, while others may be involved with projects with local industry to encourage visitors to the area.

Sample job titles

Courier, holiday representative, marketing and tourism manager, product manager, resort manager, resort representative, tourist board registered guide, tourist information centre assistant, tourist information centre manager, tourist guide, travel agent/consultant

Opportunities

Travel and tourism jobs are to be found not only in traditional tourist areas, such as the Lake District and the Cotswolds but in all parts of the UK. There are about 7,500 high street travel agencies, many of which are owned by tour operators. Some jobs are in small companies, run by one or two people, while others are in very large organisations, with thousands of employees. The larger organisations provide the opportunity to make a career by moving around and up within the organisation. Other jobs are in the public sector, for example, in local authority leisure facilities or in local tourist information centres; and others are in the private sector, with tour operators, airlines and cruise ships. Self-employment is possible, for example, some people set up as specialist tour operators.

Resort managers or representatives, tourist guides and couriers can all work overseas.

Seasonal employment can always be found in hotels as holiday representatives or tourist guides, in the UK and abroad. Tourist guides are nearly always self-employed, although some may work for tour operators or tourist boards on a seasonal basis.

Couriers are employed by the major tour operators and some winter sports companies as chalet staff or ski guides.

Other factors to consider

Anyone working in the travel and tourism industry must enjoy meeting people and helping them. Many of the jobs also require excellent selling skills, especially as overall earnings can sometimes depend on commission (for example, in travel agencies). So a friendly nature combined with the ability to be persuasive is an advantage.

Other useful attributes are a good memory and the ability to work under pressure, particularly when queues form, telephones ring and paperwork beckons. Computer skills are an advantage, particularly for travel agency work.

Although pay is not always on a par with many other jobs, there are often target-related bonuses plus perks, such as discounted travel and educationals (promotional trips), for staff working for tour operators and travel agencies, and tips for couriers or guides.

Jobs such as resort representatives are perceived to be glamorous, but a lot of the work can be hard: working hours are not set, and the representatives are always on-call for customers. Much of the work is seasonal and short-term. A willingness to be flexible and adaptable is useful.

Most tourist guides are freelance. They are expected to keep their information up-to-date. Much of the work can be tiring, particularly if walking around cities, so stamina and good health are essential. Summer is the busiest time for tourist guides so their holidays have to be taken at other times. It is also important to enjoy working with people and to understand the stresses and strains of travelling. Hours can be long.

Although there are opportunities for foreign travel, much of the work in travel and tourism can be office-based, dealing with booking, accounts or administration.

Entry and training

Various courses are on offer at different levels: some relate specifically to travel and tourism, while others major in another subject, such as business studies, with a travel and tourism option. Training is often on-the-job, although City & Guilds qualifications (for example, Certificate in Tourist Information Centre Competence, Introduction to Tourism in the UK, Certificate in Visitor Attraction Operations, Certificate in Farm Tourism), and NVQs (levels 1–4) in various aspects of travel services are also available. Local TECs/LECs or careers service companies can provide details of Modern Apprenticeships available.

Fluency in a foreign language is often required for overseas work.

Most people wanting to work in travel agencies start as juniors or apprentices. The most common route of entry into travel agencies is via the Travel Training Company's Travel Training Programme (TTP) for young people aged 16 or 17, where trainees work towards various qualifications such as NVQs in retail travel, tour operating or business travel. Those interested in this route should normally find employment with a travel agency first and ask to be nominated for a place on a TTP. This means they get structured on-the-job training while employed. Alternatively, another route to the TTP is to take the ABTA Certificate at college or via distance-learning. GCSEs are necessary for entry to the course.

Couriers and tourist/holiday representatives are usually aged over 20 and need to be proficient in at least one European language; most training takes place on-the-job. It is possible to work towards the Certificate of Overseas Resorts Representatives.

Tourist guides who pass a written and practical examination qualify as Tourist Board Registered Guides. The 'Blue Badge' is the symbol of the Tourist Board Registered Guide qualification throughout England. In order to qualify, candidates are assessed on in-depth local knowledge, national knowledge and presentation skills (on foot, on site and on a coach). The training for the London Blue Badge lasts two years (weekday evenings and some Saturdays) and costs about £2,000. Competition for entry is considerable. The ability to speak another language is an advantage. Many Blue Badge guides have a qualification in some specialist subject: art, architecture, archaeology, music, and so on.

Tourist Information Centre assistants are usually aged over 21 years, with experience in related industries, such as leisure or marketing. They often have a minimum of four GCSEs. Knowledge of a foreign language is an advantage.

Subjects

Business studies, geography and foreign languages are useful at GCSE or A-level. English and mathematics are usually important.

Further information

British Tourist Authority/English Tourist Board
Institute of Travel and Tourism
London Tourist Board and Convention Bureau
Travel Training Company

Books and leaflets

Reily Collins, V. 1997. *Careers in the Travel Industry*. Kogan Page
Working in Tourism. 1995. COIC
ABTA's Guide to Working in Travel. The Travel Training Company

Voluntary work (CLCI: A)

Voluntary work is 'any activity which involves spending time, unpaid, doing something which aims to benefit someone other than close relatives, or to benefit the environment' (National Centre for Volunteering definition). However, posts can be paid as well as unpaid. Over 300,000 people work in the voluntary sector and opportunities within it are considerable and varied.

The unpaid voluntary roles involve work such as assisting local voluntary social organisations (for example, Scope and Age Concern) that help people, especially young, disabled, disadvantaged and elderly people. Duties include home visiting and arranging meals and sports activities.

All the local, national and international specialist organisations depend on unpaid or low-paid help. The areas volunteers might work in are:

- conservation and the environment
- the arts (drama, music, dance, art, literary groups, and so on)
- sports clubs
- charities
- youth work and youth clubs.

The volunteers may only receive expenses in return for their time or in some cases a small allowance (particularly for those working full-time). These organisations also employ paid managers.

Major charity organisations, for example, Oxfam, Greenpeace, the British Heart Foundation and many more, also employ qualified staff with expert knowledge or skills, such as fund-raising, medicine, administration, secretarial work, personnel, marketing and publicity. Managers may sometimes have hundreds of volunteers working under them and many events to organise.

Volunteer help organisers (usually paid) work for agencies, not charities. They interview volunteers and try to match them with appropriate vacancies. Their role is varied and may include liaising with a wide range of organisations, managing and supervising volunteers, organising training sessions and carrying out some administrative duties.

Volunteer development officers and voluntary services managers may also do some or all of these tasks within a voluntary organisation. Titles vary according to the organisation. In some cases these posts are voluntary but coordinated by a paid staff member.

Sample job titles

Helper, trainer, volunteer development officer, voluntary help organiser, voluntary services manager, volunteer

Opportunities

Volunteers are always in demand. The work is in a variety of settings, from local charity shops and hospitals to major national organisations, and the jobs are diverse, ranging from doing conservation and community projects to fund-raising and arranging sports activities.

Voluntary work is often an excellent way to gain useful employment experience and it can also provide you with a good background to careers in environmental, conservation, social and youth work. It can be done as part of the Duke of Edinburgh's Award scheme, and many schools and colleges arrange voluntary work for their pupils. Many students consider doing it during their 'gap year' – the year between leaving school or college and starting a higher education course. The 'Youth for Britain' database (available in some careers service companies, schools and colleges as part of the ECCTIS 2000 'UK Course Discover' database – a guide to courses available) gives details of 250,000 placements with nearly 700 volunteer organisations both in the UK and overseas for students aged between 16 and 25.

Voluntary workers, particularly those with specific skills such as teaching, engineering and so on, can work abroad: this affords the opportunity to travel, to provide a service and gain worthwhile experience at the same time. Volunteers may have to pay for their own travel and insurance.

The government has pledged to develop a Millennium Volunteers organisation offering volunteer opportunities for people aged 16 to 25 in the UK. Consultation with interested bodies and voluntary organisations is currently taking place.

Other factors to consider

Voluntary work requires dedication and may sometimes require long working hours, but volunteers have the choice of doing it either full-time or part-time and on a short-term, long-term or on a one-off basis (for, say, one day or even one hour a month). Volunteers who are unemployed and receiving benefits may find that they lose their benefits if they do voluntary work because volunteers are not considered to be actively seeking employment. Check with the Benefits Agency or with the National Centre for Volunteering. Some organisations, for example, Community Service Volunteers, give unemployed volunteers free accommodation, food and a weekly allowance which is a similar amount to what they would receive through benefits.

Adaptability and flexibility are important as volunteers may have to be available whenever and wherever needed.

Voluntary work helps people to develop communication skills, teamwork and self-confidence.

Those involved in recruiting and training volunteers need to have good communication and interpersonal skills.

Entry and training

Voluntary organisations often employ qualified people with specialist skills for specific roles. However, there are usually no specific entry requirements in terms of academic qualifications or previous experience for the ordinary volunteer jobs.

Training for employees is usually on-the-job, although they may have to do relevant courses. Paid volunteer organisers sometimes recruit, train and manage unpaid volunteers.

Subjects

All subjects are relevant but languages, for example, could be useful for travel abroad.

Further information

British Trust for Conservation Volunteers (BTCV)
Community Service Volunteers
GAP Activity Project Ltd
National Centre for Volunteering
National Council for Voluntary Organisations
National Youth Agency
Voluntary Service Overseas

Books and leaflets

Hempshell, M. 1995. *How to Do Voluntary Work Abroad.* Trotman
Working in the Voluntary Sector. 1996. COIC
Youth for Britain (database of volunteer opportunities at home and abroad for 16- to 25-year-olds – available on subscription through the ECCTIS 2000 'UK Course Discover' database in many schools, colleges and careers offices).

Other sources of information

This section gives you details of careers encyclopaedias, directories and software databases which you may find helpful. You will also find sources of information given at the end of each career area in the careers guide. Many of these can be found in school or college careers libraries, your local careers office and public reference library. In addition, any good bookshop will be able to provide you with the books mentioned. The list is not exhaustive and you may find other equally useful books and software programmes during your research. Some of the publications are published annually and it is important that you use the latest editions.

Remember to use the other resources available to you – your family, teachers, careers advisers and friends. It is always helpful to talk things through with someone else and to learn from others' experiences. Remember, though, that in the end any decision to be made is yours.

Career choice and change

Davies, Laing and Dick. 1997. *Which A-levels?* Lifetime Careers Wiltshire Ltd

Dixon, B. 1994. *Jobs and Careers After A-levels*. Lifetime Careers Wiltshire Ltd

Smith, M. and Matthew, V. 1995. *Decisions 13/14+*. CRAC/Hobsons

Smith, M. and Matthew, V. 1995. *Decisions 15/16+*. CRAC/Hobsons

Straw, S. 1996. *GNVQ: Is It For You?* Lifetime Careers Wiltshire Ltd

How to Choose your GCSEs. 1995. Trotman

How to Choose Your A-levels. 1996. Trotman

The Job Book (annual). CRAC/Hobsons
Which Degree? series (annual). CRAC/Hobsons

Education

Boehm, K. and Lees-Spalding, J. 1997. The NatWest Student Book
Heap, B. 1996. *How to Choose Your Degree Course*. Trotman
Higgins, T. *How to Complete your UCAS Form* (annual). Trotman
Wittington, E. 1996. *How to Choose Your HND Course*. Trotman
A Brief Guide for Higher Education Students (annual). DfEE
College, sixth form and university prospectuses
COPE: Compendium of Post-16 Education & Training in residential establishments for young people with special needs. 1996. Lifetime Careers Wiltshire Ltd
Degree Course Guides (annual). CRAC/Hobsons
The Directory of Further Education (annual). CRAC/Hobsons
Entrance Guide to Higher Education in Scotland (annual). COSHEP/UCAS
Higher Education and Disability. 1997. Skill: National Bureau for Students with Disabilities
LASER Compendium of Higher Education (2 volumes) (annual). Butterworth Heinemann
The NATFHE Handbook of Initial Teacher Training (annual). Linneys ESL
The Potter Guide to Higher Education. 1997 (annual). Dalebank Books (Gives information on the institutions, towns/cities and social life.)
The PUSH Guide to Which University (annual). McGraw Hill Group of Companies
Sponsorships for Students (annual). CRAC/Hobsons
Springboard Sixth Form Casebook (annual). CRAC/Hobsons
University and College Entrance – the Official Guide (annual). UCAS/Sheed & Ward
What do Graduates Do? (annual). CSU/UCAS

Software

Choosing Higher Education Courses (CHEC2). Careersoft (information about course details and qualifications.)

PUSH CD – the multimedia guide to UK universities. McGraw Hill Book Co. (Researched by students and recent graduates.)

Which University on CD-Rom. CRAC/Hobsons (Key facts about accommodation, costs, environment, location.)

Youth for Britain database – a guide to voluntary work (Available in some careers service companies, schools and colleges as part of the ECCTIS 2000 *UK Course Discover* database.)

European and international

Jones, R. 1996. *How to Get a Job Abroad.* How To Books Ltd
Packer, J. 1997. *Directory of Jobs and Careers Abroad.* Vacation Work
Straw, S. 1995. *Getting Into Europe.* Trotman
Woodworth, D. 1997. *Summer Jobs Abroad.* Vacation Work

Software

Careers Europe. Bradford Careers Service (An international careers information database.)

Europe in the Round CD. Vocational Technologies Ltd (Information on study and work opportunities in Europe.)

Occupational information

Alston, A. and Daniel, A. 1996. *The Penguin Careers Guide.* Penguin
Burston, D. *The A–Z of Careers & Jobs.* 1996. Kogan Page
Lea, K. 1997. *Careers Encyclopaedia.* Cassell
Careers In . . . . series. Kogan Page
CASCAiD Careers Guide. CRAC/Hobsons
Occupations (annual). COIC
Question & Answer series. Trotman
Working In . . . series of booklets. COIC

Software

CID – Careers Information Database. Careersoft (Occupational database with a simple quiz and job suggestions linked to curriculum subjects and interest areas.)

Odyssey. Progressions Ltd (Occupational information database that was known as *MicroDOORS* and which is licensed from the DfEE.)
Subject-Wise for 13/14 year olds. CASCAiD (Links careers with subjects.)

Self-awareness (software)

CID – Careers Information Database. Careersoft (see above)
DISCOURSE. ISCO (Questionnaire linking interests to degree course suggestions.)
JIIG-CAL SubjectScan. Hodder & Stoughton (Questionnaire linking interests to year 9 option choice.)
KUDOS. CASCAiD (Questionnaire linking qualifications and interests to job suggestions.)
PROBE for years 9/10. Cambridge Occupational Analysts (Questionnaire linking interests and skills to job suggestions.)

Special needs

COPE (see under 'Education')
Disability Rights Handbook (annual). Disability Alliance (Benefits, legislation, services and a comprehensive list of organisations.)
Equal Opportunities for Disabled Graduates Casebook. Available through Future Prospects

Software

CID – Careers Information Database. Careersoft (see above)

Taking a year off

Butcher, V. 1997. *Taking a Year Off*. Trotman
Gray, P. 1997. *Opportunities in the Gap Year*. ISCO
Straw, S. 1995. *A Year Off . . . A Year On*. Lifetime Careers Wiltshire Ltd
The Gap Year Guide Book (annual). Peridot Press
Working Holidays. 1997. Central Bureau
A Year Between. 1997. Central Bureau

Voluntary work

Hempshell, M. 1997. *Doing Voluntary Work Abroad*. How To Books Ltd

Pybus, V. 1997. *International Directory of Voluntary Work*. Vacation Work

Volunteer Work. 1995. Central Bureau

Working in the Voluntary Sector. 1996. COIC

Software

Youth for Britain database (see 'Education' software). This is an information database on volunteer opportunities in the UK and abroad

Glossary

The following is a list of the more common acronyms and abbreviations used in this book and in the careers, education and training world.

ADAR Art and Design Admissions Registry (merged with UCAS)

A-level Advanced-level GCE

AS-level Advanced Supplementary (may change to Advanced Subsidiary) GCE – equivalent to half an A-level

BA Bachelor of Arts

BEd Bachelor of Education

BEng Bachelor of Engineering

BSc Bachelor of Science

BTEC Business and Technology Education Council (the validating body is the Edexcel Foundation, which awards National Diploma, HND, GNVQ, NVQ and other levels)

CAD Computer-Aided Design

CAL Computer-Aided Learning

CBI Confederation of British Industry

CCETSW Central Council for Education and Training in Social Work

C&G / CGLI City & Guilds of London Institute

CLCI Careers Library Classification Index

COIC Careers and Occupational Information Centre (DfEE)

CRAC Careers Research and Advisory Centre

CSYS Certificate of Sixth Year Studies (Scotland)

DfEE Department for Education and Employment

FE further education

GATE GNVQs and Access to Higher Education – a database

GCE General Certificate of Education (A- and AS-levels)

GCSE General Certificate of Secondary Education

GNVQ General National Vocational Qualification

GSVQ General Scottish Vocational Qualification

H-grade Higher Grade examinations and awards in Scotland

HE higher education

HMI Her Majesty's Inspectorate

HNC/HND Higher National Certificate/Higher National Diploma

LCCI London Chamber of Commerce and Industry

LEA Local Education Authority

LEC Local Enterprise Company (Scotland), similar to TECs in England and Wales

LMS Local Management of Schools

MA Modern Apprenticeships

NC/ND National Certificate/National Diploma

NCVQ National Council for Vocational Qualifications (merged with SCAA to form QCA)

NTETs National Targets for Education and Training

NRA National Record of Achievement

NVQ National Vocational Qualification

O-grade Ordinary grade examinations and awards in Scotland (largely been replaced by Standard Grade)

OC Open College

OFSTED The Office for Standards in Education

OU Open University

PSE Personal and Social Education

QCA Qualifications and Curriculum Authority (merger of SCAA and NCVQ)

RSA Royal Society of Arts

SCAA School Curriculum and Assessment Authority (merged with NCVQ to form QCA)

SCCC Scottish Consultative Council on the Curriculum

SCE Scottish Certificate of Education

SCOTVEC Scottish Vocational Education Council (used to award diplomas and HNDs in Scotland). This has now been replaced by the SQA

SEA Scottish Education Authority

Skill National Bureau for Students with Disabilities

S-grade Standard Grade examinations in Scotland

SQA Scottish Qualifications Authority

SWAS Social Work Admissions System

TAP Training Access Point

TEC Training and Enterprise Council (England and Wales)

TEFL Teaching English as a Foreign Language

TESL Teaching English as a Second Language

TQM Total Quality Management

UCAS Universities and Colleges Admissions Service

VET Vocational Education and Training

YT Youth Training

Addresses

General

Chapter 1

BTEC (Edexcel), Edexcel Foundation
Customer Response Centre, Stewart House, 32 Russell Square, London WC1B 5DN
Tel: 0171-393 4444
Fax: 0171-393 4501
Web site:
http://www.edexcel.org.uk

City & Guilds
1 Giltspur Street, London EC1A 9DD
Tel: 0171-294 2468
Fax: 0171-294 2400
Email: enquiry@city-and-guild.co.uk
Web site:
http://www.city-and-guild.co.uk

COIC (Careers and Occupational Information Centre), DfEE
Moorfoot, Sheffield S1 4PQ
Tel: 0114-259 3368
Fax: 0114-259 3439
Email: ccd.dfee.mf@gtnet.gov.uk
Web site: http://www.open.gov.uk/dfee/ccdintro.htm

COSHEP
St. Andrew House, 141 West Nile Street, Glasgow G1 2RN
Tel: 0141-353 1880
Fax: 0141-353 1881
Email: coshep@gcal.ac.uk
Web site:
http://www.coshep.gcal.ac.uk

CRAC/Hobsons
Bateman Street, Cambridge CB3 0AX
Tel: (01223) 460277
Fax: (01223) 311708
Email: enquiries@crac.org.uk
Web site:
http://www.crac.org.uk/crac

DfEE Publications
PO Box 500, Sudbury, Suffolk
Tel: (0845) 6022260
Fax: (0845) 6033360
Web site: http://www.open.gov.uk/dfee/dfeehome.htm

Future Prospects
Tel: (01229) 588166
0171-728 1914 (enquiry line)
Fax: (01299) 588225

OFSTED Publications Centre
PO Box 6927, London E3 3NZ
Tel: 0171-510 0180
Fax: 0171-510 0196
Web site:
http://www.ofsted.gov.uk

Qualifications and Skills Strategy Division
The Scottish Office, Education and Industry Department, Victoria Quay, Edinburgh EH6 6QQ
Tel: (0345) 741741 (*general enquiries*)
Fax: 0131-244 7122/7123
Web site:
http://www.scotland.gov.uk

Qualifications and Curriculum Authority (QCA) Customer Services
Newcombe House, 45 Notting Hill Gate, London W11 3JB
Tel: 0171-728 1914 (*GNVQ enquiry line*)
Fax: 0171-229 8526
Email: info@qca.org.uk
Web site:
http://www.open.gov.uk/qca/

Royal Society of Arts (RSA) Examinations Board
Westwood Way, Coventry, Warwickshire CV4 8HS
Tel: (01203) 470033
Fax: (01203) 468080
Web site: http://www.rsa.co.uk

Scottish Qualifications Authority (SQA)
Hanover House, 24 Douglas Street, Glasgow G2 7NQ
Tel: 0141-248 7900
Fax: 0141-242 2244
Email: mail@sqa.org.uk
Web site: http://www.sqa.org.uk

Student Awards Agency for Scotland
Gyleview House, 3 Redheughs Rigg, Southgyle, Edinburgh EH12 9AH
Tel: 0131-244 5823
Fax: 0131-244 5887

UCAS (University and Colleges Admissions Service)
Fulton House, Jessop Avenue, Cheltenham, Gloucestershire GL50 3SH
Tel: (01242) 222444
Fax: (01242) 221622
Email: enq@ucas.ac.uk
Web site: http://www.ucas.ac.uk

Chapter 3

Disability on the Agenda
Freepost, Bristol BS38 7DE

Disablement Advisory Service
(Northern Ireland)
Training and Employment Agency Headquarters, Adelaide House, 39–49 Adelaide Street, Belfast BT2 8FD
Tel: (01232) 257480
Fax: (01232) 257468

Society of Occupational Medicine
6 St. Andrews Place, Regents Park, London NW1 4LB
Tel: 0171-486 2641
Fax: 0171-486 0028
Email:
societyoccmed.compuserve.com
Web site:
http://www.med.ed.ac.uk/hew/som/

Careers Guide

Administration and office work

Association of Medical Secretaries, Practice Administrators and Receptionists Ltd
Tavistock House North, Tavistock Square, London WC1H 9LN
Tel: 0171-387 6005
Fax: 0171-388 2648

Institute of Agricultural Secretaries and Administrators Ltd
National Agricultural Centre, Stoneleigh, Kenilworth, Warwickshire CV8 2LZ
Tel: (01203) 696592
Fax: (01203) 417537
Email: iagsa@farmline.com

Institute of Health Service Management
7–10 Chandos Street, London W1M 9DE
Tel: 0171-460 7654
Fax: 0171-460 7655
Email: mailbox@ihsm.co.uk
Web site: http://www.ihsm.co.uk

Institute of Personnel and Development
IPD House, Camp Road, London SW19 4UX
Tel: 0181-971 9000
Fax: 0181-263 3333
Email: ipd@ipd.co.uk
Web site: http://www.ipd.co.uk

Institute of Qualified Private Secretaries
First Floor, 6 Bridge Avenue, Maidenhead, Berkshire SL6 1RR
Tel: (01628) 625007
Fax: (01628) 624990

Advertising, marketing and PR

Advertising Association
Abford House, 15 Wilton Road, London SW1V 1NJ
Tel: 0171-828 4831
Fax: 0171-931 0376
Email: ic@adassoc.org.uk
Web site: http://www.adassoc.org.uk

Chartered Institute of Marketing
Education Division, Moor Hall, Cookham, Maidenhead, Berkshire SL6 9QH
Tel: (01628) 427500
Fax: (01628) 427499
Email: marketing@cim.co.uk
Web site: http://www.cim.co.uk

Communication, Advertising and Marketing Education Foundation (CAM)
Abford House, 15 Wilon Road, London SW1V 1NJ
Tel: 0171-828 7506
Fax: 0171-976 5140
Web site: http://www.cam.uk.com

Institute of Practitioners in Advertising
44 Belgrave Square, London SW1X 8QS
Tel: 0171-235 7020
Fax: 0171-245 9904
Email: mark@ipa.co.uk
Web site: http://www.ipa.co.uk

Institute of Public Relations
The Old Trading House,
15 Northburgh Street,
London EC1V 0PR
Tel: 0171-253 5151
Fax: 0171-490 0588
Email: info@ipr1.demon.co.uk
Web site: http://www.ipr.press.net

Market Research Society
15 Northburgh Street,
London EC1V 0AH
Tel: 0171-490 4911
Fax: 0171-490 0608
Email: info@marketresearch.org.uk
Web site:
http://www.marketresearch.org.uk

Animals

Association of British Riding Schools
Queen's Chambers, 38–40 Queen
Street, Penzance,
Cornwall TR18 4BH
Tel: (01736) 369440
Fax: (01736) 351930
Web site:
http://www.equiworld.net/abrs

British Horse Society
Stoneleigh Deer Park, Kenilworth,
Warwickshire CV8 2XZ
Tel: (01203) 696697
Fax: (01203) 692351
Email: bhs@bhshorse.demon.co.uk
Web site:
http://www.equiweb.co.uk/bhs

British Veterinary Nursing Association Ltd (BVNA)
Unit D12, The Seedbed Centre,
Coldharbour Road, Harlow,
Essex CM19 5AF
Tel: (01279) 450567

Fax: (01279) 420866
Email: bvna@compuserve.com
Web site:
http://www.vetweb.co.uk

Guide Dogs for the Blind Association
Hillfields, Burghfield Common,
Reading, Berkshire RG7 3YG
Tel: 0118-983 5555
Fax: 0118-983 5433

Institute of Animal Technology
5 South Parade, Summertown,
Oxford OX2 7JL

Royal College of Veterinary Surgeons (RCVS)
Belgravia House, 62–64 Horseferry
Road, London SW1P 2AF
Tel: 0171-222 2001
Fax: 0171-222 2004
Email: admin@rcvs.org.uk
Web site:
http://www.rcvs.org.uk/rcvs

RSPCA
The Causeway, Horsham,
West Sussex RH12 1HG
Tel: (0990) 555999
Fax: (01245) 241048

Architecture, landscape architecture and housing

Architects and Surveyors Institute
15 St Mary Street, Chippenham,
Wiltshire SN15 3WD
Tel: (01249) 655398
Fax: (01249) 443602
Email: asinst@aol.com
Web site: http://www.asi.org.uk

British Institute of Architectural Technologists
397 City Road, London EC1V 1NE
Tel: 0171-278 2206
Fax: 0171-837 3194
Email: info@biat.org.uk

Chartered Institute of Housing
Octavia House, Westwood Business Park, Westwood Way,
Coventry CV4 8JP
Tel: (01203) 695010
Fax: (01203) 695110

Landscape Institute
6–7 Barnard Mews,
London SW1 1QU
Tel: 0171-738 9166
Fax: 0171-738 9134
Email: mail@l-i.org.uk
Web site: http://www.l-i.org.uk

Royal Incorporation of Architects in Scotland
15 Rutland Square,
Edinburgh EH1 2BE
Tel: 0131-229 7545
Fax: 0131-228 2188
Email: admin@risa.co.uk
Web site: http://www.ris.org.uk

Royal Institute of British Architects (RIBA)
66 Portland Place,
London W1N 4AD
Tel: (0891) 234400/234444 (Careers information – 50p per minute)
Email: admin@inst.riba.org
Web site: http://www.riba.org

Art and design and photography

Association of Illustrators
1st Floor, 32–38 Saffron Hill,
London EC1N 8FH
Tel: 0171-831 7977
Fax: 0171-831 6277
Email: a-o-illustrators.demon.co.uk

British Institute of Professional Photography
Fox Talbot House, 2 Amwell End,
Ware, Hertfordshire SG12 9HN
Tel: (01920) 464011
Fax: (01920) 487056

Chartered Society of Designers
32–38 Saffron Hill,
London EC1N 8FH
Tel: 0171-831 9777
Fax: 0171-831 6277
Email: csd@csd.ord.uk
Web site:
http://www.designweb.co.uk/csd

Institute of Ceramics
Shelton House, Stoke Road,
Shelton, Stoke-on-Trent,
Staffordshire ST4 2DR

Society of Designer Craftsmen
24 Rivington Street,
London EC2A 3DU
Tel: 0171-739 3663
Fax: 0171-739 3663

Beauty therapy and hairdressing

Beauty Industry Authority
3 Chequer Road,
Doncaster DN1 2AA
Tel: (01302) 329835
Fax: (01302) 323381
Email: enquiries@habia.org

Hairdressing Training Board
3 Chequer Road,
Doncaster DN1 2AA
Tel: (01302) 342837
Fax: (01302) 323381
Email: enquiries@habia.org

International Health and Beauty Council
46 Aldwick Road, Bognor Regis,
West Sussex PO21 2PN
Tel: (01243) 842064
Fax: (01243) 842489

Clothing, fashion and textiles industries

CAPITB Trust
80 Richardshaw Lane, Pudsey,
Leeds LS28 6BN
Tel: 0113-239 3355
Fax: 0113-239 3155
Email: capitb@capitb.co.uk

Textile Institute
10 Blackfriars Street,
Manchester M3 5DR
Tel: 0161-834 8457
Fax: 0161-835 3087
Email: tiihq@textileinst.org.uk
Web site: http://www.texi.org

Complementary medicine

Anglo European College of Chiropractic
13–15 Parkwood Road, Boscombe,
Bournemouth, Dorset BH5 2DF
Tel: (01202) 436200
Fax: (01202) 436312
Email: aecc@aecclib.demon.co.uk
Web site:
http://www.aecclib.demon.co.uk

British Acupuncture Council
Park House, 206–208 Latimer
Road, London W10 6QY
Tel: 0181-964 0222
Fax: 0181-964 0333

British Chiropractic Association
29 Whitley Street, Reading,
Berkshire RG2 0EG
Tel: 0118-975 7557
Fax: 0118-975 7257
Email: britchiro@aol.com

British College of Acupuncture
(See 'British Acupuncture Council')

British College of Naturopathy and Osteopathy
Lief House, 2 Sumpter Close,
120–122 Finchley Road,
London NW3 5HR
Tel: 0171-435 6464
Fax: 0171-431 3630

British Homoeopathic Association
27a Devonshire Street,
London W1N 1RJ
Tel: 0171-935 2163

British School of Osteopathy
75 Borough High Street,
London SE1 1JE
Tel: 0171-407 0222
Fax: 0171-839 1098
Web site: http://www.bso.ac

**Institute for Complementary
Medicine**
PO Box 194, London SE16 1QZ
(*Send an SAE with two spare stamps to
receive information.*)

**International College of Oriental
Medicine**
Green Hedges House, Green Hedges
Avenue, East Grinstead,
Sussex RH19 1DZ
Tel: (01342) 313106/107
Fax: (01342) 318302
Email: info@orientalmed.ac.uk
Web site:
http://www.orientalmed.ac.uk

**Society of Teachers of the Alexander
Technique**
20 London House, 266 Fulham
Road, London SW10 9EL
Tel: 0171-351 0828
Fax: 0171-352 1556
Email: stat@pavilion.co.uk
Web site:
http://www.pavilion.co.uk/stat

Computing

British Computer Society
1 Sandford Street, Swindon,
Wiltshire SN1 1HJ
Tel: (01793) 417417
Fax: (01793) 480270
Email: bcshq@bcs.org.uk
Web site: http://www.bcs.org.uk

**National Training Organisation for
Information Technology (ITNTO)**
16 Berners Street,
London W1P 3DD
Tel: 0171-580 6677
Fax: 0171-580 5577
Web site: http://www.itito.org.uk/

**National Computing Centre
Education Services Ltd**
The Towers, Towers Business Park,
Wilmslow Road, Didsbury,
Manchester M20 2EZ
Tel: 0161-438 6200
Fax: 0161-438 6240
Email:
enquires@ncceducation.co.uk
Web site:
http://www.ncceducation.co.uk

Construction – craft careers

**Construction Industry Training
Board (CITB)**
Bircham Newton, King's Lynn,
Norfolk PE31 6RH
Tel: (01485) 577577
Fax: (01485) 577503

Construction – professional and technician careers

Association of Building Engineers
Jubilee House, Billing Brook Road,
Weston Favell,
Northampton NN3 8NW
Tel: (01604) 404121
Fax: (01604) 784220
Email: buildengrs@aol.com
Web site:
http://www.abe.org.uk.abe

Chartered Institute of Building
Englemere, Kings Ride, Ascot,
Berkshire SL5 8BJ
Tel: (01344) 630700
Fax: (01344) 630777
Email: nameciob.org.uk
Web site: http://www.ciob.org.uk/

Chartered Institute of Building Services Engineers
Delta House, 222 Balham High
Road, London SW12 9BS
Tel: 0181-675 5211
Fax: 0181-675 5449
Email: info@cibse.org
Web site: http://www.cibse.org/

Construction Industry Training Board (CITB)
(See 'Construction – craft careers')

Institute of Building Control
92–104 East Street, Epsom,
Surrey KT17 1EB
Tel: (01372) 745577
Fax: (01372) 748282
Email:
admin@instobc.demon.co.uk
Web site:
http://www.demon.co.uk/instobc

Cultural careers

Council for British Archaeology
Bowes/Morrell House, 111
Walmgate, York YO1 2UA
Tel: (01904) 671417
Fax: (01904) 671384
Email:
archaeology@compuserve.com
Web site:
http://www.britac3.britac.ac.uk/cba

Institute of Field Archaeologists
University of Reading, 2 Earley
Gate, PO Box 239,
Reading, Berkshire RG6 6AU
Tel: 0118-931 6446
Fax: 0118-931 6446

Museums Association
42 Clerkenwell Close,
London EC1R 0PA
Tel: 0171-608 2933
Fax: 0171-250 1929
Email:
info@museumsassociation.org
Web site: http://www.museums
association.org

Museum Training Institute
Glyde House, Glydegate,
Bradford BD5 0UP
Tel: (01274) 391056
Fax: (01274) 394890
Email: peter@m-t-i.demon.co.uk
Web site:
http://www.m-t-i.demon.co.uk

Society of Archivists
40 Northampton Road,
London EC1R 0HB
Tel: 0171-278 8630
Fax: 0171-278 2107

United Kingdom Institute for Conservation of Historic and Artistic Works (UKIC)
109 The Chandlery, 50 Westminster
Bridge Road, London SE1 7QY
Tel: 0171-721 8721
Fax: 0171-721 8722

Dentistry

British Association of Dental Nurses
11 Pharos Street, Fleetwood,
Lancashire FY7 6BG
Tel: (01253) 778631
Fax: (01253) 773266

British Dental Association
64 Wimpole Street,
London W1M 8AL
Tel: 0171-935 0875
Fax: 0171-487 5232
Email: enquiries@bda-dentistry.org.uk
Web site:
http://www.bda-dentistry.org.uk

British Dental Hygienists' Association
13 The Ridge, Yatton,
nr Bristol BS19 4DQ
Tel: (01934) 876389
Fax: (01934) 876389

Charles Clifford Dental Hospital
Wellesley Road, Sheffield,
South Yorkshire S10 2SZ
Tel: 0114-271 7987
Fax: 0114-271 7855
Email: k.h.figures@sheffield.ac.uk

Dental Auxiliary School, London Hospital Medical College
36 New Road, Whitechapel,
London E1 2AX
Tel: 0171-377 7000

Dental Auxiliary School, University Dental Hospital NHS Trust
Heath Park, Cardiff CF4 4XY
Tel: (01222) 742421

Dental Technician Education and Training Advisory Board
Partners in Practice, 5 Oxford
Court, St. James Road, Brackley,
Northamptonshire NN13 7XY
Tel: (01280) 702600
Fax: (01280) 702274
Email:
100770.2526@compuserve.com

Dental Therapy Course, Liverpool University School of Dentistry
Pembroke Place, Liverpool L3 5PS
Tel: 0151-706 2000 (extn 5036)

Emergency services

Coastguard and Marine Safety Agency
Spring Place, 105 Commercial
Road, Southampton SO15 1EG
Tel: (01703) 329100
Fax: (01703) 329488
Email: email@coastguard.gov.uk
Web site:
http://www.coastguard.gov.uk

Fire Services Unit (Home Office)
Horseferry House, Dean Ryle
Street, London SW1P 2AW
Tel: 0171-217 8754
Fax: 0171-217 8789

Police – Accelerated Promotion Scheme for Graduates (APSG)
Room 466, Home Office, 50 Queen
Anne's Gate, London SW1H 9AT
Tel: 0171-273 4000
Fax: 0171-273 4031

Police Division, Scottish Home and Health Department
St. Andrew's House,
Edinburgh EH1 3DE
Tel: 0131-244 2156
Fax: 0131-244 2666

Police Personnel and Training Unit
Room 514, Home Office, Queen Anne's Gate, London SW1H 9AT
Tel: 0171-273 3684
Fax: 0171-273 2501

Scottish Office Home Department, Fire Service and Emergency Planning Division
F1 Spur, Saughton House,
Broomhouse Drive,
Edinburgh EH11 3XD
Tel: 0131-244 2187
Fax: 0131-244 2819

Engineering

Engineering and Marine Training Authority (EMTA), Engineering Careers Department
Vector House, 41 Clarendon Road,
Watford, Hertfordshire WD1 1HS
Tel: (0800) 282167 (freephone)
Fax: (01923) 337344
Email: ecis@emta.org.uk
Web site: http://www.emta.org.uk

Engineering Council
10 Maltravers Street,
London WC2R 3ER
Tel: 0171-240 7891
Fax: 0171-240 7517
Email: info@bngc.org.uk
Web site: http://www.bngc.org.uk

Institution of Chemical Engineers
Davis Building, 165–189 Railway Terrace, Rugby CV21 3HQ
Tel: (01788) 578214
Fax: (01788) 560833
Email: kallman@ichemi.org.uk
Web site: http://www.ichemi.org

Institution of Civil Engineers
1–7 Great George Street,
London SW1P 3AA
Tel: 0171-222 7722
Fax: 0171-222 7500
Email: snashfold-l@ice.org.uk
Web site: http://www.ice.org.uk

Institution of Electrical Engineers
Michael Faraday House, Six Hills Way, Stevenage SG1 2AY
Tel: (01438) 313311
Fax: (01483) 313465
Email: postmaster@iee.org.uk
Web site: http://www.iee.org.uk

Institution of Engineering Designers
Courtleigh, Westbury Leigh,
Westbury, Wiltshire BA13 3TA
Tel: (01373) 822801
Fax: (01373) 858085

Institution of Mechanical Engineers
1–3 Birdcage Walk, Westminster,
London SW1H 9JH
Tel: 0171-222 7899
Fax: 0171-222 4557
Email: cstead@imeche.org.uk
Web site:
http://www.imeche.org.uk

WISE (Women Into Science and Engineering)
10 Maltravers Street,
London WC2R 3ER
Tel: 0171-240 7891
Fax: 0171-240 7517
Email: info@engc.org.uk
Web site: http://www.engc.org.uk

Women's Engineering Society
Imperial College of Science and
Technology, Department of Civil
Engineering, Imperial College
Road, London SW7 2BU
Tel: 0171-594 6025
Fax: 0171-594 6026
Email: wes@ic.ac.uk
Web site: http://www.cant.ac.uk/
misc/wes/weshome.html

Environmental services

British Ecological Society
26 Blades Court, Deodar Road,
Putney, London SW15 2NU
Tel: 0181-871 9797
Fax: 0181-871 9779
Email:
general@ecology.demon.co.uk
Web site:
http://www.demon.co.uk/bes

British Geological Survey
Keyworth, Nottingham NG12 5GG
Tel: 0115-936 3100
Fax: 0115-936 3200
Email: wrobinson@bgs.ac.uk
Web site: http://www.bgs.ac.uk

British Trust for Conservation Volunteers (BTCV)
36 St. Mary's Street, Wallingford,
Oxford OX10 0EU
Tel: (01491) 839766
Fax: (01491) 839646

Email: info@btcv.org.uk
Web site: http://www.btcv.org.uk/

Chartered Institute of Environmental Health
Chadwick Court, 15 Hatfields,
London SE1 8DJ
Tel: 0171-928 6006
Fax: 0171-827 5865
Email: cieh@dial.pipex.com
Web site: http://www.cih.org.uk

Countryside Commission
John Dower House,
Crescent Place, Cheltenham,
Gloucestershire GL50 3RA
Tel: (01242) 521381
Fax: (01242) 584270
Email: info@countryside.gov.uk
Web site:
http://www.countryside.gov.uk

English Nature
Enquiry Service, Room 1W,
Northminster House,
Peterborough PE1 1UA
Tel: (01733) 455100
Fax: (01733) 68834
Email:
enquiries.en.nh@gtnet.gov.uk
Web site:
http://www.english-nature.org.uk

Environment Agency
Public Enquiries Department, Rio
House, Waterside Drive, Aztec
West, Almondsbury,
Bristol BS32 4UD
Tel: (0645) 333111
Fax: (01454) 624409
Email: enquiries@environment:
agency.gov.uk
Web site: http://
www.environment:agency.gov.uk

Environment Council
21 Elizabeth Street,
London SW1W 9RP
Tel: 0171-824 8411
Fax: 0171-730 9941
Email: environment.council@
ukonline.co.uk
Web site:
http://www.greenchannel.com/tec

National Trust
36 Queen Anne's Gate,
Westminster, London SW1H 9AS
Tel: 0171-222 9251
Fax: 0171-222 5097

Natural Environment Research Council
Polaris House, North Start Avenue,
Swindon SN2 1EU
Tel: (01793) 411500
Fax: (01793) 411501
Email: fisher@nerc.ac.uk
Web site: http://www.nerc.ac.uk

Scottish Natural Heritage
12 Hope Terrace,
Edinburgh EH9 2AS
Tel: 0131-447 4784
Fax: 0131-446 2277

Finance

Association of Accounting Technicians
154 Clerkenwell Street,
London EC1R 5AD
Tel: 0171-837 8600
Fax: 0171-837 6970
Email: aatuk@dial.pipex.com
Web site: http://www.aat.co.uk

Association of Chartered Certified Accountants
1 Woodside Place,
Glasgow G3 7QF
Tel: 0141-331 1046
Fax: 0141-309 4141
Email:
student.admissions@acca.co.uk
Web site: http://www.acca.co.uk

Bank of England
Head Office, Threadneedle Street,
London EC2R 8AH
Tel: 0171-601 4444
Fax: 0171-601 4771
Web site: http://
www.bankofengland.co.uk

British Bankers Association
Pinners Hall, 105–108 Old Broad
Street, London EC2N 1EX
Tel: 0171-216 8800
Fax: 0171-216 8811
Web site: http://www.bba.org.uk

British Insurance and Investment Brokers' Association
BIIBA House, 14 Bevis Marks,
London EC3A 7NT
Tel: 0171-623 9043
Fax: 0171-626 9676
Email: enquiries@biiba.org.uk
Web site: http://www.biiba.org.uk

Building Societies Association
3 Savile Row, London W1X 1AF
Tel: 0171-437 0655
Fax: 0171-734 0655

Chartered Institute of Bankers
Emmanuel House, 4–9 Burgate
Lane, Canterbury CT1 2XJ
Tel: (01227) 762600
Fax: (01227) 763788
Email: institute@cib.org.uk
Web site: http://www.cib.org.uk

Chartered Institute of Banking in Scotland
19–20 Rutland Square,
Edinburgh EH1 2DE
Tel: 0131-229 9869
Fax: 0131-229 1852
Email: info.ciobs@dial.pipex.com
Web site: http://www.ciobs.org.uk

Chartered Institute of Loss Adjusters
Manfield House, 1 Southampton
Street, London WC2R 0LR
Tel: 0171-836 6482
Fax: 0171-836 0340

Chartered Institute of Management Accountants
63 Portland Place,
London W1N 4AB
Tel: 0171-637 2311
Fax: 0171-631 5309
Web site: http://www.cima.org.uk

Chartered Institute of Public Finance and Accountancy
3 Robert Street,
London WC2N 6BH
Tel: 0171-543 5600
Fax: 0171-543 5700
Email: marketing@cipfa.org
Web site: http://www.cipfa.org.uk

Chartered Insurance Institute
31 Hillcrest Road, London E18 2JP
Tel: 0181-989 8464
Fax: 0181-530 3052
Web site: http://www.cii.co.uk

Faculty of Actuaries
17 Thistle Street,
Edinburgh EH2 1DF
Tel: 0131-220 4555
Fax: 0131-220 2280
Email: faculty@actuaries.org.uk
Web site:
http://www.actuaries.org.uk

Institute of Actuaries
Napier House, 4 Worcester Street,
Oxford OX4 2AW
Tel: (01865) 794144
Fax: (01865) 794094
Email: institute@actuaries.org.uk
Web site:
http://www.actuaries.org.uk

Institute of Chartered Accountants in England and Wales (ICAEW)
PO Box 433, Chartered
Accountants' Hall, Moorgate Place,
London EC2P 2BJ
Tel: 0171-920 8677
Fax: 0171-920 8603
Email: etdsrp@icaew.co.uk
Web site: http://www.icaew.co.uk

Institute of Chartered Accountants in Scotland
27 Queen Street,
Edinburgh EH2 1LA
Tel: 0131-225 5673
Fax: 0131-247 4872
Email:
studenteducation@icas.org.uk
Web site: http://www.icas.org.uk

Institute of Financial Accountants
Burford House, London Road,
Sevenoaks, Kent TN13 1AS
Tel: (01732) 458080
Fax: (01732) 455848
Web site: http://www.ifa.org.uk

London Stock Exchange Ltd
Old Broad Street,
London EC2N 1HP
Tel: 0171-797 1372
Fax: 0171-410 6861
Email: lse@dial.pipex.com
Web site:
http://www.londonstockex.co.uk

Securities Institute
Centurion House, 24 Monument
Street, London EC3R 8AJ
Tel: 0171-626 3191
Fax: 0171-929 2422
Email:
securitieshaydeninstitute.org.uk
Web site: http://www.securities
haydeninstitute.org.uk

Funeral directing

*British Institute of Funeral Directors
(BIFD)*
140 Leamington Road,
Coventry CV3 6JY
Tel: (01272) 673609

*National Association of Funeral
Directors (NAFD)*
618 Warwick Road, Solihull,
West Midlands B91 1AA
Tel: 0121-711 1343
Fax: 0121-711 1351

Government service

*Application Helpdesk, Recruitment
and Assessment Services Ltd* (for fast
stream entry to the civil service)
Innovation Court, New Street,
Basingstoke, Hampshire RG21 7JB
Tel: (01256) 468551
Web site:
http://www.open.gov.uk/co/fsaesd/
selfass.htm (for copy of fast-stream

self-assessment disk prior to
application)

*Economics and Business Education
Association*
1A Keymer Road, Hassocks,
West Sussex BN6 8AD
Tel: (01273) 846033
Fax: (01273) 844646
Email: ebeah@pavillion.co.uk
Web site:
http://www.bized.ac.uk/ebea/

*Graduate and Schools Liaison
Branch*
Room 127/2, Cabinet Office, Horse
Guards Road, London SW1P 3AL
Tel: 0171-270 5713
Fax: 0171-270 5764
Email:
fsesd.recruit.co@gtnet.gov.uk
Web site:
http://www.open.gov.uk/
co/fsaesd/recruit.htm

*Inland Revenue, Human Resources
Division – Graduate Recruitment*
Mowbray House, PO Box 55,
Castle Meadow Road,
Nottingham NG2 1BE
Tel: 0115-974 0603

*Local Government Opportunities,
Local Government Management
Board*
Layden House, 76–86 Turnmill
Street, London EC1M 5QU
Tel: 0171-296 6600
Fax: 0171-296 6666
Email: carol.lee@gmb.gov.uk
Web site:
http://www.datalake.com/lgo

Recruitment and Assessment Services
Tel: (01256) 383780
Fax: (01256) 373786
Web site: http://www.rasnet.co.uk

Royal Economic Society
London Business School, Sussex Place, Regent's Park,
London NW1 4AS
Tel: 0171-706 6783
Email: eburke@lbs.ac.uk
Web site: http://www.res.org.uk

Healthcare professions

British Dietetic Association
7th Floor, Elizabeth House,
22 Suffolk Street, Queensway,
Birmingham B1 1LS
Tel: 0171-323 1531
Fax: 0171-462 2620

Chartered Society of Physiotherapy
14 Bedford Row,
London WC1R 4ED
Tel: 0171-242 1941
Fax: 0171-306 6611
Email: csp@csphysio.org.uk

College of Occupational Therapists
6/8 Marshalsea Road,
London SE1 1HL
Tel: 0171-357 6480
Fax: 0171-207 9612
Web site: http://www.cot.co.uk

College of Radiographers
2 Carriage Row, 183 Eversholt Street, London NW1 1BU
Tel: 0171-391 4500
Fax: 0171-391 4504

General Optical Council
41 Harley Street, London W1N 2DJ
Tel: 0171-580 3898
Fax: 0171-486 3525

Health Service Careers
PO Box 204, London SE99 7UW

Royal College of Speech and Language Therapists
7 Bath Place, Rivington Street,
London EC2A 3DR
Tel: 0171-613 3855
Fax: 0171-613 3854
Email: postmaster@rcslt.org
Web site: http://www.rcslt.org.uk

Society of Chiropodists and Podiatrists
53 Welbeck Street,
London W1M 7HE
Tel: 0171-486 3381
Fax: 0171-935 6359

Hospitality industry

Brewers and Licensed Retailers Association
42 Portman Square,
London W1H 0BB
Tel: 0171-486 4831
Fax: 0171-935 3991
Email: mailbox@brla.co.uk
Web site: http://www.brla.co.uk

British Institute of Innkeeping
Park House, 24 Park Street,
Camberley, Surrey GU15 3PT
Tel: (01276) 684449
Fax: (01276) 23045
Email: careers@bii.org

Hospitality Training Foundation
International House, High Street,
Ealing, London W5 5DB
Tel: 0181-579 2400
Fax: 0181-840 6217
Email: helpline.htf@tcom.co.uk
Web site: http://www.htf.org.uk

*Hotel and Catering International
Management Association
(HCIMA)*
191 Trinity Road,
London SW17 7HN
Tel: 0181-672 4251
Fax: 0181-682 1707
Email: sabine@hcima.org.uk
Web site: http://
www.hcima.org.uk/

Land-based industries

Arboricultural Association
Ampfield House, Ampfield,
Romsey, Hampshire SO51 9PA
Tel: (01794) 368717
Fax: (01794) 368978
Email: freehouse@dial.pipex.com
Web site:
http://www.dspace.dial.pipex.com/
treehouse/

ATB-Landbase
NAC, Kenilworth, Warwickshire
CV8 2LG (the National Training
Organisation for agriculture and
commercial horticulture)
Tel: (0345) 078007 (*training helpline*)
Fax: (01203) 696732
Email: atb.landbase.training@
farmline.com
Web site:
http://www.atb-landbase.co.uk

Farming Press
2 Wharfdale Road, Ipswich,
Suffolk IP1 4LG
Tel: (01473) 241122
Fax: (01473) 240501
Email:
farmingpress@dotfarming.com
Web site:
http://www.dotfarming.com

*Food and Farming Information
Service*
The National Agricultural Centre,
Stoneleigh Park,
Warwickshire CV8 2LZ
Tel: (01203) 696966
Fax: (01203) 696732

Forestry Commission
231 Corstorphine Road,
Edinburgh EH12 7AT
Tel: 0131-334 0303
Fax: 0131-314 6174
Web site: http://
www.forestry.gov.uk

Institute of Horticulture
14/15 Belgrave Square,
London SW1X 0PS
Tel: 0171-245 6943
Fax: 0171-245 6943
Email: ioh@horticulture.org.uk
Web site: http://
www.horticulture.demon.co.uk

*Institute of Leisure and Amenity
Management*
ILAM House, Lower Basildon,
Reading, Berkshire RG8 9NE
Tel: (01491) 874800
Fax: (01491) 874801
Email: info@ilam.co.uk
Web site: http://www.ilam.co.uk

National Association of Agricultural Contractors
Huts Corner, Tilford Road,
Hindhead, Surrey GU26 6SF
Tel: (01428) 605360
Fax: (01428) 606531
Email: naac@farmline.com

National Trust
(see 'Environmental Services')

Royal Forestry Society
102 High Street, Tring,
Hertfordshire HP23 4AF
Tel: (01442) 822028
Fax: (01442) 890395
Email: rfs_tring@compuserve.com
Web site: http://www.rfs.org.uk

Royal Horticultural Society Garden
Wisley, Woking,
Surrey GU23 6QB
Tel: (01483) 224234
Fax: (01483) 212382
Email: rhs@rhs.walk.uk
Web site: http://www.rhs.org.uk

School of Horticulture, Royal Botanic Gardens, Kew
Richmond, Surrey TW9 3AB
Tel: 0181-332 5545
Fax: 0181-332 5574
Email: i.leese@rbgq.org.uk

Soil Association
86 Colston Street, Bristol BS1 5BB
(*organic farming information*)
Tel: 0117-929 0661
Fax: 0117-925 2504
Email: soilassoc@gn.apc.org

Timber Growers Association
5 Dublin Street Lane South,
Edinburgh EH1 3PX
Tel: 0131-538 7111
Fax: 0131-583 7222
Email: tga@ednet.co.uk

Willing Workers on Organic Farms
19 Bradford Road, Lewes,
East Sussex BN7 1RB
Tel: (01273) 476286
Web site: http://www.phdcc.com/sites/wwoof

Woodland Trust
Autumn Park, Dysart Road,
Grantham, Lincolnshire NG31 6LL
Tel: (01476) 581111
Fax: (01476) 590808

Language-based careers

Centre for Information on Language Teaching and Research
20 Bedfordbury,
London WC2N 4LB
Tel: 0171-379 5110 (resources library)
Fax: 0171-379 5082
Email: library@cilt.org.uk
Web site:
http://www.campus.bt.com/campusworld/pub/cilt

Institute of Linguists
Saxon House, 48 Southwark Street,
London SE1 1UN
Tel: 0171-940 3100
Fax: 0171-940 3101
Email: info@iol.org.uk
Web site: http://www.iol.org.uk

*Institute of Translation and
Interpreting*
377 City Road, London EC1V 1NA
Tel: 0171-713 7600
Fax: 0171-713 7650
Email: iti@compuserve.com
Web site: http://iti.org.uk

*International Association of
Conference Interpreters*
12 Vicars Road, London NW5 4NL
Tel: 0171-284 3112
Fax: 0171-284 0240

The legal profession

Faculty of Advocates
Parliament House,
Edinburgh EH1 1RF
Tel: 0131-226 2881
Fax: 0131-225 3642

General Council of the Bar
2–3 Cursitor Street,
London EC4 1NE
Tel: 0171-440 4000
Fax: 0171-440 4002

Inns of Court School of Law
4 Grays Inn Place, Grays Inn,
London WC1R 5DA
Tel: 0171-404 5787
Fax: 0171-831 4188
Email: bvc@icsl.ac.uk

Institute of Legal Executives
Kempston Manor, Kempston,
Bedfordshire MK42 7AB
Tel: (01234) 841000
Fax: (01234) 840373
Web site: http://www.ilex.org.uk

Law Society
Ipsley Court, Berrington Close,
Redditch, Worcestershire B98 0TD

Tel: 0171-242 1222
Fax: (01527) 510213
Web site:
http://www.lawsociety.org.uk

Law Society of Northern Ireland
Law Society House, 98 Victoria
Street, Belfast BT1 3JZ
Tel: (01232) 231614
Fax: (01232) 232606

Law Society of Scotland
26 Drumsheugh Gardens,
Edinburgh EH3 7YR
Tel: 0131-226 7411
Fax: 0131-225 2934
Email: lawscot@lawscot.org.uk
Web site:
http://www.lawscot.org.uk

Library, information and archive work

Institute of Information Scientists
44 Museum Street,
London WC1A 1LY
Tel: 0171-831 8633
Fax: 0171-430 1270
Email: iis@dial.pipex.com
Web site: http://www.iis.org.uk

Library Association
7 Ridgmount Street,
London WC1E 7AE
Tel: 0171-636 7543
Fax: 0171-436 7218
Email: info@la-hq.org.uk

*Records Management Society of
Great Britain*
Woodside, Coleheath Bottom,
Speen, Princes Risborough,
Buckinghamshire HP27 0SZ
Tel: (01494) 488599

Fax: (01494) 488590
Email: rms@awdry.demon.co.uk
Web site:
http://www.rms.gb.org.uk

Society of Archivists
(See 'Cultural careers')

The media

BBC Corporate Recruitment Services
PO Box 7000, London W12 8GJ
Tel: 0181-225 9874
Fax: 0181-225 9877
Web site:
http://www.bbc.co.uk/jobs

Cyfle
Llawr Uchaf, Gronant Penrallt Isaf,
Caernarfon, Gwynedd LL55 1NW
Tel: (01286) 671000
Fax: (01286) 678890
Email:
cyfle@cyfle-cyf.demon.co.uk
Web site:
http://www.cyfle-cyf.demon.co.uk

ft2 – Film and Television Freelance Training
Warwick House, 9 Warwick Street,
London W1R 5RA
Tel: 0171-734 5141
Fax: 0171-287 9899

Gaelic Television Training Trust, Sabhal Mor Ostaig College
Teangue, Sleat,
Isle of Skye IV44 8RU
Tel: (01471) 844373
Fax: (01471) 844383
Email: oifis@smo.uhi.ac.uk
Web site:
http://www.smo.uhi.ac.uk

National Council for the Training of Broadcast Journalists (NCTBJ)
188 Litchfield Court, Sheen Road,
Richmond, Surrey TW9 1BB
Tel: 0181-940 0694
Fax: 0181-940 0694

National Council for the Training of Journalists (NCTJ)
The Laton Bush Centre, Southern
Way, Harlow, Essex CM18 7BL
Tel: (01279) 430009
Fax: (01279) 438008
Email: nctj@itecharlow.co.uk
Web site:
http://www.itecharlow.co.uk/nctj/

Periodicals Training Council
Queens House,
55–6 Lincolns Inn Fields,
London WC2A 3LJ
Tel: 0171-404 4168
Fax: 0171-404 4167
Email: training@ppa.co.uk
Web site: http://www.ppa.co.uk

Scottish Newspaper Publishers' Association
48 Palmerston Place,
Edinburgh EH12 5DE
Tel: 0131-220 4353
Fax: 0131-220 4344

Scottish Screen
74 Victoria Crescent,
Glasgow G12 1LN
Tel: 0141-302 1700
Fax: 0141-302 1711
Email:
info@scottishscreen.demon.co.uk
Web site: http://
www.scottishscreen.demon.co.uk

Skillset (National Training Organisation for Broadcast, Film and Video)
2nd Floor, 91–101 Oxford Street,
London W1R 1RA
Tel: 0171-534 5300
Fax: 0171-534 5333
Email: info@skillset.org
Web site: http://www.skillset.org

Medicine and nursing

British Medical Association
BMA House, Tavistock Square,
London WC1H 9JP
Tel: 0171-387 4499
Fax: 0171-383 6400
Email: cmay@bma.org.uk
Web site: http://www.bma.org.uk

English National Board for Nursing, Midwifery and Health Visiting
Careers Section, PO Box 2EN,
London W1A 2EN
Tel: 0171-391 6200 (*careers line*)
Fax: 0171-391 6207
Email: enb.careers@easynet.co.uk
Web site: http://www.enb.org.uk

Health Service Careers
(See 'Healthcare professions')

National Board for Nursing, Midwifery and Health Visiting for Northern Ireland
RAC House, 79 Chichester Street,
Belfast BT1 4LR
Tel: (01232) 238152
Fax: (01232) 333298

National Board for Nursing, Midwifery and Health Visiting for Scotland
Careers Information Service,
22 Queen Street,
Edinburgh EH2 1NT
Tel: 0131-225 2096
Fax: 0131-226 2492

Nursing and Midwifery Admissions Service (NMAS)
Fulton House, Jessop Avenue,
Cheltenham,
Gloucestershire GL50 3SH
Tel: (01242) 544949
Fax: (01242) 263555

Welsh National Board for Nursing, Midwifery and Health Visiting
Golate House, 101 St Mary's Street,
Cardiff CF1 1DX
Tel: (01222) 261400
Fax: (01222) 261499
Email: anne.duggan@wnb.org.uk

Performing arts

Arts Council
14 Great Peter Street,
London SW1P 3NQ
Tel: 0171-333 0100
Fax: 0171-973 6590
Email: information.ace@artssb.org.uk
Web site: http://www.artscouncil.org.uk

Association of British Theatre Technicians
47 Bermondsey Street,
London SE1 3XT
Tel: 0171-403 3778
Fax: 0171-378 6170
Email: office@abtt.org.uk
Web site: http://www.abtt.org.uk

British Actors' Equity Association
Guild House, Upper St. Martin's
Lane, London WC2H 9EG
Tel: 0171-379 6000
Fax: 0171-379 7001
Email: equity@easynet.co.uk
Web site:
http://www.equity.org.uk

**Council for Dance Education and
Training (UK)**
Conference of Drama Schools,
Riverside Studios, Crisp Road,
London W6 9RL
Tel: 0181-741 5084
Fax: 0181-748 7604

Incorporated Society of Musicians
10 Stratford Place,
London W1N 9AE
Tel: 0171-629 4413
Fax: 0171-408 1538
Email: membership@ism.org
Web site: http://www.ism.org

**National Council for Drama
Training**
5 Tavistock Place,
London WC1H 9SS
Tel: 0171-387 3650
Fax: 0171-387 3650

National Youth Music Theatre
Fifth Floor, The Palace Theatre,
Shaftesbury Avenue,
London W1V 8AY
Tel: 0171-734 7478
Fax: 0171-734 7515
Web site: http://www.nymt.org.uk

National Youth Theatre
443–445 Holloway Road,
London N7 6LW
Tel: 0171-281 3863
Fax: 0171-281 8246

Post Office

Assessment Consultancy
FREEPOST, Coton House
Management Centre, Rugby,
Warwickshire CV23 0BR
(*for graduate enquiries*)

Printing and packaging

**British Printing Industries
Federation**
11 Bedford Row,
London WC1R 4DX
Tel: 0171-242 6904
Fax: 0171-405 7784
Email: info@bpif.org.uk
Web site: http://www.bpif.org.uk

Institute of Packaging
Syonsby Lodge, Nottingham
Road, Melton Mowbray,
Leicestershire LE13 0NU
Tel: (01664) 500055
Fax: (01664) 64164
Email: info@iop.co.uk

Scottish Print Employers Federation
48 Palmerston Place,
Edinburgh EH12 5DE
Tel: 0131-220 4353
Fax: 0131-220 4344

Publishing and
bookselling

**Booksellers Association of Great
Britain**
272 Vauxhall Bridge Road,
London SW1V 1BA
Tel: 0171-834 5477
Fax: 0171-834 8812
Email:
100437.2261@compuserve.com

London College of Printing and Distributive Trades
Elephant and Castle,
London SE1 6SB
Tel: 0171-514 6500
Fax: 0171-514 6535

Oxford Centre for Publishing Studies
Oxford Brookes University,
Richard Hamilton Building,
Headington Hill Campus,
Oxford OX3 0BP
Tel: (01865) 484951
Fax: (01865) 484952
Email: ptrichardson@brookes.ac.uk

Oxford Publicity Partnership
12 Hid's Copse Road, Cumnor
Hill, Oxford OX2 9JJ
Tel: (01865) 865466
Fax: (01865) 862763
Email: opp@opp.i-way.co.uk

Periodicals Training Council
(See 'Media')

PMA Training
PMA House, Free Church Passage,
St. Ives, Cambridgeshire PE17 4AY
Tel: (01480) 300653
Fax: (01480) 496022
Email: admin@pma.group.com
Web site:
http://www.pma.group.co.uk

Publishers Association
19 Bedford Square,
London WC1B 3HJ
Tel: 0171-565 7474
Fax: 0171-836 4543
Email: mail@publishers.org.uk
Web site:
http://www.publishers.org.uk

Publishing Training Centre
45 East Hill, London SW18 2QZ
Tel: 0181-874 4608
Fax: 0181-870 8985
Email: publishing.training@
bookhouse.co.uk

Scottish Publishers Association
Scottish Book Centre, 137 Dundee
Street, Edinburgh EH11 1BG
Tel: 0131-228 6866
Fax: 0131-228 3220
Email: enquiries@scottishbooks.org

Society of Indexers
Mermaid House, 2 Mermaid Court,
London SE1 1HL
Tel: 0171-403 4947

Religious work

Baptist Union of Great Britain
Ministry Office, Baptist House,
PO Box 44, 129 Broadway,
Didcot, Oxfordshire OX11 8RT
Tel: (01235) 512077
Fax: (01235) 811537
Email:
baptistuniongb@compuserve.com

Catholic Church, Diocesan Vocations Service of England and Wales
39 Eccleston Square,
London SW1V 1BX
Tel: 0171-630 8220
Fax: (01772) 558552 (*answerphone*)

Catholic Church, Scottish National Vocations Office
2 Chesters Road, Bearsden,
Glasgow G61 4AG
Tel: 0141-943 1995 (*answerphone*)/
0141-772 8912
Fax: 0141-943 1995

Christians Abroad
1 Stockwell Green,
London SW9 9HP
Tel: 0171-346 5950
Fax: 0171-346 5955
Email: wse@cabroad.org.uk

Church of England, Vocations Adviser
Advisory Board of Ministry,
Church House, Great Smith Street,
London SW1P 3NZ
Tel: 0171-222 9011
Fax: 0171-976 7625

Church of Ireland
Church of Ireland House, Church
Avenue, Rathmines, Dublin 6,
Republic of Ireland
Tel: (00 353) 1497 8422
Fax: (00 353) 1497 8821
Email: rcbdvb@iol.ie
Web site:
http://www.ireland.anglican.org

Church of Scotland
Dept of Education, Church of
Scotland Office, 121 George Street,
Edinburgh EH2 4YN
Tel: 0131-225 5722
Fax: 0131-220 3113
Email: kirkeculink@gn.apl.org

Church in Wales
39 Cathedral Row, Cardiff,
South Glamorgan CF1 9XF
Tel: (01222) 704007
Fax: (01222) 712413
Email: office@mission.
churchinwales.org.uk

Congregational Federation
Congregational Centre, 4 Castle
Gate, Nottingham NG1 7AS
Tel: (01865) 514358 (*answerphone*)

**Elim Pentecostal Church,
Ministerial Training and Selection
Board**
Regents Theological College,
Regents Park, London Road,
Nantwich, Cheshire CW5 6LW
Tel: (01270) 610800
Fax: (01270) 610013

Jews' College (University of London)
44a Albert Road,
London NW4 2SJ
Tel: 0181-203 6427
Fax: 0181-203 6420
Email: jewscol@clus1.ulcc.ac.uk

Methodist Church
Division of Ministries, Candidates'
Office, Room 509, 25 Marylebone
Road, London NW1 5JR
Tel: 0171-467 5187
Fax: 0171-935 2104

Office of the Chief Rabbi
735 High Road, London N12 0US
Tel: 0181-343 6301
Fax: 0181 343 6310

United Free Church of Scotland
General Secretary, 11 Newton
Place, Glasgow G3 7PR
Tel: 0141-332 3435
Fax: 0141-333 1973

United Reformed Church in the UK
Ministries Dept, 86 Tavistock Place,
London WC1H 9RT
Tel: 0171-916 2020
Fax: 0171-916 2021
Email: ministries@urc.cix.co.uk
Web site:
http://www.cix.co.uk/~urc

Retail

British Display Society
70a Crayford High Street,
Dartford, Kent DA1 4EF
Tel: (01322) 550544

National Retail Training Council
5 Grafton Street, London W1X 3LB
Tel: 0171-647 1500
Fax: 0171-647 1581

Science and technology

Chemical Industries Association
Kings Buildings, Smith Square,
London SW1P 3JJ
Tel: 0171-834 3399
Fax: 0171-834 4469

Institute of Biology
Tel: 0171-581 8333
Fax: 0171-823 9409

**Institute of Food Science &
Technology**
5 Cambridge Court, 210 Shepherd's
Bush Road, London W6 7NL
Tel: 0171-603 6316
Fax: 0171-602 9936
Web site:
http://www.easynet.co.uk/ifst/

**Institute of Mathematics and its
Applications**
Catherine Richards House,
16 Nelson Street,
Southend on Sea, Essex SS1 1EF
Tel: (01702) 354020
Fax: (01702) 354111
Email: post@ima.org.uk
Web site: http://www.ima.org.uk

Institute of Physics
76 Portland Place,
London W1N 3DH
Tel: 0171-470 4800
Fax: 0171-470 4848
Email: physics@iop.org
or education@iop.org
Web site: http://www.iop.org

Royal Society of Chemistry
Burlington House,
London W1V 0BN
Tel: 0171-437 8656
Fax: 0171-734 1227
Email: chemistry.rsc.org
Web site:
http://www.chemistry.rsc.org

Royal Statistical Society
12 Errol Street,
London EC1Y 8LX
Tel: 0171-638 8998
Fax: 0171-256 7598
Email: rss@rss.org.uk

Society of Occupational Medicine
6 St. Andrews Place,
Regent's Park,
London NW1 4LB
Tel: 0171-486 2641
Fax: 0171-486 0028
Email:
societyoccmed@compuserve.com
Web site: http://
www.med.ed.ac.uk/hew/som/

Security services

Prison Service
Directorate of Personnel, The Home Office, Room 403, Cleland House, Page Street, London SW1P 4LN
Tel: 0171-217 6633
Fax: 0171-828 8692

Probation Board for Northern Ireland
80–98 North Street, Belfast, County Antrim BT1 1LD
Tel: (01232) 262400
Fax: (01232) 262470
Email: pbni@nics.gov.uk
Web site: http://www.nics.gov.uk/pbni/index.htm

Probation Unit
The Home Office, Room 444, 50 Queen Anne's Gate, London SW1H 9AT
Tel: 0171-273 2675
Fax: 0171-273 3944

Social and related work

Advice, Guidance, Counselling and Psychotherapy Lead Body
40a High Street, Welwyn, Hertfordshire AL6 9EQ
Tel: (01438) 840511
Fax: (01438) 840576

British Psychological Society (BPS)
St. Andrew's House, 48 Princess Road East, Leicester LE1 7DR
Tel: 0116-254 9568
Fax: 0116-247 0787
Email: mail@bps.org.uk
Web site: http://www.bps.org.uk

Central Council for Education and Training in Social Work (CCETSW)
Information Service, Derbyshire House, St. Chad's Street, London WC1H 8AD
Tel: 0171-278 2455
Fax: 0171-278 2934

CCETSW Information Service (Scotland)
5th Floor, 78/80 George Street, Edinburgh EH2 3BU
Tel: 0131-220 0093
Fax: 0131-220 6717

CCETSW Information Service (Wales)
2nd Floor, South Gate House, Wood Street, Cardiff CF1 1EW
Tel: (01222) 226257
Fax: (01222) 884764

CCETSW Information Service (Northern Ireland)
6 Malone Road, Belfast BT9 5BN
Tel: (01232) 665390
Fax: (01232) 669469

Council for Awards in Children's Care and Education (CACHE)
8 Chequer Street, St. Albans, Hertfordshire AL1 3XZ
Tel: (01727) 847636
Fax: (01727) 867609

Institute of Careers Guidance
27a Lower High Street, Stourbridge, West Midlands DY8 1TA
Tel: (01384) 376464
Fax: (01384) 440830
Email: hq@icg_uk.org
Web site: http://www.icg.uk.org

National Youth Agency
17–23 Albion Street,
Leicester LE1 6GD
Tel: 0116-285 6789
Fax: 0116-247 1043
Email: nya@nya.org.uk
Web site: http://www.nya.org.uk

Royal Anthropological Institute of Great Britain and Ireland
50 Fitzroy Street, London W1P 5HS
Tel: 0171-387 0455
Fax: 0171-383 4235
Web site: http://lucy.ukc.ac.uk/rai

Sport and leisure

English Sports Council
16 Upper Woburn Place,
London WC1H 0QP
Tel: 0171-273 1500
Fax: 0171-383 5740
Email: info@english.sports.gov.uk

Institute of Leisure and Amenity Management
(See 'Land-based industries')

Institute of Professional Sport
Francis House, Francis Street,
London SW1P 1DE
Tel: 0171-828 3168
Fax: 0171-630 8820

Institute of Sport and Recreation Management (ISRM)
Giffard House, 36–38 Sherrard Street, Melton Mowbray,
Leicestershire LE13 1XJ
Tel: (01664) 65531
Fax: (01664) 501155
Email:
ralph@instofsportrec.demon.co.uk

National Coaching Foundation
114 Cardigan Road, Headingley,
Leeds LS6 3BJ
Tel: 0113-274 4802
Fax: 0113-275 5019
Email: coaching@ncf.org.uk
Web site: http://www.ncf.org.uk

Scottish Sports Council
Caledonia House, South Gyle,
Edinburgh EH12 9DQ
Tel: 0131-317 7200
Fax: 0131-317 7202
Email: ssclis@easynet.co.uk

Sports Council for Northern Ireland
House of Sport, Upper Malone
Road, Belfast BT9 5LA
Tel: (01232) 381222
Fax: (01232) 682757
Email: sportscouncil_ni.org.uk

Sports Council for Wales
Sophia Gardens, Cardiff CF1 9SW
Tel: (01222) 300500
Fax: (01222) 300600

UK Outdoor Institute
Eastgate House, Princesshay,
Exeter EX1 1LY
Tel: (01392) 272372
Fax: (01392) 413163
Email: cg@ukoi.demon.co.uk
Web site:
http://www.ukoi.demon.co.uk

UK Sports Council
Walkden House, 10 Melton Street,
London NW1 2EB
Tel: 0171-380 8000
Fax: 0171-380 8010

Women's Sport Foundation
Hither Green Lane,
London SE13 6TJ
Tel: 0181-697 5370
Fax: 0181-697 5370

Surveying and planning

Architects and Surveyors Institute
St. Mary House, 15 St. Mary Street,
Chippenham, Wiltshire SN15 3WD
Tel: (01249) 655398
Fax: (01249) 443602
Email: ASInst@all.com

British Cartographic Society
53 Rownhams Road,
Southampton,
Hampshire SO16 5DX
Tel: (01703) 781519
Fax: (01703) 781519
Email: rownhams@aol.com

Institution of Civil Engineering Surveyors
26 Market Street, Altrincham,
Cheshire WA14 1PF
Tel: 0161-928 8074
Fax: 0161-941 6134
Email: icesurco.demon.co.uk
Web site:
http://www.icesurco.demon.co.uk

Institute of Revenues, Rating and Valuation (IRRV)
41 Doughty Street,
London WC1N 2LF
Tel: 0171-831 3505
Fax: 0171-831 2048
Email: enquiries@irrv.org.uk
Web site: http://www.irrv.org.uk

ISVA (the Professional Society for Valuers and Auctioneers)
3 Cadogan Gate,
London SW1X 0AS
Tel: 0171-235 2282
Fax: 0171-235 4390
Email: isva.co.uk

National Association of Estate Agents
Arbon House, 21 Jury Street,
Warwick CV34 4EH
Tel: (01926) 496800
Fax: (01926) 400953
Email: naea@dial.pipex.com
Web site:
http://www.propertylive.co.uk

Royal Institution of Chartered Surveyors (RICS)
Surveyor Court, Westwood Way,
Coventry CV4 8JE
Tel: (01203) 694757
Fax: 0171-334 3800
Email: rics.org.uk
Web site: http://www.rics.org.uk

Royal Town Planning Institute (RTPI)
26 Portland Place,
London W1N 4BE
Tel: 0171-636 9107
Fax: 0171-323 1582
Email: online@rtpi.org.uk
Web site: http://www.rtpi.org.uk

Society of Surveying Technicians (SST)
(see 'Royal Institution of Chartered Surveyors')

Society of Town Planning Technicians
c/o 7 Kingsway, Ferndown,
Dorset BH22 9QN
Tel: (01202) 886201
Fax: (01202) 849863
Email: stpt@eastdorsetdc.gov.uk

Teaching and lecturing

Bench Marque Ltd
(*Graduate and Registered Teacher Programmes*)
1st Floor, 5 Euston Place,
Leamington Spa,
Warwickshire CV32 4LN
Tel: (01926) 330006
Fax: (01926) 330094
Email:
106310.444@compuserve.com
Web site:
http://www.benchmarque.co.uk

Department for Education in Northern Ireland
Rathgael House, Balloo Road,
Bangor, Co. Down BT19 7PR
(*for teaching in Northern Ireland*)
Tel: (01247) 279537
Fax: (01247) 279100
Web site: http://www.deni.gov.uk

Graduate Teacher Training Registry (GTTR)
Fulton House, Jessop Avenue,
Cheltenham,
Gloucestershire GL50 3SH
(*for application form and handbook for PGCE entry*)
Tel: (01242) 544788 (general enquires)
(01242) 223707 (application pack)
Fax: (01242) 263555

Maryvale Institute
Maryvale House, Old Oscott Hill,
Birmingham B44 9AG
Tel: 0121-360 8118
Fax: 0121-366 6786
Email:
maryvale.institute@dial.pipex.com

National Association of Teachers of Further and Higher Education (NATFHE)
27 Brittania Street,
London WC1X 9JP
Tel: 0171-837 3636
Fax: 0171-837 4403

Teacher Education Admissions Clearing House (TEACH)
PO Box 165, Edinburgh EH8 8AT
(*for teaching in Scotland*)
Tel: 0131-558 6170
Fax: 0131-558 6180

Teacher Training Agency Communication Centre
PO Box 3210, Chelmsford,
Essex CM1 3WA (*for teaching in England and Wales*)
Tel: (01245) 454454
Fax: (01245) 261668
Email:
teaching@ttainfo.demon.co.uk
Web site: http://www.teach.org.uk

Teaching Information Line
Tel: (01245) 454454
Web site: http://www.teach.org.uk

UCAS
(See 'General')

Transport

Chartered Institute of Transport
80 Portland Place,
London W1N 4DP
Tel: 0171-467 9400
Fax: 0171-467 9440
Email: gn@citrans.org.uk
Web site:
http://www.citrans.org.uk

**Civil Aviation Authority (CAA)
(Air-traffic control)**
CAA House, 45–59 Kingsway,
London WC2B 6TE
Tel: 0171-379 7311
Fax: 0171-240 1153

Institute of Chartered Shipbrokers
3 St. Helen's Place,
London EC3A 6EJ
Tel: 0171-628 5559
Fax: 0171-628 5455
Email: isclon@dial.pipex.com

Institute of Road Transport Engineers
22 Greencoat Place,
London SW1P 1PR
Tel: 0171-630 1111
Fax: 0171-630 6677
Email: gmo7@dial.pipex.com

**Merchant Navy Careers, The
Chamber of Shipping**
Carthusian Court, 12 Carthusian
Street, London EC1M 6EB
Tel: 0171-417 8400
Fax: 0171-796 1810
Web site:
http://www.british.shipping.org

**National Air Traffic Services Ltd
(NATS)**
Recruitment Services, T1213,
CAA House, 45–59 Kingsway,
London WC2B 6TE
Tel: 0171-497 5555
Fax: 0171-832 6633

**Office of the Commodore, Royal
Fleet Auxiliary Flotilla**
Lancelot Building, Postal Point 29,
HM Naval Base,
Portsmouth PO1 3NH
Tel: (01705) 722351
Fax: (01705) 726021

Travel and tourism

**British Tourist Authority/English
Tourist Board**
Thames Tower, Blacks Road,
London W6 9EL
Tel: 0181-846 9000
Fax: 0181-563 3062
Email: nmcain@mail.bta.org.uk
Web site:
http://www.visitbritain.com

Institute of Travel and Tourism
113 Victoria Street, St Albans,
Hertfordshire AL1 3TJ
(Send a large SAE plus £3 for
information)
Tel: (01727) 854395
Fax: (01727) 847415

**London Tourist Board and
Convention Bureau**
6th Floor, Glen House, Stag Place,
London SW1E 5LT
Tel: 0171-932 2000
Fax: 0171-932 0222

Travel Training Company
The Cornerstone, The Broadway,
Woking, Surrey GY21 5AR
Tel: (01483) 727321
Fax: (01483) 756698
Email: tttc@dial.pipex.com

Voluntary work

British Trust for Conservation Volunteers (BTCV)
36 St. Mary's Street, Wallingford,
Oxford OX10 0EU
Tel: (01491) 839766
Fax: (01491) 839646
Email: information@btcv.org.uk
Web site: http://www.btcv.org.uk/

Community Service Volunteers
237 Pentonville Road,
London N1 9NJ
Tel: 0171-278 6601
Fax: 0171 833 0149
Email:
106337.3060@compuserve.com
Web site: http://www.csv.org.uk

GAP Activity Project Ltd
44 Queen's Road, Reading,
Berkshire RG1 4BB
Tel: 0118-959 4914
Fax: 0118-957 6634

National Centre for Volunteering
Carriage Row,
183 Eversholt Street,
London NW1 1BU
Tel: 0171-388 9888
Fax: 0171-383 0448
Email: vol_uk@aol.com

National Council for Voluntary Organisations
8 All Saints Street,
London N1 9RL
Tel: 0171-713 6161
Fax: 0171-713 6300
Email:
106007.1315@compuserve.com
Web site:
http://www.vois.org.uk/ncvo

National Youth Agency
(see 'Social and related work')

Voluntary Service Overseas
317 Putney Bridge Road,
London SW15 2PN
Tel: 0181-780 2266
Fax: 0181-780 7576
Email: b.luther@vso.org.uk
Web site:
http://www.oneworld.org

Index